MAKING A SOCIAL BODY

Making a Social Body

British Cultural Formation
1830–1864

Mary Poovey

The University of Chicago Press
Chicago & London

MARY POOVEY, professor of English at the Johns Hopkins
University, is the author of *Uneven Developments* and *The Proper
Lady and the Woman Writer*, both published by the University of
Chicago Press.

The University of Chicago Press, Chicago 60637
The University of Chicago Press, Ltd., London
© 1995 by The University of Chicago
All rights reserved. Published 1995
Printed in the United States of America
04 03 02 01 00 99 98 97 96 95 1 2 3 4 5

ISBN 0–226–67523–8 (cloth)
ISBN 0–226–67524–6 (paper)

Library of Congress Cataloging-in-Publication Data

Poovey, Mary.
    Making a social body: British cultural formation, 1830–1864 /
Mary Poovey.
        p.   cm.
    Includes bibliographical references and index.
    1. Great Britain—Civilization—19th century.   2. National
characteristics, British—History—19th century.   3. Great Britain—
Social conditions—19th   century.   4. Great Britain—History—
Victoria, 1837–1901.   5. Arts,   Modern—19th century—Great
Britain.   6. Arts, British.   I. Title.
    DA533.P66 1995
    941.081—dc20   95-4153
                                                        CIP

⊗ The paper used in this publication meets the minimum requirements
of the American National Standard for Information Sciences—
Permanence of Paper for Printed Library Materials, ANSI Z39.48–1984.

FOR MY PARENTS

Contents

ACKNOWLEDGMENTS

It seems as if it has taken me years to understand what these essays are about, and I am grateful to all those who have helped me in this effort. I especially appreciate several crucial conversations I have had with my closest friends and colleagues: Margie Ferguson, John Guillory, Emily Martin, and David Simpson. As always, my students have been instrumental in helping me clarify my thoughts; Johannah Bradley and Daniel Denecke particularly deserve my gratitude for their helpful comments on the first essay in this volume, and Lara Kriegel for her help in the last stages of the project. I've inflicted various versions of these essays on more audiences than I can name here, but I would like to single out for special thanks John Lamb and the participants in the Summer Seminar in Literary and Cultural Studies at the University of West Virginia. Several of these essays were written while I held a fellowship from the John Simon Guggenheim Memorial Foundation, and I am grateful for this support, and for the assistance of The Johns Hopkins University.

Versions of five of these essays have already appeared in print, and they appear here with the permission of their publishers. "Curing the Social Body in 1832: James Phillips Kay and the Irish in Manchester" was published in *Gender & History* 5, no. 2 (Summer 1993); "Anatomical Realism and Social Investigation in Early Nineteenth-Century Manchester" appeared in *differences: A Journal of Feminist Cultural Studies* 5, no. 3 (Fall 1993); "Domesticity and Class Formation: Chadwick's 1842 *Sanitary Report*" was published in *Subject to History: Ideology, Class, Gender,* edited by David Simpson, pp. 65–83 (Ithaca: Cornell

University Press, 1991), © 1991 Cornell University; a very different version of "Homosociality and the Psychological: Disraeli, Gaskell, and the Condition-of-England Debate" appeared in *The Columbia History of the English Novel,* edited by John Richetti (New York: Columbia University Press, 1994), © 1994 by Columbia University Press; and "Speculation and Virtue in *Our Mutual Friend*" was published in *Historical Criticism and the Challenge of Theory,* edited by Janet Levarie Smarr (Urbana: University of Illinois Press, 1993).

One

MAKING A SOCIAL BODY: BRITISH CULTURAL FORMATION, 1830–1864

I

Although composed over a period of five years for various volumes or occasions, all of the essays in this collection undertake two tasks: to recover some of the dynamics of British cultural formation in the first half of the nineteenth century, and to show that it makes a difference to treat history-writing and textual analysis as facets of a single enterprise. To so designate the primary aims of these essays is, of course, already to take positions in contemporary literary debates about the relationship between literary texts and historical contexts, the functions of criticism, and the boundaries of the canon. In the pages that follow, I will indirectly specify the positions I take in these debates. In this introduction I want to focus primarily on three issues: the historical problematic that governs these essays—cultural formation; the phrase that best captures this phase of cultural formation—*making a social body;* and the historiographical enterprise to which this discussion contributes—historical epistemology.[1]

The emphasis in the subtitle of this book should fall on *formation* as an active concept—the process of forming—not on *culture* or *formation* as nouns of stasis or realization.[2] I emphasize the active sense of *formation* because, from one perspective, we can see that culture is never fully formed, never achieved as a unified, homogeneous whole. Even though a British national identity was widely proclaimed to exist by 1830,[3] we can identify the persistence of competing cultural strains within the kingdoms of Great Britain. The most pronounced cultural differences probably corresponded to what had once been national (and racialized) distinctions: even when living in England, the Irish were consistently said to have their own (inferior) culture; Scots celebrated a distinct legal system and defended a variant of the state church sufficiently different from Anglicanism for its clergy to defy the British government in the early 1840s; the Welsh, although more thoroughly integrated into the British whole, retained their own language and customs, especially in remote areas.[4]

Other kinds of difference, which have assumed increasing prominence in work by Western academics in the last two decades, also make the concept of a single British culture difficult to defend. Many of these diacritical marks were also visible to contemporaries, although the importance ascribed to them varied according to the position of the speaker and the context in which the differences were noted. During the 1830s, for example, contemporaries repeatedly remarked on both the existence of what many (reluctantly) called *class* and the differences class made: the 1842 *Sanitary Report* gave this difference physical as well as economic meaning when its tables showed workers in certain trades living less long than did their leisured governors.[5] Gender, which had long been an important legal, medical, and occupational marker, achieved new prominence during this period.[6] Certainly, by the late 1850s, when the Ladies of Langham Place organized an initiative to challenge existing property laws, it had become clear that some women were questioning the age-old truism that women's interests were naturally "covered" by men's.[7] The notion of a unitary British culture was also strained in the period by the geographical dispersal of an empire whose rulers rarely agreed on how various possessions should be governed. Add to this the varieties of attitudes toward "race," which was a concept only just beginning to be stabilized in the 1840s,[8] and we have a situation in which many historians would quite rightly feel hard-pressed to define—much less defend—the notion of a single British culture.[9]

Despite what we (and some contemporaries) can identify as competing and sometimes overlapping communities within the political entity of early nineteenth-century Britain, the implicit argument of the following essays is that in these decades the groundwork was laid for what would eventually assume the appearance of a single, "mass" culture.[10] Partly because of the dominance of categories like class, gender, and race, this process of homogenization has not received as much attention recently as has the history of internal fragmentation to which I have been alluding. Indeed, in order to raise this other history to the level of visibility, we must supplement the identity categories I have used in the preceding paragraphs with categories that illuminate not the positionality or identity of groups or individuals but the assumptions and conventions that constitute the epistemological field that underwrites the salience acquired by identity categories at various times. As the object of analysis at the heart of what Lorraine Daston has called *historical epistemology*, this epistemological field allows for the production of what counts as knowledge at any given moment.[11] This field changes over time—it has a history—and it has its own distinctive categories— categories like domains, genres, discourses, disciplines, and specific rationalities. I'll discuss some of these epistemological categories in a moment. For now, let me just say that, while positional and identity differentiations intersect with the epistemological categories I will focus on here, the former seem paradoxically both epiphenomenal and narrowly material when viewed against the backdrop of epistemology. That is, while gender and race are often obvious factors in the way individuals are treated, these differences tend to imply that identity is a function of some deeper determinant, like the body or economics. They also imply that identity is always more decisive than are questions about how social authority is distributed, how institutions formalize and divide knowledge, and what, at any given moment, constitutes "the true."[12] Focusing on epistemological categories, by contrast, enables us to understand why some distinctions (like race, for example) became visible at certain times, as well as to measure the impact (or lack thereof) that identity determinants have had on the differentiation of one domain of knowledge from another. These introductory remarks, then, are intended to begin mapping our current vocabulary (which governs some of my own essays as well) onto an epistemological vocabulary so as to make visible the process by which what looks like homogeneity was written into modern mass culture.

Let me begin to explore historical epistemology by way of a brief narrative that will frame the moment of cultural formation with which I am most directly concerned. The culture whose early stage of formation I want to examine here is the "mass culture" that characterizes modernity. In its late twentieth-century form, mass culture appears as an aggregate of individuals and a series of domains that seem more alike than different: individuals seem alike because they are all apparently animated by the same desire, the desire to consume products that take the form of commodities; domains, such as the aesthetic or the theological, seem alike because they all resemble the economic domain of commodity production. As Adorno and Horkheimer have argued, mass culture is organized by a "culture industry," a series of institutions that discipline desire and subordinate difference to homogeneity through technologies that reach (nearly) everyone.[13] Thus mass culture, which is the historical outcome of the mid-nineteenth-century developments I'll turn to in a moment, presents itself as a series of repetitions—individuals who assert their "individuality" by consuming products that are ever more precisely differentiated yet always already the same, domains that mirror each other even as their practitioners proclaim the esoterica of specialization. Epistemologically, mass culture is characterized by the dominance of images. More real in many ways than material "determinations," the images that constitute mass culture as a mode of production and consumption are increasingly generated by multinational corporations whose reach penetrates every part of the globe illuminated by electricity and possessed of a market for the fantasies that have become necessary to national and personal well-being.[14]

The nineteenth-century conditions that laid the groundwork for mass culture also consisted of interdependent relays of images and institutions. Because the epistemological field in which this culture was constituted was not yet completely dominated by representation, however, this period enables us to identify the dynamics by which representation gradually—and unevenly—acquired its prominence. As early as the 1860s, for example, members of the influential National Association for the Promotion of the Social Sciences represented Britain as a single culture, whose individual members could "better themselves" by consuming the products their nation produced.[15] This representation of a single culture competed with and then gradually replaced another representation, which emphasized the differences among various groups within England. The image of a single culture had begun to seem plausible in 1860—even though different subgroups continued to exist—because the technologies capable of materializing an aggregate known as the "population" had been institutionalized for several decades. These technologies included the census, which was first conducted in England in 1801, and statistics, which had begun to be institutionalized in the early 1830s. Along with material innovations like affordable transportation, cheap publications, and national museums, these technologies of representation simultaneously brought groups that had rarely mixed into physical proximity with each other and represented them as belonging to the same, increasingly undifferentiated whole.[16]

The dynamic by which representation gradually came to dominate modern epistemology, then, involved a complex process by which concepts like that of "population" took on some of the properties of material entities, largely as a consequence of the institutionalization of protocols for knowing and technologies of representation. The process I am describing here bears affinities to what Marx called "simple" or "general" abstraction, but whereas Marx offered only a rather schematic description of this process, I want to give it institutional specificity. Here is Marx on this form of abstraction: "The most general abstractions arise on the whole only when concrete development is most profuse, so that a specific quality is seen to be common to many phenomena, or common to all."[17] I want to argue, along with but more specifically than Marx, that the institutionalization or codification of protocols for knowing and representing facilitates the perception that certain characteristics are common to a number of discrete practices. The reified abstractions that standardized modes of knowing generate then produce effects that are simultaneously symbolic and material—as we see, for example, in the case of the census, where abstractions like "minorities" (however defined) receive differential symbolic and material treatment according to prevailing assumptions about their relative value to society as a whole.

As I conceptualize them, institutions are best understood as subsets of domains. Since domain is a crucial category of the historical epistemology I am advocating, it seems important to specify what I mean by this term. Etymologically, *domain* comes to us through two intersecting routes, from the Latin *dominium* and the Old French *demaine*. In common usage, *domain* refers to a geographical territory that has been appropriated as property, as well as to the absolute ownership of that property (which reaches its logical extreme in private property). In adopting the term *domain*, I want to signal the transformations that occur when land becomes property: territory is appropriated; boundaries are drawn; rules governing usage are established; unequal privileges are codified by law and then naturalized by repetition.

As a category that helps define an epistemological field, *domain* signals the outcome of a similar transformation. This transformation also involves the drawing of boundaries and the codification of rules in such a way as to create from what once seemed to be an undifferentiated continuum of practices and ideas new and more specialized conceptual—or imaginary—entities. This transformation occurs both in the register of representation (what Foucault calls the "order of discourse") and in the register of materiality, producing effects that can be measured or felt. Of course, what I am calling the registers of representation and materiality are not actually separate, and the impression that they are is one effect of the history I am trying to describe. Nevertheless, because slippage does occur between language and what (for want of a better phrase) we can call *material reality*, I want to preserve for now the concept of different "registers" to convey this slippage.

To further explain the concept of domain, let me take as an example the domain of the economic. As the etymology of *economy* suggests, practices that we now associate with finance and commerce were once conceptualized as part of a more capacious social relation. The term *economy* initially referred to the management of a household, with all of the financial, ethical, and domestic responsibilities that an early modern household entailed.[18] In the course of the eighteenth century, the word *economy* was yoked to the term *political* and used to signal the management of national resources. This linguistic innovation suggests—and helped stabilize—some of the changes wrought by the emergence of a civil society in the early eighteenth century—both the continuity between modes of governance developed in the aristocratic household and the kind of management that could produce national prosperity through commerce *and* the gradual separation of specifically financial activities from practices that had once seemed related to finance, such as ethical instruction and military prowess. From our perspective, the domain—in this case, the economic domain—can be seen as an imaginary entity that is governed by a specific rationality—in this case, the logic and procedures by which productivity and financial security are thought to be ensured. Here we enter the register of materiality, however, for the domain also comes into being through institutions, which actualize the domain's rationality—its logic—in representations that everyone can see and in protocols that are increasingly specialized and refined. The study of a domain and its institutions is eventually formalized in a discipline governed by an identifiable set of questions and a protocol of inquiry.

"The economic," then, can be said to have constituted a domain when commercial and financial transactions that were once viewed as part of a complex system of management began to seem different from other kinds of practices to which they were once related. "The economic" can also be said to have constituted a domain when the abstraction of the "economy" began to seem as real as individual acts of commercial exchange *because* these exchanges all seemed like each other and different from other household transactions such as providing ethical instruction for servants or children. Institutionally, the rudiments of what eventually became the economic domain were established in England in the late seventeenth century, in the Bank of England, the national debt, and the stock exchange. These institutions, along with the discipline by which they were detailed and naturalized— political economy—constituted the first of many concrete forms in which individuals encountered and imagined the economic to exist.

As this description suggests, the creation of modern domains was a process of disaggregation or specialization. This historical process of disaggregation accelerated in the late seventeenth century with the demotion of the monarchy and the development of modern civil society.

During the course of the eighteenth century, emergent domains, like the economic, were gradually specified as separate from residual domains, like the political, the theological, and the ethical.[19] These emergent domains did not immediately replace their predecessors, however, but were mapped onto them in a process that entailed the negotiation and eventual redrawing of the boundaries between kinds of knowledge, kinds of practice, and kinds of institutions. This process of negotiation was complex and uneven, not only because old ways die hard, but also because, as I have already suggested, the emergence and consolidation of modern domains entailed the production of abstractions alongside and through the establishment of institutions. The unevenness, or slippage, that both separates and connects representation and institutions was sometimes registered as variations in linguistic usage. Thus, words like *economy* were still used, often metaphorically, in the more general sense of "the administration of resources" long after what *we* can identify retrospectively as "the economic" had acquired a rationality sufficiently specific to the administration of national resources to warrant calling it a domain. I will argue in a moment that the complex process by which the boundaries of domains are negotiated through the uneven relationship between language and institutional practice introduces fissures that undermine the coherence of what otherwise seem to be self-consistent, even totalizing domains. For now, let me turn to the domain in which I am most interested here—the social domain.

What we can identify as a specifically social domain was a relative latecomer to the array of modern domains I have been describing.[20] As with the economic domain, we can see that the process of disaggregation had begun with a linguistic change—the waning importance of the phrase to which *the social body* is historically related, the *body politic*.[21] By the seventeenth century, one of the uses to which the medieval metaphor of the body politic was put was to indicate the political subjects of English society. The political subjects, members of Parliament and gentlemen, were held to constitute the "second body" of the king. Unlike these political subjects, the poor were not usually considered members of the body politic. Indeed, as "diseased" (unproductive, criminal, plague-ridden) members, the poor were considered inimical to the health of the body politic.

By 1776, the phrase *body politic* had begun to compete with another metaphor, the *great body of the people*. As Adam Smith used this phrase in the *Wealth of Nations*, it referred not to the well-to-do but to the mass of laboring poor. By the early nineteenth century, both of these phrases were joined by the image of the social body, which was used in two quite different ways: it referred either to the poor in isolation from the rest of the population or to British (or English) society as an organic whole. The ambiguity that this double usage produced was crucial to the process of cultural formation I am describing, for it allowed social analysts to treat one segment of the population as a special problem at the same time that they could gesture toward the mutual interests that (theoretically) united all parts of the social whole. The phrase *social body* therefore promised full membership in a whole (and held out the image *of* that whole) to a part identified as needing both discipline and care.

The nineteenth-century concept of a social body carries traces of both the political domain, to which the concept of a body politic properly belongs, and the economic domain, to which the "great body of the people" referred. The substitution of *social* for *politic,* however, and the disappearance of *the people* suggests that a new conceptual entity had begun to emerge by the early nineteenth century. The gradual consolidation of a distinctively "social" domain was facilitated by efforts to comprehend—to understand, measure, and represent—the poverty that seemed increasingly visible in the last three decades of the eighteenth century. Adam Smith had argued that the productivity of the laboring poor was essential to national prosperity and security; by the 1790s, with economic depression at home and revolutionary ferment abroad, this link seemed both more crucial and more tenuous than ever before.

The last decades of the eighteenth century witnessed the first modern efforts to represent all—or significant parts—of the population of Britain as aggregates and to delineate a social sphere distinct from the political and economic domains. These two developments—the aggregation of distinct populations and the conceptual disaggregation of a social domain—were intimately connected, for identifying the problems that afflicted the nation involved isolating the offending populations, abstracting from individual cases the general problems they shared, and devising solutions that would not contradict the specific rationalities of those domains by which British social relations had traditionally been organized. Central to current political rationality was the idea that political power should reflect property ownership, and increasingly central to economic rationality was the notion that commerce should be freed from government control. The emergence of the social domain thus involved the specification of a set of problems that was related to but not coincident with political and economic issues. This specification occurred in texts like Sir John Sinclair's 1791 *Statistical Account of Scotland,* which was organized into sections dealing with "the Population, the Political Circumstances, [and] the Productions of a Country."[22] In

the 1830s, the statistical societies founded throughout Great Britain repeated and elaborated this categorization by separating "social" topics
like education and crime from economic subjects like imports and
exports.[23]

In the disaggregation of the social we see once more the role that a
particular kind of abstraction played in the constitution of modern domains. Abstraction has always played a crucial role in the production of
what counts as truth, of course. Indeed, it is a historical commonplace
that the challenge posed to Aristotelian philosophy by probabilistic
thinking in the seventeenth century was a challenge to a particular kind
of abstract reasoning. Here, I simply want to make that commonplace
more specific. During the course of the seventeenth and eighteenth centuries, the kind of abstraction associated with deduction or scholasticism began to be rewritten in relationship to the version of empiricism
that we associate with Bacon and the kind of sensationalism that we associate with Locke. While I can't rehearse the complexities of this revision here, let me just say that the version of abstraction that dominated
truth-claims by the end of the eighteenth century had begun to manifest
three salient characteristics. First, it tended to be instantiated—by
which I mean both related, in some fashion or another, to the concrete
instances of the phenomenal world and institutionalized as codified
practices that are confirmed and then naturalized through the social relations established by people working together. Second, and largely as a
consequence of this instantiation, modern abstraction tends to be susceptible to the process of vivification that nineteenth-century writers
like Marx and Freud referred to variously as reification, commodification, and fetishization. This vivification, in turn, is the basis for what has
gradually become the almost complete domination of representation—
of appearances—in modern mass culture.[24] Third, modern abstraction
tends to generate norms that are typically defined as such by numerical
calculation. Modern abstraction, in other words, as the product of the
spatialization of Euclidean geometry that I discuss in "The Production
of Abstract Space," derives from the imposition of a conceptual grid that
enables every phenomenon to be compared, differentiated, and measured by the same yardstick. Such comparisons and measurements, of
course, produce some phenomena as normative—ostensibly because
they are more numerous, because they represent an average, or because
they constitute an ideal towards which all other phenomena move.[25]

It might be helpful at this point to provide a concrete example of the
specific dynamic by which the domain of the social was disaggregated in
the early nineteenth century. I'll turn, then, to the New Poor Law, for in
it we see the complex interaction of material reality, ideas, institutions,

technologies, and abstraction that I have been presenting as characteristic of the formation of modern culture.

Agitation for poor-law reform accelerated dramatically after 1770, partly in response to a proliferation of pamphlets exposing the abuses of the present system and partly in response to the publication, beginning in 1775, of reliable figures for national expenditures on poverty.[26] During the period between 1770 and 1830, writers like Jonas Hanway, Thomas Gilbert, Robert Malthus, Jeremy Bentham, and Thomas Chalmers reformulated the problem of poverty in the context of the domains to which it had traditionally been relegated—the theological, the political, and the economic. These reformulations, however, brought out potential discrepancies among these domains, thereby pointing out contradictions inherent in the current treatment of poverty. Thus Bentham's 1795 National Charity Company sought unsuccessfully to remove poverty from the domain of religion and to subject it completely to economic rationality, while efforts by Malthus and Chalmers to preserve a religious framework for understanding poverty highlighted natural tendencies that, according to Malthus, would lead to economic ruin.[27] In his response to Malthus, Robert Southey focused on the political ramifications of excessive poor relief: if traditional paternalism was disrupted, he argued, political instability would soon follow.

By the third decade of the nineteenth century, then, poor-law reform was demanded on evangelical, economic, and political grounds and by groups as different as the Benthamite editors of the *Westminster Review* and Tory landowners.[28] The tensions among these groups, which could have stymied reform, were effectively neutralized, however, by the representational technology used to pursue reform. This technology, which can be summarized as "fact-gathering," drew its prestige from the authority granted certain natural philosophical (scientific) practices, which were being refined in the late eighteenth and early nineteenth centuries as natural philosophy diverged from its disciplinary twin, moral philosophy. These "scientific" practices, which I discuss further in "Anatomical Realism and Social Investigation," centered on the use of "experts" to gather and analyze "facts" from extensive empirical observations. In the making of the New Poor Law, the influence of science can be identified most generally in the appointment, in 1830, of a Royal Commission.[29] The influence of science is also apparent in the kind of knowledge these facts produced. This knowledge, as exemplified in the commission's report, claimed to be objective, in the sense of being politically disinterested, and to derive its central abstractions from empirical observations. In keeping with the scientific protocol, the knowledge produced by the report tended to aggregate its object of analysis and to yield general "laws" about regularities rather than detailed pictures of individual cases.[30]

The knowledge produced by the Royal Commission also contributed to the delineation of a social domain. Largely as a consequence of the report, for example, *pauperism* came to be distinguished from *poverty*.[31] Pauperism was a moral and physical designation, which encompassed all of the components eventually relegated to the social domain: criminal tendencies, bodily health, environmental conditions, education, and religion. Poverty, by contrast, was an economic category. It referred not only to the prosperity of individuals or of the poor as a group, but also to a structural part of the national economy that some, including Edwin Chadwick, conceptualized as essential to capitalist production.[32] This distinction, which was instituted along with—indeed, as a critical component of—the New Poor Law of 1834, insisted that morality and health were separable from one's economic situation *and* that the poverty of some individuals was essential to the prosperity of the nation. As a consequence of this rhetorical distinction, which was materialized and enforced through the workhouse test, pauperism, which belonged to the emergent social domain, could be subjected to government oversight, while poverty, which was relegated to the economic, was left to the operations of a free market. In the decades that followed, we can see in the transformation of pauperism the complete disaggregation of the social, and then its reformation in the very image of the economic. In the 1830s, that is, pauperism was treated as a moral problem that had social and economic components; in the 1840s, it was expanded (or perhaps refined) to encompass the physical aspects of poor people's bodies and living conditions, while the economic was relegated to the status of effect. By the 1850s, pauperism had disappeared as a problem, *not* because there were no poor people but because the social sphere, to which pauperism had been assigned, had come to *mirror* the economic domain, where individuals appeared as independent, self-regulating agents.

If the use of an apparently disinterested apparatus of fact-gathering produced abstractions about an aggregate whose social components could be isolated from its political and economic dimensions, then the machinery of the New Poor Law produced an avalanche of new information that mandated more—and more far-reaching—fact-gathering, inspection, and legislation. In this sense, the law was relatively autonomous and self-propelling. This autonomy was simultaneously an early sign that the social domain was being separated from the political domain and an instrument that specified the two domains and formalized their relationship to each other. In 1834, for example, as soon as the act was implemented, disturbances broke out in some parts of the south. The Poor Law Commissioners attributed these disturbances to uncertainty about the amount of relief allowable under the law (not to the law itself or to the interruption of traditional social relations caused by the law). Because they read the disturbances as lack of information, their solution was to initiate a "renewed and more detailed inquiry."[33] This inquiry proved what the commissioners already assumed—that "although the investigations of the late Commissioners of Inquiry were more extensive than any preceding, and were fully adequate to the purposes of legislation," they did not yield sufficient information for implementing the law. "We felt," the commissioners explained in 1835, "that until we could reexamine the parishes or districts in question by our Assistant-Commissioners, our instructions to the local officers must of necessity be general and discretionary, and could not be safely extended to numerous details."[34] Thus the Central Board sent out another, more specialized circular, which was overseen by the newly appointed assistant commissioners, and which generated enough information to determine where unions should be established. The formation of these unions was duly recorded in tables and monitored by more questionnaires and more inspectors.

Eventually, all this poor-law information generated not *coverage* of that entity known as the social body (much less control over poor rates) but a new picture of an adjacent problem that also needed to be surveyed, tabulated, legislated, and administered by representatives of the political domain. The problem of public health, which became visible as poor rates increased in urban areas, directed official attention to poor urban neighborhoods, which had been the object of concern for medical men since the early years of the decade. Thus, as I argue in "Curing the Social Body in 1832" and "Domesticity and Class Formation," both the amateur surveys written by doctors like James Phillips Kay and Chadwick's government-sponsored *Sanitary Report* of 1842 contributed to the project of cultural formation by extending the domain of the social and by specifying the relationship between its management and the other domains I have been discussing. Not incidentally, the appointment of Kay (soon Kay-Shuttleworth) to the positions of assistant poor-law commissioner in 1835, then first secretary to the Committee of Council on Education in 1839, makes it clear that the domains I have been discussing did not correspond to either of the senses in which contemporaries used the categories of private and public spheres. Not only was the social a domain overseen by both governmental and private initiatives, but the boundary between the private (voluntary *or* domestic) and the public (governmental *or* market-related) was permeable (for some individuals more than others) in a way that did not exactly correspond to the permeability of the boundary between the social and the political domains.[35]

The example of the New Poor Law, along with the migration of James Phillips Kay from the social to the political domain, calls attention to one of the key concepts that governs the historical narrative I have been constructing. This is the concept of relative autonomy, which has been developed by Louis Althusser and elaborated by Pierre Bourdieu.[36] This concept glances two ways at once: toward the *autonomy* that institutionalization gives the concepts and practices associated with various domains, and toward the *relative* or partial nature of this autonomy. This double emphasis suggests that while extrainstitutional determinants will always be mediated through the language, practices, and priorities of an institution, that institution will never free itself completely from the various domains from which it emerged and in which it continues to operate.[37] Thus the concept of relative autonomy enables us to register both a historical process—the gradual disaggregation of domains and the specification of relationships among the institutions that reified this disaggregation—*and* a continuing structural interdependence—the retention of traces of the originary affiliation that bound one domain to another and the permanent influence that domains exercise over the institutions that give them life. Both of these movements—the disaggregation of domains and the continuing structural interdependence—are best seen retrospectively and through theoretical analysis, although both can also be glimpsed in the uncertain status of terms like *economy* or even *body.*

The concept of relative autonomy proves useful at a number of levels. In addition to specifying the historical and structural differences among domains as capacious as the economic, the political, and the social, the concept can help indicate that the various kinds of disaggregation and reification I have been discussing—the separation of a social domain from an economic one, for example—were themselves merely the local dynamics of a historical process that must also be described more abstractly. At this more abstract level, the history I have been presenting as a process of disaggregation assumes the appearance of consolidation or self-duplication. At the most abstract level, in other words, and in the register of representation, the disaggregation of domains, the specification of discourses and kinds of practice, and the institutionalization of protocols associated with specific rationalities constitute facets of what appears as a single tendency—a tendency whose terminus has been variously described as formal rationality, commodity fetishism, modernity, and what I have called mass culture.

The argument I have been developing may seem at this point simply to coincide with other theoretical attempts to define modernity: as the emergence of fully differentiated domains whose fundamental dynamics precisely replicate each other; as the decisive transfer of meaning from the realm of material production to that of representation; as the repetition at the level of subjectivity and the body of the disciplinary dynamics played out more ostentatiously in various domains.[38] Especially given the emphasis I have just placed on a "single tendency," moreover, my argument may also seem to dovetail with New Historicist representations of modern power as a totalizing force. In this account, the distinctively modern form of power/knowledge subsumes potential opposition by proliferating ever more differentiated versions of itself.[39] Although some of my earlier work leans toward this representation of power as hegemonic, here and in the essays that follow I suggest that no theoretical position that credits modernity with totalization is adequate to the historical record. In recent years, several theorists have offered explanations for the limitations or failures of modern rationality. Following Foucault's late work on "governmentality," for example, Ian Hunter has emphasized that even if domains have their own institutions, "forms of calculation," and political programs, the implementation of these programs depends on specific, piecemeal, and local measures whose success is contingent on other factors.[40] Working from theorists as diverse as Max Weber, Jürgen Habermas, and Leo Strauss, by contrast, Anthony Cascardi has suggested that the incoherences of modern culture, which show up primarily as contradictions in the subject, emanate from the conflict among separate "value spheres, each one of which tends to exclude or attempts to assert its priority over the rest."[41]

My own contribution to this growing dissent from the view that modern culture's imaginary totality is effective emphasizes not so much the contingency that governs the implementation of specific rationalities or the clash among "value spheres" as the incoherence that results from the uneven process of disaggregation itself. Because emergent domains develop out of and retain a constitutive relationship to preexistent, or residual, domains, the rationalities and forms of calculation that are institutionalized in new domains tend to carry with them traces of the rationality specific to the domain in which they arise. In the context of the new domain, however, the specific rationality of the residual domain may seem distinctly irrational—as, for example, when mathematical calculations about risk that are specific to discussions of uncertainty in the economic domain retain traces of the language of providence, which is specific to the treatment of uncertainty (miracles) in the theological domain.[42]

As the essays that follow suggest, the incoherences generated by dis-aggregation often show up at the site of the modern identity categories that have dominated so much recent literary criticism. This should not be surprising, for the constitutive inequalities that were written into the modern domains typically mobilized assumptions about gender, racial, and status inequality naturalized in the older theological and juridical domains. Another way to describe the source of this incoherence is to agree with Mitchell Dean that the disaggregation of modern domains was a development *within* patriarchy (and racism and elitism).[43] It is important to emphasize, however, that even though the gender inequal-ity of patriarchal relations, for example, was initially carried over from the theological into the modern economic domain, this inequality soon manifested itself as *irrational* in relation to the claim that economic indi-viduals were structurally equivalent in the marketplace. This irra-tionality was recognized by women like Barbara Bodichon and the Ladies of Langham Place, who argued in the late 1850s that if men could own property, then married women—who were *economically struc-tural equivalents*—should be able to own property too.[44] Because Bod-ichon capitalized on the Benthamite project of formally rationalizing the legal system, moreover, she and her colleagues were able to bolster their economic arguments with arguments drawn from the Law Amendment Society's claim that modern laws should not preserve an-cient irrationalities. The failure of attempts to pass a married women's property bill in 1857 allowed one kind of rationality (theological) to persist, then, but only as an increasingly obvious *ir*rationality when judged in the context of emergent modern domains (the juridical, the economic).

Thus what theorists have described as the totality of modern forms of power must be seen as subject not only to imperfect implementation but also to the contradictions that the disaggregation of domains inev-itably produced. In each of the following essays I devote some attention to both parts of this dynamic, by which the appearance of totality was generated alongside—but in tension with the persistence of and conflict among—specific rationalities. Thus, in "The Production of Abstract Space," I argue that the institutionalization of a Euclidian view of space as empty and amenable to mathematical calculation was crucial to the constitution of the social body, because this concept of space authorized treating the poor as an aggregate whose neighborhoods should be pene-trated and subjected to statistical analysis by clergymen and doctors. In this essay, however, I also point out that the very image of a social body authorized individuals who were not connected with the Church or pro-fessional medicine to participate in social reform. Because they had been assigned the care of young and ailing bodies by scripture and by tradition, that is, women were able to enter the social domain not only as mothers, but as nurses and educators too.

Similar contradictions emerge in every essay in this volume. Thus, in "Anatomical Realism and Social Investigation," the clash between the specific rationality of medical science and evangelical theology became especially obvious in the treatment of prostitution, for sexuality, which was a fit subject for the former, was considered antithetical to the moral program of the latter. In "Curing the Social Body in 1832," the racialized Irish constitute the site at which specific rationalities conflict. In order to argue that the Irish should be excluded from the English labor market, James Phillips Kay mobilized the stereotype of the Irish as uncivilized "barbarians," yet because he also used the medical image of "contagion" to describe the "pauperizing" influence these workers had on the English, Kay exposed the contradiction between a medical rationality that emphasized physiological "cure" and an older, ethnological rationality that insisted on racial inferiority. The poor constitute another site where rationalities came into conflict. In the account I provide of government growth in "Thomas Chalmers, Edwin Chadwick, and the Sublime Revolution in Nineteenth-Century Government," I show that debates about how to manage poverty pitted proponents of an evangelical variant of laissez-faire against advocates of government-supervised poor relief. While the logics of both evangelical theology and the Benthamite science of administration can be seen in retrospect to have contributed to the modern form of liberal government and disciplinary individualism, to many contemporaries, the Benthamite scheme of government reform seemed dangerously at odds with the divinely appointed paternalism that had traditionally informed poor relief.

In the last three essays in this volume ("Domesticity and Class Formation," "Homosociality and the Psychological," and "Speculation and Virtue in *Our Mutual Friend*"), I identify gender as the fault that exposes the contradictions among rationalities and domains. To a certain extent, then, these essays extend the concerns I addressed in *Uneven Developments,* but they are more concerned with the relationship between gender and the epistemological process I have been describing than with what I called "ideological work" per se.

"Domesticity and Class Formation," for example, deals specifically with the 1842 *Sanitary Report* as a text that specified the rationality of the social domain as distinct from the rationalities of the political and the economic domains. This text also reveals, however, that Edwin Chadwick undermined working-class men's political aspirations by mobilizing older (theological) assumptions about the proper role that women should play. My essay on Disraeli and Gaskell, which also focuses on the 1840s, pursues the relationship between the discourse about social reform and the specific rationality of the political domain in two literary texts. As contributions to the "condition-of-England" debate, *Coningsby* (1845) and *Mary Barton* (1848) suggest how differently assumptions about masculinity (or "manliness") and femininity contributed to (and were influenced by) a form of social analysis that spoke to a political debate in a genre that rejected the abstractions produced by political theorists. In so doing, these texts also suggest the specific protocols that literature brought to this discussion, for the conventions of literature elevated individualizing narratives over the kind of aggregation used in government blue books. "Speculation and Virtue," in which I examine the relationship between Dickens's *Our Mutual Friend* (1863—65) and patterns of capital investment in the late 1850s, shows how assumptions about femininity, which were inherited from the old theological domain, could be used to offset the ethical dilemmas posed in an economic domain now completely disaggregated from theological concerns. This essay also shows how assumptions about gender were used to stabilize another identity category that had become prominent (again) in the 1860s. Managing the category of race was to become increasingly critical to the legitimation of imperialism, which accelerated dramatically after 1865. Paradoxically, whereas colonial administration (especially in India) provided the testing ground for rationalizing the domain of governmentality, the category of race— which seemed to mandate the bureaucratic apparatus of indirect rule[45]—ultimately proved impossible to police, not least because of the "hybridity" that mixed-race sex soon produced. The vicissitudes of imperialism, which show the geographical unevenness of the disaggregation of domains, constitute the horizon of the essays in this volume. This important subject clearly deserves its own epistemological history to supplement the identity paradigm in relation to which its history has thus far been written.

My emphasis on the faultlines generated by the imposition of one rationality upon other, preexisting rationalities helps explain why I do not examine what are generally thought of as oppositional cultures. Certainly, studies of working-class cultures, especially by historians working in the tradition of E. P. Thompson,[46] have enabled me to recognize the limits of the cultural project I examine here. In the essays that follow, however, I do not contribute to this historiographical enterprise. I have not written essays about working-class attitudes to the sanitary movement or working-class women's response to respectability partly because I am more interested in the epistemological changes I have been describing than in a history that privileges identity categories like class. The most important reason I focus on the dominant rather than the oppositional side of what is too often construed as a binary configuration of power, however, is that the epistemological history I have sketched out here explodes the idea that power could ever be monolithic or merely repressive.[47] Certainly, in the decades I examine here, some individuals and groups could do and buy and publish things that other individuals could not. White, propertied men, especially those who were or had access to Members of Parliament, could participate in shaping legislation, for example, in a way that most working-class men and all women could not. To acknowledge this, however, is not to say that all white, propertied men enjoyed the same kind of influence, nor is it to say that those ascriptions of identity—white, propertied, male—always outweighed the determinants that irradiated the epistemological field where kinds of knowledge were distinguished from each other and various degrees of social authority were accorded to each.[48]

To suggest how "power" is exploded by focusing on the relative autonomy and intersection of domains of activity and meaning, let me return once more to the period at hand. I have argued that, by 1830, the economic had become a relatively autonomous domain that, while still overseen by the English government, was increasingly analyzed and treated as a realm in which the state should not interfere. The autonomy of the economic was *only* relative, however, not only because individual commercial activities were freighted with religious significance, but also because a strictly economic analysis could not account for the interests of all of the parties involved in the debate. While the economic arguments offered by David Ricardo, in other words, conveyed the financial interests of manufacturers and many commercial men, they did not capture or advance the interests of landowners, who wanted to retain trade restrictions to maximize their own profit from grain. Many, but not all, of these landowners were Tories; many, but by no means all, were M. P.s; some were also religious evangelicals, which meant (among other things) that their paternalism was not merely self-interested (economic) but humanitarian (theological and social) as well. In the context of such complexities, which make it impossible to equate "the state" with "the economy" with "middle-class ideology," it makes no sense to talk of individual writers wielding "power" in some univocal way. If power is organized and wielded differently within—and *between*—various domains that were relatively autonomous with respect to each other, then we need more nuanced ways to describe the roles played by various kinds of texts in the production, maintenance, and erosion of cultures that are always internally fissured and contradictory.

II

In this introduction, I have suggested that we can best capture these nuances by directing our critical gaze beyond the identity categories to which we have become accustomed, beyond an image of power as monolithic, and toward the horizon of historical epistemology. I admit that the following essays do not uniformly deploy the terms of this epistemological analysis, for (as is so often the case) the theoretical trajectory of my own work is only becoming visible to me as I reflect on what I have already done. With the exception of "Homosociality and the Psychological," which bears almost no resemblance to the essay on Gaskell and Disraeli from which it was derived, I have made only slight—if significant—revisions in the five essays that have already been published. As a consequence, some of the essays suffer from a certain theoretical indecision; although I now see the epistemological history to which they all belong, I wrote many of these essays under the sign of identity or the influence of the New Historicism, and I have chosen not to efface all of the traces of the theoretical conditions that made their writing possible.

It might be helpful, then, by way of a final introductory note, to sketch out the historical narrative I construct in these essays and to suggest once more how each constitutes an episode in the epistemological history I would now write. After "The Production of Abstract Space," which provides an overview of the period, the essays are arranged chronologically, according to their subjects. "The Production of Abstract Space" highlights the role played by the distinctively modern form of abstraction in the disaggregation of the domains that constitutes the history of modernity. This essay also introduces the theme of contradiction, which appears when rationalities that are being specified to delineate discrete domains come into conflict with each other. In it I argue that the conflicts generated by the uneven specification of the modern domains not only produced what look like irrationalities but also created what amount to opportunities that were at odds with the intentions of individual writers and with the general tendency of each domain of modern rationality as well.

In "Curing the Social Body in 1832," I describe in some detail the image of the social body constructed by early social analysts. Focusing on a study of cotton operatives by James Phillips Kay, I demonstrate that the epistemological field in which the social body was constructed did not yet conform to the modern configuration of domains. Kay presented the "ills" of the social body as simultaneously moral, physical, and economic, and he conflated political with economic analysis when he tried to diagnose its "maladies." For Kay, who sought to treat problems soon to be relegated to the social while freeing the economic domain from government interference, the Irish immigrants who populated Manchester seemed to epitomize what was wrong with England. In his pamphlet, the Irish constitute the site where social, economic, and political problems cannot be separated. Once the Irish are returned to Ireland, Kay maintains, the social will become what it should always have been—separable from but supportive of an economic domain that operates independently of political oversight.

I connect Kay's concern with the social body to modern abstraction in "Anatomical Realism and Social Investigation" by demonstrating more precisely how social analysts' use of anatomical techniques spatialized and specified the social body. I also point to the relationship between modern abstraction and the logic of equivalence that governed the formal rationality of market relations. At the same time that anatomical analysis began to specify the social, then, as a domain that could be separated from the economic, this mode of analyzing the urban residents in particular also began to construct the social in the image of the economic, to the extent that both were subject to the logic of formal and instrumental rationality. In this essay I also show that analysts' attempts to apply this investigatory technique to prostitution brought the rationality associated with the economic and scientific domains into conflict with the rationality specific to the theological realm. According to this rationality, whose contemporary articulation was evangelicalism, things that could be described by scientists (natural philosophers and political economists) were too immoral to be named.

In "Thomas Chalmers, Edwin Chadwick, and the Sublime Revolution in Nineteenth-Century Government," I begin to explore another feature common to the modern and increasingly disaggregated domains. On the one hand, this feature appeared as a new form of individualism, the paradoxical configuration that Michel Foucault called *disciplinary individualism,* whereby individuals express their freedom through voluntary compliance with some greater law. On the other hand, and as the necessary counterpart to disciplinary individualism, this feature manifested itself as a distinct form of administration, which governed through incitement rather than coercion and which offered rationalized procedures and predictable laws as guarantors for individual liberties. My treatment of disciplinary individualism focuses on Thomas Chalmers and Edwin Chadwick because the charisma exercised by the great Scottish divine seems so antithetical to the impersonal bureaucracy that Chadwick celebrated in the New Poor Law of 1834. Far from being opposites, I argue, charisma and bureaucracy should be seen as two faces of the modern form of administration, which combines tutelage with routine to incite normalized behaviors in every subject. Disciplinary individualism, which both facilitated and drew from this form of administration, constitutes a crucial bridge between institutional apparatuses, like the modes of investigation and enforcement I discuss in the first four essays in this volume, and subjectivity, to which I turn in the last two essays.

"Domesticity and Class Formation" extends my concern with the relationship between the newly emergent social sphere and the nation as an imagined community. In this essay, which deals specifically with Edwin Chadwick's 1842 *Sanitary Report,* I show how incorporating the problem of public health into the social domain helped depoliticize working-class men in the name of national well-being. Extending the "social body" to include—indeed, to focus on—the physical bodies of workers and the poor helped define "reform" as sanitary improvement, not the extension of the franchise or a revision of capitalist relations. Separating the social domain from the political and economic—while still subjecting the former to government oversight—enlisted assumptions about gender in the defense of national unity, even as it materially restricted the kinds of relationships one working-class man could have with another.

In "Homosociality and the Psychological," I begin to specify the contribution made by literary works to the disaggregation of the social and to the gendering of the social body. While both Disraeli's *Coningsby* and Gaskell's *Mary Barton* participated explicitly in the debate about poverty conducted more generally in the 1840s, they did so through the conventions specific to the novel as a genre. This means, on the one hand, that the aggregation so essential to the constitution of the social body in the 1830s was supplemented in the 1840s by an individualizing elaboration of subjectivity. The interiority implied by this subjectivity was an extension of disciplinary individualism; as such, it underwrote the stability of modern, liberal government and further consolidated the normalization of emotional and sexual behaviors increasingly conceptualized as "private." This model of interiority thereby constituted the prototype for another domain—the psychological—the dynamics of which were specified later in the century. On the other hand—and because of the individualizing tendency conventional to novels—the prominence of literature in the specification of a private sphere also means that gender began to play an even more prominent role in the constitution of the social domain.

The final essay in the volume, "Speculation and Virtue in *Our Mu-*

tual Friend," further elaborates the contribution that novels made to the constitution of the modern subject. Because this is the only essay that suggests what had happened to the social body by the 1860s and because my reading does not focus on issues that could be—and have been—read as facets of the nineteenth-century debate about the social body,[49] I want to specify in some detail the relationship of this essay to the others in the volume.

This relationship is most importantly historical. By this, I do not mean simply that *Our Mutual Friend* bears the latest publication date of the materials I analyze in this collection. I mean first that the subject Dickens raises in his last completed novel only became visible as an effect of the developments I discuss in earlier essays in this volume. Specifically, I suggest that Dickens's anxiety about the relationship between economic speculation and masculinity could only emerge after the economic domain was relieved of its moral component—a component that, by 1860, had been anchored in the social and theological domains. Secondly, I want to suggest that the problematic that engages Dickens here—the possibility that every man is an instance of the same self-managing entity—was available as a formulation because the social domain had begun to be reconceptualized as a collection of responsible, disciplined individuals, not as an aggregate that should be policed by the government. The reconceptualization of the social domain—its dissolution into similar, self-regulating individuals—was partly the effect of the popularity of individualizing technologies like the serial novel; partly, it was the outcome of the government promotion of self-help programs like savings banks, friendly societies, and insurance schemes; and partly, this individualization was the result of the creation, through legislation like the Public Health Act, of a new realm of interests, centered on laborers' "standard of living," most generally conceived, instead of on political reform or economic equity more narrowly conceived.[50] Whatever its causes, by 1860, the idea that individuals were alike in being responsible (economic and moral) agents was being advanced as a substitute for the tutelary role that the metaphor of the social body had initially assigned to the state. "In plain terms," Robert Chambers announced in 1861, "on every man, no matter what his position, is imposed *Individual Responsibility. . . .* from the power of universal self-management and self-reliance . . . must ever spring the chief glory of a state."[51]

The possibility that every individual is an instance of the same, self-managing entity, then, was being promoted by members of the influential National Association for the Promotion of the Social Sciences as a formulation that could make government intervention even in social affairs seem unnecessary (if always a possibility). To Dickens, the fact that every individual might be an instance of the same was *not* a matter for celebration. In order to understand why, it is helpful to detour briefly through the writing of Thomas Chalmers. In 1832, Chalmers, the Scotsman who was arguably the most famous clergyman of the first half of the nineteenth century, turned his attention to political economy. It seemed reasonable for him to do so, because, as we have seen, in the 1830s the economic was still not completely disaggregated from adjacent domains; in particular, and despite the efforts of Ricardo, the economic domain was still enmeshed in the theological domain, so that bankruptcy, for example, could still be read as the sign of divine punishment. By the late 1850s, this was no longer true—a fact that was signaled by the demise of Chalmers's brand of Christian economics and by the passage of the limited liability legislation in 1855–56. As Boyd Hilton has argued, limited liability had many meanings as well as far-reaching material effects.[52] One of its most important effects, from the perspective of the disaggregation of domains, was that the legislation severed the link between business failure and personal ruin. This legislation, in other words, stripped the economic domain of its theological overtones, for it meant that because company failures would not necessarily spell bankruptcy for investors who had overreached themselves, these failures could not be read as divine retribution.[53]

The scathing portrait of Mrs. Clennam in *Little Dorrit* is evidence enough of Dickens's distaste for the evangelical bookkeeping of the soul associated with Thomas Chalmers. Even though Dickens despised Chalmers's "flogging theology,"[54] however, he shared with the Scottish divine both a distrust of central government (caricatured in the incompetent Circumlocution Office) and the suspicion that individual men were insufficiently moral to regulate themselves. Dickens sided with Chalmers, then, in arguing that British men required some mechanism for regulating morality; he just did not believe that the economic domain provided this mechanism, in the form of retributive bankruptcies or anything else. Instead, Dickens offers an idealized version of femininity, firmly located in the domain of the social, to shore up both individual morality and masculinity in particular.

By 1863, when Dickens began *Our Mutual Friend,* his position was already somewhat anachronistic. Not only was his defense of masculinity grounded on a definition of femininity whose place within the traditional patriarchal order was being challenged by the claim of middle-class women to be responsible individuals too, but his skepticism about the ability of the market individual to discipline him- (and sometimes her-) self was increasingly a minority concern. When Robert Lowe introduced the limited liability legislation into Commons, for example, he chastised nay-sayers for their unwarranted pessimism: "You must deal on the basis of confidence," he urged fellow lawmakers.

"Fraud and wickedness are not to be presumed in individuals."[55] Lowe's optimism, which was corroborated by the passage of the legislation, was one sign that the aggregate—and problematic—social body had begun to be dissolved into its constitutive members. As early as 1849, the economist John Hill Burton had warned against the metaphors by which the poor were conventionally designated. "Calling them 'the mass of the people,' the 'great body of the people,' 'the bulk of society'—indicate[s] an inert body, not acting from within," Burton wrote. Burton thought that social analysts should "throw light into this dark mass, [so] that it may be able to shake off the despotism of its ignorance"[56] By 1860, Sir James Emerson Tennent announced to the SSA that this "mass" had been sufficiently enlightened to be treated as something other than a body: members of what had once seemed a social body now appear as disciplinary individuals capable of governing themselves in a society that is perfectly "free." In this society, Tennent proclaimed,

> the condition of the people and all that affects their individual happiness and social progress are more directly dependent on their own conduct than on any policy of the rulers, however enlightened. Where industry has been rendered free, life and property safe, taxation moderate, and public expenditure judicious, the utmost has been done that it is within the power of Government to achieve for those that work. It then rests with the labouring classes, by availing themselves of these advantages, to contribute to their own happiness;—and no Government, however liberal, can counteract the consequences of idleness and vice, nor avert the amount of misery which is the unfailing result of ignorance and error.[57]

The image of this "free" society constitutes the terminus of the essays in this book. As Tennent's comment suggests, this society was "free" in the sense that government interfered with the economic not at all and with the social as little as possible. It was "free," in other words, in the sense that its members constituted individualized instances of a single, self-regulating subject, whose life was subdivided among the domains that claimed autonomy but appeared to be alike. The paradoxes and contradictions of this "liberal" society were numerous. As the essays in this volume suggest, they were forged in the institutions, legislation, and imaginative texts that gave the "social body" a local habitation and a name.

Two

THE PRODUCTION OF ABSTRACT SPACE

Without the concepts of space and its production,
the framework of power (whether as reality or concept)
simply cannot achieve concreteness.[1]

The foundational assertion of this essay is that modern industrial capitalism was characterized by a new organization of space and of bodies in space. The formation of the culture attendant upon modern capitalism therefore entailed the naturalization of these spatial arrangements as well as the mystification of the "framework of power" inherent in—and enforced by—the new organization of space. The most symptomatic instantiation of this new form of space, the factory, has long been the object of critical analysis.[2] For all our knowledge about the factory system, however, the distinctively modern form of abstraction that this system embodied remains relatively unexplored. As the elusive heart of the epistemology associated with modernity, this form of abstraction—and its historical production as abstract space—facilitated the disaggregation of conceptual and spatial domains: the nineteenth-century institutionalization of separate social sciences (economics, anthropology, sociology) owes as much to the naturalization of abstract space as does the physical reordering of London (the building of the Embankment, the laying of surface and underground rails, the hygienic reform of urban neighborhoods like St. Giles).

The first purpose of this essay is to explore this modern form of abstraction, its production in theoretical treatises and homely metaphors,

I would like to thank Kirstie McClure for her effort to help me salvage an earlier version of this essay. A still earlier version was written for a conference, held at the University of Arizona in Tucson, entitled "Making Worlds: Metaphor and Materiality in the Production of Feminist Texts." I would like to thank the conference organizers for their support.

and its maintenance through specific systems of administration and oversight. Its second purpose is to suggest some of the reasons why the modern form of abstraction epitomized in the factory system failed to penetrate all segments of English society in the nineteenth century. If the modern form of abstraction *had* been successfully implemented, as some of its most visionary champions dreamed it could be, we would now live in the totalized field of power some late twentieth-century commentators seem to experience.[3] I contend that power has never assumed such a totalized form and that the "framework" through which modern power was institutionalized was supported as much by the local circumstances in which abstraction was applied as by the theories with which it was perfected. These local circumstances affected the production of abstract space not merely because specific circumstances posed special problems, but also because in some circumstances, rationalities that pertained to earlier social forms tended to persist and in some cases actually impeded the implementation of abstraction.[4]

In keeping with the nature of my subject, I have organized this essay into four sections, the analytic biases of which tend from the relatively more to the relatively less abstract. The first section offers a general description of the ideal of abstract space and some preliminary observations about the analytic process by which it was produced between the sixteenth and the nineteenth centuries in the West. In section 2 I suggest that the production of abstract space entailed a new, liberal mode of administration as well as a new arrangement of bodies in space. Adam Smith is a crucial spokesperson for the kind of (self-) government we associate with liberal society, for Smith not only defended laissez-faire but also argued that some segments of the population required the kind of oversight that others did not need. I conclude this section with a brief discussion of some of the ways that self-government was supplemented in the early nineteenth century, as implicit acknowledgements that liberal government could not be universally applied.

Section 3 focuses on two of the metaphors by which defenders of abstraction represented the society that was being (re)formed in early nineteenth-century Britain. While these metaphors, which depicted society as a machine and as a body, were not the only images used to characterize modern society, they assumed particular prominence because they carried with them assumptions about how to govern that were compatible with liberal theories of society. As early nineteenth-century champions of these two metaphors, Charles Babbage and Thomas Southwood Smith provide compelling accounts of the contributions of each metaphor to the realization of abstract space.

Even as the images of the machine and the social body contributed to the production and administration of abstract space, however, each figure also revealed some of the problems inherent in the assumption that abstract space was essentially self-governing. These limitations were partly a function of irrationalities or inconsistencies implicit in the images themselves and partly the unanticipated effects of superimposing a liberal mode of government onto older assumptions about social relations. Thus, for different reasons, the images of the machine and the social body were both used to sanction women's participation in social reform, *even though,* according to scripture and conventional wisdom, women were by nature unsuited to such work. In the final section of this essay, I explore the unintended consequences of the metaphorical defense of abstract space by examining in some detail Ellen Ranyard's adaptation of the figures of the machine and the body in her theory of the "missing link." To a certain extent, in appropriating and adapting these images to authorize women's participation in the social domain, Ranyard undermined the tendencies of abstract space, for her emphasis on women's bodies and on founding knowledge on personal experience ran counter to dematerialization and generalization, both of which were central to the logic of modern, spatialized abstraction.

I

Henri Lefebvre's concept of "(social) space" is difficult to grasp because it drifts, on the one side, toward physical space as defined by nature and, on the other, toward ideas about space as defined by philosophers.[5] This conceptual difficulty is compounded when one's object of analysis is the distinctively modern form of "(social) space" that Lefebvre calls "abstract" space, because one of the characteristics of abstract space is its ontological dependence on representation, which functions to obscure its own material conditions of possibility: history, nature, and technology. Within abstract space, Lefebvre explains, "lived experience is crushed, vanquished by what is 'conceived of.' History is experienced as nostalgia, and nature as regret—as a horizon fast disappearing behind us."[6]

Given the importance of representation for modern "(social) space," it seems that the best way to understand its production might be to identify the representational assumptions by which key conceptual abstractions—for example, the idea that space itself is abstract or empty—acquired sufficient authority to influence the treatment of physical spaces and human relations. Historically, these representational assumptions are all associated with the modern scientific method. As it was formalized in the seventeenth century by Robert Boyle and

René Descartes among others, the scientific method was governed by three assumptions about the relationships among phenomena, representation, and knowledge: (1) complex phenomena or problems should be approached through *analysis,* which consists of reducing observed complexities into simpler elements or problems; (2) solutions to complex problems should then be reached through *synthesis,* which recombines the results of analysis into a new, comprehensible (mental) whole; and (3) these methods are independent of their subject matter and can therefore be applied to any phenomenon, including social problems.[7] During the late seventeenth century and for much of the eighteenth, analysts of society as different in their philosophies as Thomas Hobbes, William Petty, Adam Smith, and Jeremy Bentham all elaborated the relationship between this analytic method (which is also a mode of representation) and the emergent problems of civil society.

A proper analysis of the institutions and protocols by which the scientific method acquired sufficient authority to challenge scholasticism and theological tenets about innate ideas lies beyond the scope of this essay.[8] I will return in a moment to the all-important subject of *consensus,* for the homogenization of public opinion was critical both to the authorization of science and to the effective administration of abstract space in the nineteenth century. For now, however, it is important to identify some of the effects produced by transferring the epistemological assumptions associated with the scientific method from discussions of the natural world to debates about social relations. These effects, which were simultaneously symbolic and material, can best be understood by their relationship to two corollaries of modern abstraction: geometry and the peculiar form of abstraction variously designated the *commodity, reification,* and the *fetish.*[9]

René Descartes's influential arguments about scientific method drew heavily upon geometry, the form of mathematics long considered successful in producing compelling truths about the physical world.[10] As both a means of measuring physical distances and a source for visual models of the world, Euclidean geometry could be considered as either mimetic *or* abstract.[11] Whether mimetic or abstract, geometric models assumed that space was continuous and uniform in all directions (isotropic) and that it was therefore uniformly subject to mathematical laws. In the late seventeenth century, Sir Isaac Newton recast the notion of isotropic space as absolute space, which, in addition to its mathematical regularity, was held to be independent of all time, matter, and motion.[12]

When Thomas Hobbes applied geometrical principles to the state in his *Leviathan* (1651), he transported elements of Euclidean geometry into (what would become) social-scientific knowledge. For my purposes, the most critical components of Hobbes's geometrical formalism were its tendency to render every subject of the state functionally equivalent and its equation of value with quantity.[13] The notion of functional equivalence—which has also been called the theory of *interchangeable participants, analytic equality,* and *species equality*[14]—was quickly taken up by apologists for trade like Sir Josiah Child.[15] As a repudiation of the early-modern politico theological theory of God-given "stations" or "orders," the idea of functional equivalence helped underwrite the new economic arrangements that facilitated both social mobility and capital accumulation in the early eighteenth century. As the theoretical underpinning of Adam Smith's *homo economicus,* functional equivalence also became a cornerstone of political economy, the new eighteenth-century science of wealth.[16]

Hobbes's assertion that individuals are functional equivalents within the state was closely tied to the notion that value is a function of quantity, which can be signified by another sign of equivalence—money. "The *Value,* or WORTH of a man, is as of all other things, his Price; that is to say, as much as would be given for the use of his Power; and therefore it is not absolute; but a thing dependant on the need and judgement of another."[17] William Petty elaborated this assertion in 1665, when he set out to calculate the monetary value of "the People" of England in an attempt to convince Charles II to rationalize tax collection.[18] Petty developed the science of political arithmetic in order to enumerate what was otherwise unmeasurable. To reach a meaningful figure, Petty calculated the average worth of each individual by subdividing the product of the estimated total population and the per diem wage; then he estimated the number and value of the individuals lost to the plague, and applied these figures to the expenditures he estimated the crown would need. In making these complex calculations, Petty implicitly argued that national productivity was more important than individual well-being, that aggregates were more telling than individual case histories, and that all individuals counted (only) in so far as they were productive members of society.[19]

From the geometric lineage of early social analysis, we can identify one set of features that eventually came to characterize abstract space. Like Hobbes's image of the individual, modern space was conceptualized as isotropic (as everywhere the same) and as reducible (or already reduced) to a formal (that is, empty) schema or grid. Partly as a consequence, abstract space was symbolically and materially associated with homologies: seriality; repetitious actions; reproducible products; interchangeable places, behaviors, and activities. Like the geometry that so influenced Hobbes, abstract space was also dominated by visuality, the technical analogue of which was the camera obscura.[20] Visuality dominated abstract space in at least two senses: (1) because "realization" tended to be associated with literal or imaginative seeing, plans or diagrams typically preceded the inauguration of such projects as the laying of modern streets; and (2) because the visible, finished product tended to be the center of attention, this concrete realization of an imaginary plan tended to obscure both the social labor by which this plan was realized and the repetitiousness that characterized all the implementations of the originary plan.[21]

I have already noted that geometric figures are both mimetic (their angles correspond to those of actual entities) and abstract (they embody mathematical formulas). The double nature of geometric forms points to another feature of modern space: it was inseparable from the peculiar form of abstraction whose cognate manifestations have been called *commodification, reification,* and *fetishization.* This characteristically modern form of abstraction was produced not by classical deduction or by simple induction but by a double gesture that moved back and forth between thought and practice. In this double gesture, which was both derived from real phenomena and productive of real effects, some feature was extracted from observations of material things, isolated from its context, and then invested with a life of its own—a life so vivid that it dwarfed the complexity of the phenomenon from which it was derived.

In his analysis of this modern form of abstraction, Marx pointed out that such vivified concepts were inextricably bound up with the modern reorganization of material space. The commodification of "labor," for example, and the reification of "production" were simultaneously facilitated (as ideas) and actualized (as practices) by spatial arrangements that divided and isolated the complex functions of laboring individuals.[22] As it was manifested in such spatially and functionally divided sites as the factory, moreover, the modern form of abstraction revealed its own inherent logic: the priority of product over process; the cultivation of efficiency, functional specificity, and thrift; and the maximization of profits through the production of surplus value. The rational or functional arrangements of space and of bodies in space appeared simply as the means toward these ends, but these arrangements also created new modes of producing more of the valuable ends with which they were associated.[23] "Though a *product* to be used," Lefebvre explains, abstract space is also "*a means of production;* networks of exchange and flows of raw materials and energy fashion space and are determined by it. Thus this means of production, produced as such, cannot be separated either from the productive forces, including technology and knowledge, or from the social division of labour which shapes it, or from the state and the superstructures of society. . . . As it develops, then, the concept of social space . . . infiltrates, even invades, the concept of production, becoming part—perhaps the essential part—of its content."[24]

Three further corollaries of modern abstraction need to be noted. First, the homogeneity of abstract space, which was dramatized in the repetitiousness of rationally divided labor, contributed to the banishment of time from modern life.[25] Second, and despite its dependence on the labor of literal bodies, modern abstraction tended to deemphasize or even eliminate bodies as objects of analysis and as the authoritative basis of personal experience.[26] Third, modern abstraction tended to produce the kind of normative thinking that Foucault associates with "disciplinary power."[27] Against an imaginary geometric grid, which was conceptually imposed upon people and behaviors as well as space, productivity became the measure of value, repetition made time stand still, bodies disappeared into labor power, and norms began to dictate the criteria by which individuals were evaluated.

II

The modern system of abstraction, which I have been describing abstractly (and as if fully realized), was produced in relation to a complex set of problems, which were simultaneously economic, political, and administrative. These problems arose from developments long underway in early modern Europe: the (uneven) prosperity derived from trading expeditions to the New World; the institutionalization of financial arrangements developed in part to underwrite (or manage) these colonial enterprises; the splintering of the Catholic Church and the reformulation of ecclesiastical power; the emergence, in England in particular, of a political body capable of rivaling the monarch's power; and the ramification of civil society as a set of institutions that supported the state but were not directly controlled by the crown. Because of their massive impact on everyday life and matters of state, these developments mandated a reformulation of the relationship between the modern state and the individuals who were its subjects. As Foucault has suggested in his late work on governmentality, these developments challenged state officials to discover ways to integrate concrete aspects of individuals' lives into the pursuit of the state's objectives, which can be roughly defined as maintaining security and increasing prosperity.[28]

By the early eighteenth century, British political theorists had begun to formulate a mode of governing that was (supposedly) capable of enhancing both the "happiness" of individuals and the prosperity—and therefore the security—of the state. We associate this mode of governing with modern liberal society, because it assumed that semi-autonomous realms like the economy or the population would govern themselves as long as society was organized to conform to specific natural laws. As this formulation suggests, the political theorists who defended this form of government tended to model their analysis on those of natural philosophers (scientists); that is, they claimed to have discovered natural laws whose operations were as regular as the force of gravity. If the political theorists were right—if society was as lawful as the natural world— then monarchs should not interfere in realms like the economy, because they could not possibly know enough to make constructive decisions. To enable society to achieve its natural state, governments should simply remove restrictive legislation and inculcate habits of self-government in individuals, not try to enforce discipline from above. In support of this liberal mode of government, David Hume argued that England's modern commercial society constituted a more-or-less harmonious whole dominated by sympathy, sociability, and civility; this society, Hume suggested, required a government that simply marshaled and directed public opinion, that restrained "enthusiasm" and "faction" by the promotion of rational and civil "conversation."[29]

Like the methodological innovations of early-modern scientists, such political justifications of liberalism contributed directly to the production of abstract space. At the same time, the institutionalization of these theories began to reveal the inconsistencies (or irrationalities) within modern abstraction. During the eighteenth century, for example, we see both the institutionalization of measures that enabled members of the middling ranks to enrich themselves, and the erection of purpose-built workhouses designed to extract labor from the unemployed poor. Whereas the former (regularized systems of banking and credit, for example, as well as improved roads and canals) assumed that the efforts of (some) individuals automatically benefitted society, the latter implied that (other) individuals would not work if they were not forced. In other words, whereas liberal measures designed to incite self-government might suffice for one segment of the population, other segments seemed to require the coercion that properly belonged to an earlier time.

Adam Smith's contribution to the theory of liberal government is particularly important, because it provided both an explanation of why (some) individuals naturally benefitted society and an acknowledgement that the prosperity that strengthened the state also debased some segments of the population. Initially, Smith advocated the state's withdrawal from civil affairs by arguing that all individuals were governed by natural laws, which Smith claimed to discover by observing himself. If left alone, Smith asserted, individuals would exercise virtue because they naturally sought social approval and because they naturally sympathized with others like themselves. As he developed this argument in his *Theory of Moral Sentiments* (1759), Smith suggested that each individual is actually a miniature of the larger self-governing society, for each individual is not one, but two.

> When I endeavour to examine my own conduct, when I endeavour to pass sentence upon it, and either to approve or condemn it, it is evident that, in all such cases, I divide myself, as it were, into two persons; and that I, the examiner and judge, represent a different character from that other I, the person whose conduct is examined into and judged of. The first is the spectator, whose sentiments with regard to my own conduct I endeavour to enter into, by placing myself in his situation, and by considering how it would appear to me, when seen from that particular point of view. The second is the agent, the person whom I properly call myself, and of whose conduct, under the character of a spectator, I was endeavouring to form some opinion.[30]

According to Smith, the human capacity for self-government both derived from and underwrote the sociality of human nature. When Smith reformulated this universal sociality as universal self-interest in *The Wealth of Nations,* he simply substituted another (more Hobbesian) form of equivalence for the moral interchangeability implied by this theory of serial (and self-governing) subjectivity.[31] The universal propensity to "truck, barter, and exchange one thing for another" provided a second rationale for liberal government, for it linked the universal tendency to seek approval to the desire to seek socially constructive wealth.

As a contribution to the elaboration of abstract space, Smith's work also helps explain the relationship between liberal government and visuality. The passage I have just quoted suggests that Smith's morality was founded on specular relations: he assumed that imaginative identification was modeled on seeing and that virtue depended upon (literally or imaginatively) being seen. The importance that Smith attributed to seeing, in fact, led him to acknowledge that modern society prohibited some individuals from realizing the state of natural virtue even as it facilitated this for others. Because the prosperity of modern society depended upon the proliferation of large towns, Smith admits, some individuals were bound to disappear from the moralizing gaze of others. "Sunk in obscurity and darkness," the poor city dweller fails to develop the specular morality that Smith considered the essence of human nature. "His conduct is observed and attended to by nobody, and he is therefore very likely to neglect it himself, and to abandon himself to every sort of low prodigality and vice."[32]

Smith's elaboration of the role that visuality played in modern liberal government revised older, theological arguments that God simply assigns some individuals the tasks of hewing wood and drawing water. For Smith, social inequality was inevitable, but he considered it a side-effect of civilization, not a repetition of the great chain of being. For Smith, in fact, the inequity that cities exacerbated was rooted in the principle that enabled prosperity (and therefore civilization) to grow: the division of labor. At the same time that it increased the wealth of some individuals (and the nation as a whole), the division of labor also rendered the worker as "stupid and as ignorant as it is possible for a human creature to become."[33] In Smith's revision of theological explanations, in other words, all individuals (men) were theoretically capable of self-government because they were theoretically able to work. In practice, however, the very division of work that enabled the nation to prosper under a liberal government also kept the poor man from becoming a self-governing individual. In order to counteract the dehumanizing effects of modern society, Smith argued that the working poor must be treated differently from those individuals capable of specular morality: because their literal bodies could no longer be seen, the former had to be conceptualized as an aggregate; because they could not govern themselves, they had to be governed from above.

The complexities of Smith's analysis underscore some of the paradoxes written into the modern form of abstraction, and into abstract space more specifically. These paradoxes center on Smith's treatment of the material body, and in this example they carry what we would call class implications.[34] When Smith imagines working men disappearing into cities or into the more specialized operations of mechanized labor, he imagines them as simultaneously more material (in the sense of being embodied, not imaginative, creatures) and more amenable to aggregation (in the sense of being less individualized or particularized). At the same time, however, Smith was abstracting all social relations and all individuals—even, or especially, the well-to-do. Social relations became abstract in the sense that Smith reduced them all to versions of measurable exchange, and individuals became abstract in the sense that he represented "everyone" as an instance of the same abstract entity, a representative of "human nature" that wants only to truck, barter, and exchange.

Smith's uneven and paradoxical application of abstraction to the problems of government and wealth is obviously related to the geometric analytic I have associated with Hobbes and to the scientific method more generally. Smith thought he was creating a science of wealth, after all, and he argued that this science had both descriptive and predictive validity. The fact that this "science" (political economy) offered a new explanation for existing social inequities only enhanced its cultural authority. The fact that these inequities seemed to be an inevitable aspect of national progress, paradoxically, seemed to draw the working poor into the emergent community of the nation at the same time that it set them apart. According to Smith, the living conditions of "the great body of the people" would improve along with the wealth of the nation, but in order to insure that the poor would contribute to this wealth (and therefore to their own improvement), they had to be treated differently: their education and their morality had to be overseen; their neighborhoods and their bodies had to be inspected.[35]

During the next half century, this logic governed the implementation of abstraction and the production of abstract space. Even though it was occasionally reinforced by coercive legislation like the Six Acts of 1819, the government of rich and poor alike was generally exercised in the service of inciting consensus, so as to make of the nation a single, homogeneous whole. Because morality was conceptualized within a problematic of visuality, however, and because the poor were considered to be different from, as well as a part of, the national whole, surveillance and ocular penetration of poor neighborhoods were generally considered to be as critical to the inculcation of virtue as was the cultivation of taste.[36] Indeed, surveillance and the cultivation of taste were assumed by many to be facets of the same project of incorporating the poor into the nation. Such projects as the home-visiting scheme implemented in Scotland by Thomas Chalmers, for example, were specifically designed to correct the "low and grovelling taste" of the poor by "inducing" in them habits that would make them more like their well-to-do neighbors. We can see in Chalmers's instructions to the clergy the extent to which values associated with modern abstraction and economic rationality had begun to permeate moralizing projects by the second decade of the century. Chalmers commanded the clergy "to go forth among the people; and there to superinduce the principles of an efficient morality . . . to work a transformation of taste and of character . . . to deliver lessons, which, of themselves, will induce a habit of thoughtfulness, that must insensibly pervade the whole system of man's desires and his doings . . . infusing into every practical movement, along with the elements of passion and interest, the elements of duty, and of wisdom, and of self-estimation."[37]

If inducing "efficient morality" in the poor constituted one mode of liberal government, then implementing a scientifically precise scheme of efficient education constituted another. In theory at least, both modes of administration were designed to acknowledge—but also to overcome—the inequities associated with modern society. To the extent that they aspired to make all segments of the population functional equivalents (self-governing individuals), that is, plans for moralizing poor adults and educating poor children sought to eliminate what could be seen as the irrationalities of modern society—which were most painfully felt as unnecessary expenditures of public funds. We see this tendency toward a rationality that was both scientific and economic in the pedagogical program that James Phillips Kay outlined for the workhouse poor in 1838. Kay's immediate goal was to increase pedagogic efficiency; to that end, he suggested classifying students (by age, sex, and future occupation), so that children could receive instruction calibrated to their needs.[38] Because the number of children in any single workhouse was insufficient for such classification, Kay suggested combining unions to support a single, purpose-built school.[39] Kay also recommended that teachers keep precise accounts to measure the productivity of each child and that any profits obtained from school gardens be returned to the school; the former was intended to encourage hard work, the latter to discourage a child's aspiration beyond the station designated by the school's guardian (p. 24).

In Kay's plan, the problem of the poor's invisibility was solved by the application of accounting: written records made virtue visible as they rendered labor quantifiable and diligence a matter for certification.[40] The problem of government was solved by incarceration: poor children were to be confined until they (or their parents) could work. The problem of inequity was solved by habituating the poor to what Kay presented as necessity. In the workhouse, children were offered this (as) freedom: an education that "inculcate[s] the great practical lesson for those whose sole dependence for their living is on the labour of their hands, by early habituating them to patient and skilful industry" (p. 23).

The use of ocular inspection, quantification, and calculation to administer liberal government to the poor reached its logical extreme in Edwin Chadwick's *Sanitary Report* of 1842. The *Sanitary Report,* which summarized the outcome of hundreds of firsthand inspections of thousands of poor neighborhoods and homes, also signaled the extent to which the scientific method and economic rationality had come to dominate social analysis by the 1840s. The survey, the scale of which was previously impossible (and quite possibly unimaginable), deployed the administrative apparatus institutionalized by the New Poor Law of 1834 to produce detailed accounts of facts as various as the insalubrity of individual neighborhoods, the general tendency of poor lodging houses to breed crime, and both the individual daily average and the yearly aggregate productions of excrement.[41] All these calculations were intended to make the least liberal institution of the British state—the New Poor Law—more efficient and thus less costly. Because illness among the poor undermined their ability to work, Chadwick declared that insanitary living conditions increased poor rates to unnatural levels. According to this logic, more government intervention in the realm of public health would free the economy to govern itself, just as more government intervention in the area of poor relief was (supposedly) freeing "labor" to go where it could find work. In order to promote liberal government, then, Chadwick repeated the paradoxes we saw in Smith's work: he designated the poor a distinct population (whose difference could be precisely quantified), and he treated this population as simultaneously more material (in the sense of being embodied) and more amenable to aggregation (in the sense of only counting when taken en masse).

Even though Chadwick's descriptions focused more relentlessly on the details of bodily processes than had any previous government report, these descriptions tended to obliterate specific poor individuals in the service of specifying quantifiable bodily products. The critical products that interested Chadwick were labor and waste; in the overall social calculus he recommended, the object of government was to increase the former by efficiently eliminating or redistributing the latter. In theory at least, this would have made various segments of the population more like each other by reducing the discrepancy between the "comparative chances of life in different classes of the community" (chapter 4). This, in turn, would theoretically have reduced poor rates, which would have decreased the need for further government interference. Chadwick's reification of "life," not incidentally, linked abstraction back to space, for it allowed him both to correlate longevity to particular neighborhoods and to blur the boundary between individual people and the spaces they occupied.[42]

III

As even this brief discussion of the *Sanitary Report* should suggest, Chadwick's plan for improving the sanitary conditions, and hence the productivity, of Britain's working poor cast the city (and society more generally) as a giant body that required a physician's care. The image of the social body was one of the two principle images used to depict society in the 1830s. The other was the figure of the social machine. Even when these metaphors remained implicit, they informed the way that analysts approached new urban problems, the solutions they recommended, and, more often than not, the rationales they offered for defending—or defending against—government intervention. In this section I will discuss a proponent of each of these metaphors in order to suggest how each figure contributed to the production (and delimitation) of abstract space.

In 1832, Charles Babbage, the mathematician and inventor of the difference engine, published his celebration of modern industry, *On the Economy of Machinery and Manufactures.* According to Babbage, the popularity of this book reflected the curiosity with which his contemporaries viewed "the pursuits and interests of that portion of the people which has recently acquired so large an accession of political influence."[43] The political influence of manufacturers, Babbage suggested, was largely a function of the success with which they governed their own affairs; hence their political influence could be understood by examining how they governed factories. Indeed, Babbage suggested that the well-run factory—or the efficient machine, for that matter—could serve as a paradigm for an efficient, productive society.[44]

In Babbage's account, the factory system and the machine epitomized systems in which all working parts were subordinated to the productivity of the whole, discipline triumphed over disorder, and regular procedures compensated for individual failings, inattention, and variations in strength or skill. As concrete embodiments of the division of labor, the well-run factory and the well-made machine simplified the process of production; concern for the latter, moreover, enabled the former to expand. In an effort to keep their machinery running efficiently, in other words, manufacturers tended to increase their factories' working hours, and hence the number of workers they employed. As size increased, it generated an additional benefit: an increase in the "value of character," which resulted from the premium the manufacturer placed upon his reputation. Eventually, the "high character" of a large manufacturer could even supplement his capital investment; the factory's good name, Babbage explained, "supplies the place of an additional portion of capital; and the merchant . . . is saved from the expense of verification [of the quality of manufactured goods], by knowing that the loss . . . of the manufacturer's character, would be attended with greater injury to himself than any profit upon a single transaction could compensate" (p. 157).

The association between character and the investment represented by an efficient and honest factory elaborates a point Babbage made more concisely elsewhere: as "beautiful contrivances," well-run factories and productive machines epitomized moral agency, for their uniform and steady operations counteracted the dishonesty or carelessness of individual workmen (p. 54). In fact, far from reducing human beings to "hands," as some critics charged, machines could even transform individuals who were otherwise incomplete—who lacked hands, for example—into complete (that is, productive) members of society. Thus, Mr. Brunel's "fertile invention" enabled armless and legless operators to make shoes with the aid of mechanical prostheses (p. 15). Far from alienating workers from their masters, as critics also charged, the efficient administration of efficient machinery—a scheme that Babbage designated the "New System of Manufacturing"—would eventually convert workmen and capitalists into two parts of a single entity. In this "beautiful" system, "the workmen and the capitalist would so shade into each other . . . that . . . the only combination that would exist would be a more powerful union *between* both parties to overcome their common difficulties" (p. 258).

Ideally, then, the well-run factory would need no more administrative meddling than did the efficient machine, which corrected itself by means of internal "regulators" and "governors" (p. 27). As for the role of state government in industrial management, Babbage was adamant: "*Government ought to interfere as little as possible between workmen and their employers,*" he insisted (p. 363). In the examples he cites, however, the system does not seem quite as rational, fair, or self-sufficient as he suggested it should be. Thus, for example, the same expansion of factories that enhanced the "value of character" for the large capitalist also eliminated the jobs of an entire "class of middle-men [who were] formally interposed between the maker and the merchant" to verify the quality of piecework (p. 157). Beyond eliminating some jobs, Babbage's system also failed to register inequities that already existed. The table by which Babbage calculated the "Price of making each Part of a single Pin, in Millionths of a penny" led him to measure the skill of each worker by the wages he or she received per day. This circular reasoning, however, which equated wages received with the value of a skill, overlooked the fact—which his table also explicitly recorded—that men consistently received higher wages than women for performing the same task (p. 176).[45]

According to his stated goal of maximizing productivity while minimizing cost, these miscellaneous effects constituted an inefficient use of resources and an irrational application of funds. The self-correcting self-sufficiency of Babbage's system was also impeded by persistent attachments to preferences that the overall aim of efficiency should have rendered obsolete. In his discussion of bookmaking, for example, Babbage calculated the charge an author had to pay for corrections and alterations made to text already set in type. The high cost of these changes made it clear that "if the author study economy, he should make the whole of his corrections in the manuscript." In practice, however, this foresight rarely triumphed, because, Babbage admitted, "there are few subjects, upon which an author does not find he can add some details or explanation, when he sees his views in print." Even his own volume, Babbage explained, which was set in "slips" in hopes of holding revision charges to a minimum, cost more than it might have: "the corrections have been unusually large and the revises frequent" (pp. 207–8). Workers in factories might also resist the "New System of Manufacturing," Babbage acknowledged, because their preference for receiving daily wages sufficient to supply the day's food could obscure the fact that—in the long run and overall—the benefit of the workers (taken as a whole) was undeniably linked to the profits the owner enjoyed (pp. 257–58).

The image of the social body offered its own advantages and shortcomings. In general, the image produced a more dynamic picture of the relationship between organisms and their physical environment than did the image of the machine. As employed by pioneers of the sanitary movement, like Chadwick and reform-minded medical men, the image of the social body tended to differentiate between the experts who analyzed society and the poor objects of their analysis; however, when it was invoked by radicals like Robert Owen or Frederick Engels, it could also promote sympathetic identification between reformers and the poor. Like the metaphor of the machine, the image of the social body could support a politics of laissez-faire, because contemporary medical theories tended to represent the organism as naturally healthy. In general, however, the image of the social body tended to be used to defend some form of government-sponsored medical intervention, because, especially in densely occupied poor neighborhoods, nature was obviously impeded by bad air, poor sanitation, and inadequate supplies of fresh water. The image of the social body did provide a model for intervention and cure, then, but it could not specify who should have the final say in social reform, much less what form interventions should assume.[46]

Although his achievements have been dwarfed by those of Chadwick, Thomas Southwood Smith has been called the "intellectual founder of the sanitary movement" by at least one modern historian.[47] A student of the influential W. P. Alison at the University of Edinburgh, Smith was also a Unitarian minister and, after 1817, a participant in Bentham's circle in London. He served as physician to the Fever Hospital and the Eastern Dispensary, and published the influential *Treatise on Fever* in 1830 and the even more successful *Philosophy of Health* in 1835. In 1824, Smith had presided over the public dissection of Bentham's body; that same year he defended easing restrictions on the supply of corpses to medical schools in an article published in the *Westminster Review*.[48]

The heart of Smith's physiology, and therefore the heart of his understanding of society, was the idea that living organisms were inextricably bound up with their physical environments. On the one hand, therefore, Smith thought that people fell ill because they breathed fetid air in waste-saturated, overcrowded neighborhoods. On the other hand, his miasmatic theory of disease also implied that legislators could help foster health by passing sanitary measures. Smith called the dynamic that connected organisms to the environment "vital process." His theory of vital process essentially decomposed individual human bodies into their constitutive "particles," then recomposed a social body that contains the particles that enter and leave all living creatures. "Every moment old particles are carried out of the system," Smith explains; "every moment new particles are introduced into it. The matter of which the body is composed is thus in a state of constant flux."[49]

In modern cities, more often than not, the "new particles" introduced into poor bodies were contaminated, and the "old particles" had nowhere to go. Luckily, the social organism, like the individual body, produced signs, or symptoms, that something was wrong. It was the task of trained observers, especially medical men knowledgeable about sanitary reform, to identify those symptoms for what they were so that government officials could intervene before congested lungs bred epidemic fevers. In the city, signs of disease took the form of clogged drains and overcrowded tenements; these problems also forecast social disorder, because, in an analysis that conflated physical with moral "debility," environmental factors were thought capable of eroding self-discipline and moral rectitude: insalubrious living conditions, in short, could breed prostitution, trade unionism, and revolutionary politics.[50]

As Southwood Smith's contributions to the sanitary movement suggest, the image of the social body did imply a model of administration that allowed for government surveillance and even intervention in the name of prevention and cure. The problem this metaphor posed, for Smith and other medical men, was that it did not justify a medical monopoly in the arena of social reform. Granted, the miasmatic theory of disease called for diagnoses by medical men, but if society's ills were moral as well as physiological, then why weren't clergymen—or even self-proclaimed prophets like Thomas Carlyle—as qualified to take society's pulse as were doctors like Southwood Smith? Granted as well, contemporary social problems required decisive intervention, but why weren't trained bureaucrats more appropriate administrators of new legislation than medical men? For Southwood Smith, this problem arose most painfully when Edwin Chadwick excluded him (and other medical men) from the Board of Public Health. A less public competition for authority—but one that might well have been painful too—occurred in the arena of child care. If the child grew healthy or ill in direct relation to its environment, after all, why weren't mothers more important than doctors? Unable adequately to justify the physician's importance, Smith was reduced in his *Philosophy of Health* to hectoring his female readers and to rhetorically eliminating the mother from his account of the baby's environment.[51]

IV

The images of society as a machine and as a social body were both offered as symbolic representations of a system that was too large and complex to comprehend except through some kind of abstraction, which often took the form of statistical tables.[52] While they conveyed different pictures of the social whole, both images could be used to support variants of the liberal form of (self-) government theorized by Adam Smith. Both implied, in other words, that society *could* be grasped as a whole through the use of numerical representations, that semi-autonomous domains like the economy *were* lawful, and that, even if the knowledge of no individual (including the monarch) could encompass the whole, knowledge of social regularities *could* support policies that would enhance "civilization"—which was measured, most typically, by the quantifiable productivity of Britain as a whole.

Despite the eminent rationality of such views of modern society, almost none of the projects conceptualized in the name of the social machine or the social body was implemented quite as its architects planned. Partly, this was the result of political and religious differences among the would-be reformers, which often overrode their commitments to any theoretical system. Thus, for example, sectarian disagreement about the proper relationship between organized religion and education delayed the national educational act until 1870, and political differences about the relative power of local and central governments led to the abolition of the Board of Public Health in 1854. Partly, the uneven implementation of policies associated with modern abstraction resulted from popular resistance. Chalmers's generally upbeat descriptions of the welcome that home visitors were likely to receive are punctuated with begrudging references to "painful repulses," for example, and the

1834 New Poor Law proved so unpopular that it was effectively impossible to implement throughout England.[53]

The technologies of inspection and regulation associated with abstract space were never completely institutionalized, partly because the assumptions that underwrote them conflicted with the assumptions inherent in existing social relations. Such conflicts produced what looked like contradictions from the perspective of modern abstraction. Viewed from the perspective of more traditional modes of social organization, these conflicts suggested the threat of unnatural changes in a God-given order. The dispute about the meaning of change, which was actually a sign of conflicting rationalities, also signaled the susceptibility of modern society to developments that proponents of neither the old nor the new rationality anticipated. Among these was a development that all but the most radical social analysts deplored: the entry of women into the field of social reform.

To a certain extent, both the image of society as a machine and the figure of the social body authorized an expansion of the informal role that women of the middle ranks had long played in social work. Because the metaphor of the machine implied that analysis should be dispassionate, even mechanical, its proponents tended to efface all distinguishing characteristics of the social analyst—even, by implication at least, the otherwise disqualifying characteristic of sex.[54] Because the metaphor of the social body highlighted intimate bodily processes and championed the feminized epistemology of sympathy, its proponents inadvertently reinforced women's claims to be naturally suited to work that could be seen as an extension of domestic offices. Not unexpectedly, when women adapted these metaphors to sanction their participation in the social domain, they often altered the terms of social work enough to revise the form in which abstraction was institutionalized.

The activities of the most prominent female reformers have attracted considerable attention from feminist scholars.[55] Here I want to focus on a woman whose work is now less well-known than are Barbara Bodichon's efforts to expand female employment or Frances Power Cobbe's campaign against domestic violence. Ellen Ranyard enjoyed a less formal relationship than these prominent feminists did to powerful reform organizations like the National Association for the Promotion of the Social Sciences, which was so supportive of women's issues. Ranyard did position her work self-consciously in relation to a campaign for improvement that was already underway; in taking up a self-proclaimed subsidiary position, however, and in conceptualizing her work as distinctly different from the work of more elaborate organizations,

Ranyard transformed the terms in which at least one version of social work was conducted.

The daughter of a London cement maker, Ellen Henrietta White Ranyard founded the Female Bible Mission in 1857 in Seven Dials, one of London's poorest slums. Ranyard also wrote and published a cheap monthly magazine about the mission, *The Book and its Missions,* and in 1859 she published a popular volume of essays from the magazine under the title of *The Missing Link; or Bible-Women in the Homes.*[56] From its humble beginning, the Female Bible Mission grew into an organization that employed 170 Bible women in 1879, each of whom worked under the direction of an (unpaid) "lady" supervisor.[57]

In order to appreciate the distinct nature of Ranyard's work, it is helpful to place the Female Bible Mission in the context of a similar philanthropic missionary society, the London City Mission. The primary purpose of each society was to "extend the knowledge of the Gospel among the inhabitants of London" (to quote the constitution of the London City Mission[58]). Both societies were nondenominational; both subdivided their regions into manageable districts, which were "penetrated" by one or more agents on a regular basis; both derived some financial support from the powerful British and Foreign Bible Society; both kept extensive records; and both yielded books about the slums that belonged to the genre of social anatomy that James Phillips Kay helped create in 1832.

The two societies differed markedly in many respects, however, beginning with their origins and their modes of administration. The London City Mission, which was founded in 1835, was simply the latest branch of an international enterprise that already had missions in Glasgow, Cork, Limerick, Belfast, Londonderry, Birmingham, Manchester, Paris, and Havre. All of these missions were founded by a single individual, David Nasmith, the scope of whose ambition seems to have rivaled that of the founders of the British and Foreign Bible Society.[59] The first thing Nasmith did in each of his target cities was to draft a board of managers for the fledgling branch. Before authorizing agents to visit impoverished neighborhoods, this board mapped the territory to be visited, and established protocols for choosing missionaries, keeping records, and conducting financial affairs. In London, this scheme proved extraordinarily successful, despite the daunting scope of the problem and some preliminary bickering about the composition of the board. By the end of six months, the London City Mission employed fifteen missionaries and had raised £300 in contributions. By the end of a year, Sir Thomas Fowell Buxton had agreed to serve as the organization's treasurer, the mission's elaborate "machinery of mercy" consisted of forty-

nine agents, and the records showed a balance on hand of £1600 (p. 19).
Shortly thereafter, the increasingly prominent organization suffered a
temporary setback when disputes about denominational imbalance led
to the resignation of the mission's founder and the reorganization of the
board along more strictly proportioned denominational lines.

The Female Bible Mission, by contrast, had a double and much
more adventitious origin. On the one hand, it emanated from the desire
of Ellen Ranyard (here referred to only as a "lady") to continue "promoting the circulation of the word of God," which she had first undertaken in Kent. On the other hand, the mission originated in a request by
an unnamed poor woman (who is referred to as "Marian B.") to be allowed to "testify her thanks to God" for forgiving some unspecified sin.
These independent and initially unrelated impulses were joined through
the offices of one of the missionaries of the district (probably an agent of
the London City Mission), who showed the letter Marian had written
him to Ranyard. Even though Marian offered to distribute Bibles without remuneration, Ranyard arranged for a grant of £5 from the British
and Foreign Bible Society; this was used to pay Marian at the rate of 10
shillings a week for three to five hours of work a day. During the mission's first year, the Bible Society made additional grants, in the sums of
another £5, then £10, £30, and £60; seven more Bible women were
hired, and during the mission's second year, the Bible Society disbursed
£128 to agents for the sale and distribution of what Ranyard estimated
as between 7000 and 8000 Bibles (pp. 236–37).

In addition to being a smaller organization than the London City
Mission and one created ad hoc rather than according to a master plan,
the Female Bible Mission also took some of its protocols from workers
rather than imposing them from above. Thus Marian was allowed to
choose the neighborhood in which she began and, to a certain extent,
she dictated the nature of her own work. The decision to devote the mission's attention "not so much to the decent poor . . . but to the lost and
degraded of [her] own sex" originated in Marian's initial letter, for example, and what emerged as the two-part aim of the mission—"to supply the very poorest of the population with copies of the Holy
Scriptures, and also to improve their temporal condition"—reflected
Marian's perception that spiritual improvement was inseparable from
physical assistance (pp. 12, 275). Indeed, the letter in which Marian offered her services subordinates Bible distribution to the supply of more
material aid: "No matter how degraded she may be," Marian writes, "it
will be enough for [a poor woman] to require my aid—such as cleansing
and washing her, and repairing her garments. If she can, by your means,
obtain admission to a hospital, I will, by frequent visits, take care that

she has a change of linen, and in all ways endeavor to win such erring sister back to virtue and to peace" (p. 13).

Ranyard's account of the mission's first two years reveals that keeping what she insisted was the "chief aim" of the mission—the distribution of Bibles—separate from "domestic mission work" was nearly impossible (p. 201; see also p. 258). In an attempt to enforce this distinction, to make sure that the Bible women spent five hours a day doing Bible work and not simply cleaning or teaching poor women to care for children, Ranyard established two separate funds to pay her agents; she specified in her "Directions to the Bible-Women" that "Bible Work" and "Domestic Mission Work" must be conducted at different times; and she even established a specific "Mission-room" where the latter should be undertaken. In her "Suggestions to Proposed Superintendents," Ranyard reiterated this administrative principle.

> It is very important for the superintendent to understand the due administration of these respective funds. The Bible-woman may be employed for two, three, four, or five days, ONLY IN SELLING BIBLES, according to the needs of the particular district, and for this ONLY the Bible Society can pay her. She must not do any other work at the same time. If the people offer to subscribe for clothing and beds, she will say, "I only do one thing at a time," and "the right thing first. I bring you now the Message from God. I shall be glad also to provide you with clothing, &c., at the lowest prices, and for this you can pay as you do for the Bibles, in small sums weekly; but you must COME TO ME to do this, at a certain hour, in my Mission-room." There would be great evil in mixing the two departments of labor; the Bible Society would never know what they paid for and mistakes would be made in the accounts; while a particular benefit to be gained, by assembling the Women at a given hour at one place, would be lost likewise.[60] (p. 300)

We glimpse in Ranyard's description the tension between the conditions of almost limitless need that Bible women encountered in poor homes and a system that sought to rationalize poor women's efforts to help each other. Ranyard reveals in passing that the Bible Society had mandated this strict division of labor as a condition of its support (p. 258). Her willingness to go along with the Bible Society's rule, however, was consistent with her commitment to administer aid exclusively in cases where individuals were willing to help themselves. Only if the poor women were willing to discipline themselves, to come to a certain place at a certain time, could they demonstrate their willingness to contribute to their own improvement.

Ranyard's commitment to the principle of self-help echoes a truism of the Victorian period, which was repeated in countless schemes designed to promote saving and self-discipline among the poor.[61] In this sense, Ranyard's willingness to enforce the Bible Society's mandate supported both the ideal of consensus, by which modern society was theoretically governed by the 1850s, and the production of abstract space, according to which designated areas (in this case, the Mission-room) helped rationalize the use of space and correlate specific activities with specific places. What distinguishes Ranyard's implementation of the self-help principle from many similar schemes, however, is her recognition that the poor could best be encouraged to help themselves if they were initially helped by another like themselves. In the program of the Female Bible Mission, these two principles were inextricably bound together: the poor recipients of aid had to pay for the Bibles and clothes they received, and the agents who encouraged them to invest in improvement were always drawn from the ranks of the poor.

In both of these arrangements, the Female Bible Mission departed from the practice of the London City Mission. The goal of the latter was to "extend the knowledge of the Gospel." To this end, missionaries read Scripture to impoverished auditors, left instructive tracts in the homes they visited, and when they did distribute Bibles, they did so for free. Not only did the London City Mission thereby neglect the opportunity to promote financial self-discipline, but its managers' assumption that the poor should be read to and given charity belonged to a theory of improvement that rested on and reinforced the superiority of the agents administering help. Indeed, the London City Mission did everything it could to insure that its agents would be morally and educationally superior to the poor residents they visited. While the organization's first historian, John Weylland, does not specify the class of the missionaries, the fact that they had to demonstrate extensive knowledge of the Scriptures, flawless character, and overall competency for the work suggests that the London City Mission accepted no agents below the better-educated segment of the working class. Would-be missionaries faced a private interrogation by a staff of clerical examiners appointed by the mission's managers. So exacting were the standards that only two of the first thirty applicants were accepted (p. 15).

Ellen Ranyard's effort to describe her society's selection process reveals a very different protocol. Initially, she deferred the judgment to the highest power: "We believe that God finds [Bible-women], and we perpetually ask Him for a right judgment concerning those who present themselves" (p. 253). As she elaborated the process, the criteria for selection became clearer, even if the machinery for selection did not. Ranyard cited a litany of desirable virtues—"piety, humility and docility . . . courage and common sense . . . a bright, cheerful view of things . . . a quiet, energetic missionary spirit . . . trust[worthiness], conscientious[ness], honest[y], and truthful[ness]" (p. 254). Ranyard finally acknowledged, however, that each of the Bible women was flawed in some way. Indeed, Ranyard defended these flaws, which were the signs of the suffering they had endured, as rendering the Bible women teachable and therefore fit to teach: "In every one of our present forty women there is something that one might wish otherwise . . . but God works often with very imperfect instruments, or he would not work with any of us. The teachable person accomplishes most on the whole, especially if she has a large and loving heart that has itself known much affliction. We want these women for a practical purpose from a practical school" (p. 255).

The advantage these women gave the Female Bible Mission over organizations like the London City Mission is that they could gain access to homes barred to more respectable visitors. Ranyard underscored this point repeatedly:

> Educated ladies would not have been the Missionaries for these Magdalens, whose doors were closed against all respectable approach. "Out," "out," "out," is said of them day after day to the Clergyman, the City Missionary, and the Lady Visitor—all too holy, and good, and clean for *them*—of no use to *them,* except as persons from whom they might beg. But let a woman draw near them just like themselves—not an ecclesiastical agent—coming from no Church or party—without costume; not one of any sisterhood—simply a kind, good, motherly woman—and she may come and welcome. . . . She may point them to their forgotten duties, or to acts which they never saw to be duties; may shew them how their children look when they are clean; may teach them the use of soap; instruct them in the preparation of food; get their windows opened and their floors purified; teach them the comfort of clean linen and clean beds; and bring them eventually "clothed, and in their right mind," to sit at the feet of all and any who may be in their degree "the ministers of Christ." These people are tired of what they call "parsons" and "humbug," but they are not tired of kindness and sympathy. . . . Those who would be ashamed to be seen by a Clergyman, a City Missionary, or a Lady Visitor, have no objection to be a little cleared and set straight in their afflictions by one like themselves. (pp. 246, 247; see also pp. 36–37)

This description reveals Ranyard's awareness that, in practice, the administrative division between Bible work and domestic mission work could not be upheld. The very quality that enabled the Bible women to enter the poorest houses—that they were like the poor—grounded their knowledge of how to help the poor help themselves.[62] Purchasing and reading the Bible were aspects of a self-help program, but so was learning to remedy one's children's bodily ills and to improve domestic comfort. Ranyard instructed her Bible women to gain admission to homes with the Bible, but then to demonstrate "that THE BODY WAS THOUGHT OF AS WELL AS THE SOUL, for human souls live in bodies, and the bodies of these 'lowest of the low,' were very wretched" (p. 255).

To Ranyard, the success of the Female Bible Mission stemmed from its double emphasis on spiritual and bodily improvement, both of which were fostered through enforcing the discipline of small subscriptions and punctual attendance at "Mothers' classes" held in the Mission-room. The administrative apparatus that guided the Female Bible Mission was also double, "the DOUBLE agency of the lady and the poor woman." The lady was to instruct, find supplies and funds, keep accounts, and dispense "the sympathy and counsel which are indispensable" (p. 241); but the poor woman was the hitherto "MISSING LINK," the "NATIVE FEMALE AGENCY drawn from the classes we want to serve and instruct" (p. 234).

Ranyard's metaphor of a missing link is reminiscent of some of Babbage's descriptions of factory organization. Ranyard's image is not exclusively, or even primarily, mechanical, however. Even though her allotment of tasks according to ranks endorsed both class hierarchy and the division of social labor, her image of a chain derived from a theological rather than a political-economic context.[63] Ranyard made her theological conceptualization of society clear when she described the supplementary nature of her Bible women's work: "such supplementary work may now perfect the heavenly chain which shall lift the lost and the reckless from the depths of their despair. It should be forged by the universal Church of Christ" (p. 234).

Ranyard also invoked the metaphor of the social body in her effort to explain her mission's work. In justifying the alliance between poor Bible women and lady superintendents, she insisted that the two must work together: "The foot and the hand cannot say to the eye or the head, 'We have no need of you'" (p. 234). Ranyard's alternation between quasi-mechanical principles like that of the division of labor and organic metaphors like this one is not unusual in women's efforts to define their contributions to social reform during this period.[64] Partly, this alternation suggests the compatibility we have already identified between the two sets of images. Partly, it suggests that the theological rubric within which most women positioned their activities accommodated both organic notions of social relations and the pre-industrial definition of *machine,* which simply meant "contrivance."[65]

Ellen Ranyard specifically rejected Babbage's idea that an effective administrative apparatus would automatically lead an organization to expand (a principle borne out by the London City Mission). Not that she lacked the encouragement to extend her little operation. As she reported, her friends were forever inciting her: "Well, then, if the work is genuine and good, we must surely extend it. Shall we not have a great society, a great Female City Mission, with the usual apparatus for collecting money, public meetings, committees, secretaries, and reports?" (p. 258). To this, Ranyard's answer was an adamant defense of simplicity, localism, privacy, and the self-sufficiency of an organization that was actually administered by God:

> The work is His own, and He has used apparently weak instruments, that all the glory may be given to Himself. He has found the women, and pointed out the willing and devoted Lady Superintendents, and sent the funds to commence each Mission, often in the course of one week. The minute leadings of His providence have been unmistakable, and the answers to prayer innumerable. The machinery is so simple and so local wherever it arises, and it is of such importance that the work be secret and silent, that there is no necessity to clog it with extra apparatus, or to spoil it with platform compliments of man's device. (p. 257)

The mission's "ONE resolve," she continued, was not to become ensnared in the web of worldly obligations: "our ONE resolve is, *never to get into debt*: therefore, if the supplies cease, the work could always be transferred to those who will take it up, according to the rules of present routine" (p. 258).

I do not want to give the impression that the Female Bible Mission defied the economic rationality that dominated the administration of abstract space by midcentury. On the contrary, in many ways, the mission can be seen to have contributed to the rationality associated with abstraction. Ranyard presented one of the mission's triumphs, for example, as the successful promotion of credit-worthy habits among the very poorest of the poor. When individuals who lacked sufficient security even to obtain "a loan of a blanket . . . or a box of linen in their hour of need" returned these items to the mission "at the appointed season," they not only confirmed the wisdom of the mission's judgment but also advanced a step into the elaborate network of modern financial relations (pp. 193–94). Ranyard's emphasis on strictly dividing Bible work from mission work, especially because it resulted in her establishing separate Mission-rooms in which to conduct the latter, also contributed to the institutionalization of abstract space. So, for that matter, did her insistence that self-help be encouraged and measured by the willingness of poor women to apply their pittance toward their own salvation.

Despite the undeniable affinities between the Female Bible Mission and modern abstraction, we should nevertheless note Ranyard's insistence that the rationality associated with abstraction had its limits. In recognition of the peripatetic lives of the poorest poor, the irregularity of their employment, and their dependence on the *ir*rational booms and busts of the capitalist economy, Ranyard was adamant about drawing the line on extending credit; not every needy person could be moralized by incurring obligations (p. 197). Ranyard was also determined that the knowledge generated by the mission *about* the poor should not be used to facilitate either the kind of aggregation that led Chadwick to calculate the tons of waste produced by poor bodies each year or the kind of science whose systematic nature was its chief criterion for success. "It was not the first aim to secure such knowledge," Ranyard insisted (p. 29); "whatever small practical advances we may make in 'social science,' which is the study of the day, we hope always to connect them with the BIBLE" (p. 196). In Ranyard's account, in fact, missionary work was not intended to emphasize the difference between the objects of knowledge and those who produced (and dispensed) superior abstractions. Instead, it was intended to enhance that from which it fed: the *identification* of one woman with another. The lady superintendent "identif[ies] herself with the labours of the Bible-woman," Ranyard explained (p. 235); in so doing, she came as close as class society would allow her to knowing this other who was (in some ways but not others) like herself.

The kind of knowledge such enterprises could produce was strictly limited, of course, both because Ranyard resisted drawing generalizations about the poor individuals her Bible women visited and because the information they brought their superintending ladies was presumably cast in the language and categories of their own class, which Ranyard had no interest in translating. For the most part, the accounts Ranyard provided of the homes her Bible women visited take the form of dramatic tableaux rather than catalogues of aggregates; although it does contain tables of expenditures, the text contains no statistical data. Given Ranyard's principled resistance to expansion, the effects of the Female Bible Mission were by definition limited anyway. The 170 Bible women who represented the mission at the time of Ranyard's death must have strained the administrative coherence of a system based on individual supervision, but it did not approach the number of agents much more efficiently managed by the London City Mission or by the British and Foreign Bible Society, whose scope and complexity dwarfed them both. If her own account of the Female Bible Mission can be trusted, Ranyard was content to keep the enterprise relatively small and to restrict its impact to the individuals her Bible women actually visited. Imagining herself God's "weak instrument," Ranyard seems to have aspired to maintain God's order, which she understood to be hierarchical and only incidentally amenable to calculation, rather than wanting to extend to all of society an abstract system capable of establishing the ratio between Bibles sold and productivity increased.[66]

CONCLUSION

The trajectory of this essay, from a relatively theoretical discussion of the nature of modern abstraction to a more detailed account of a single philanthropic enterprise, may seem to reanimate a controversy that has been current in the American feminist community during the last decade. This controversy weighs the politics of an epistemology rooted in theory against an experience-based epistemology in hopes of finding a truly "feminist way of knowing."[67] Instead of waking this momentarily dozing giant by choosing between the theory associated with abstraction and the experience associated with bodies, I want to use the overview I have provided to draw two conclusions about the historical production of abstract space.

My first conclusion is that the codification of numerical, then statistical modes of abstract analysis, the institutionalization of protocols for inspecting, aggregating, and managing ever larger segments of the population, and the subordination of other definitions of value to quantification were unevenly produced alongside established ways of understanding, governing, and evaluating that did not simply vanish before some superior or more compelling rationality. Indeed, some facets of existing rationalities initially seemed compatible with the emergent, instrumental rationality, so that the institutionalization of the latter was actually facilitated by the persistence of the former.[68] At the same time, the fact that individuals traditionally excluded from the production of knowledge retained vestiges of the logic that excluded them *paradoxically* enabled these individuals to participate in producing knowledge that was (and was not) new. These complex effects of the interplay between existing and emergent domains are part of what we see in the case of Ellen Ranyard. When Ranyard attributed the selection of her agents to God, for example, or when she refused to subordinate the personal contact between Bible women and other poor women to the production of statistics, she actually made her organization more palatable to larger philanthropic organizations run by men, even though—or precisely

because—the Female Bible Mission did not reproduce all of the epistemological assumptions more modern organizations embodied. Yet
Ranyard's acceptance of—indeed, her aspiration to—a specifically
"supplementary" position in a hierarchy that she understood in theological terms also meant that her organization could actively contribute
to the disciplining of the very poor, even though whatever knowledge
they brought back was not presented in the modern form of statistics or
abstractions.

The second conclusion I want to draw from the example of Ellen
Ranyard is that the persistence of older rationalities, despite the authority increasingly accorded to instrumental rationality, ensured the appearance of contradictions and what look to us like resistances *even as*
more segments of the population were drawn into the emergent logic.
Partly, this is simply an effect of the incompatibility between the rationalities specific to residual and emergent domains. Ellen Ranyard's refusal to expand the Female Bible Mission along the lines of a successful
corporation must have seemed irrational to the "friends" whose encouragement she cites. In terms of the theological rationality she embraced,
however, it made perfect sense, for, just as the Heavenly Spirit worked in
highly specific, mysterious, and largely invisible ways, so did her Bible
women. To expand and publicize these efforts, to streamline their administration and tabulate their results would have been to depart from
the heavenly example upon which Ranyard modeled her enterprise.

Partly, the appearance of contradictions along with the institutionalization of modern abstraction is an effect of the fact that incorporating
more segments of the population and more aspects of everyday life into
the instrumental logic proper to the economic domain facilitated—even
encouraged—the adaptation of practices authorized by a residual rationality in contexts dominated by the emergent rationality. In the case of
the metaphors that underwrote these practices—such as those of the social machine or the social body (both of which Ranyard used)—such
adaptation was relatively unproblematic. In the case of practices, by
contrast, adaptation was not always possible. In these cases, traditional
practices preserved old rationalities, like undigestible bits of bone, in the
craw of modernity. This was the case, for example, with Ellen Ranyard's
effort to import the age-old dictate that women should care for the
bodies of others into the context of an increasingly bureaucratized
model of social reform. On the one hand, the practice of caring for impoverished bodies preserved the theological definition of women's
work. On the other hand, however, the fact that her Bible women
washed clothes and floors and bodies ran counter to the rationality of
modern abstraction, both because such physical contact undermined

the premium most reform initiatives placed on marginalizing the body or translating it into an abstraction and because this contact did not yield generalizations *about* poverty. Indeed, the physical contact Ranyard encouraged challenged the authority of abstraction and encouraged the cultivation of another approach to knowing, understanding, and improving the lives of the poor. In adapting a practice associated with women to a science dominated by men, Ranyard actually preserved an alternative model of knowledge that challenged the claim to superiority advanced by the science she practiced. Records even as perishable as *The Missing Link,* that is, keep alive the possibility of a kind of knowledge that is based not on generalizations abstracted from disinterested observation but on personal experience, preferably gained by one body's immediate contact with another.

As this last point should make clear, I am suggesting that the late twentieth-century feminist debate about whether experience is a more politically acceptable basis than theory for feminist analysis is one legacy of the preservation of an alternative mode of knowing *within* the epistemology of modern abstraction. The preservation of this alternative and its current appeal to so many of us is *not* proof of its superiority, however, or even of its ability to survive outside the context of modern abstraction in which it has come down to us. Instead, the preservation of an alternative mode of knowing is simply one sign that the power distributed through the institutions associated with modern abstraction will never be as total as its early theorists dreamed it could be.

Three

CURING THE SOCIAL BODY IN 1832: JAMES PHILLIPS KAY AND THE IRISH IN MANCHESTER

The consolidation of a national identity or national character is necessarily a protracted and uneven process, just as its maintenance is always precarious and imperfect. These generalizations rest upon two assumptions, which constitute the theoretical bedrock of my argument in this essay. My first assumption is that national identity—like nationalism, the movement by which such identity is politicized—only becomes available as a salient cultural concept at certain historical conjunctures.[1] Such historical moments are sometimes marked by explicit conflict with another country or by enhanced imperial ambitions, and they are generally characterized by a widespread perception that not everyone who lives in the country embodies its national virtues.[2] My second assumption is that such differentiation within the nation is repeated within individuals or groups that seem united by a single interest. That is, the process by which individuals or groups embrace the concept of the nation as the most meaningful context for self-definition necessarily involves temporarily marginalizing other categories that could also provide a sense of identity. Because other categories and interests persist even in periods of nationalistic fervor, however, and because they often compete with or even contradict national values, national identity is always a precarious formulation for every individual who shares the nationalist sentiment as well as for the nation as a whole.[3]

The process by which a national identity is consolidated and maintained is therefore one of differentiation and displacement—the differentiation of the national *us* from aliens within and without, and the displacement of other interests from consciousness. Because the consolidation of any national identity occurs over time and therefore in the midst of changing historical circumstances, moreover, this process may also involve alternative inclusions and exclusions of the *same* group from the idea of the nation. Such alternations are partly signs of the persistent competition of categories and interests to which I have just alluded. Partly, they reflect the fact that the consolidation of national identity does not always take center stage in a national or individual agenda. That is, sometimes the idea of a national identity is deployed to support another political or social campaign; sometimes an apparently unrelated political or social cause may also contribute to the formation of national values.

In this essay I offer a detailed analysis of this dynamic as James Phillips Kay described it in his 1832 pamphlet, *The Moral and Physical Condition of the Working Classes . . . in Manchester.* (Page references to this work are cited parenthetically in the text.) My justification for such radical selectivity is that Kay's text materially influenced how what Carlyle was to call the "condition of England" was conceptualized by Whig ministers and their publicists in the 1830s and 1840s. My rationale for the method of this essay—close textual and historical analysis—is twofold. First, I suggest that the narrative logic of this text—its contradictions and ostentatious omissions as well as its explicit argument—exposes the cultural logic by which certain attitudes and habits that we associate with the middle class were successfully elevated over other concerns as *the* characteristic values of the English. Second, I suggest that the complex conjuncture of issues in Kay's text provides an example of how thoroughly imbued with its immediate historical context is every text or event that is retrospectively assimilated to nationalism. Detailed analyses of symptomatic texts and events should remind us that the consolidation of nationalism and the construction of national identities are marked at every moment by competing currents whose energy derives from—and might return to—interests only incidentally related to the nation or national issues.

James Phillips Kay (1804–77) is best known for his contributions to educational reform, which he undertook as secretary to the Committee of Council on Education beginning in 1839.[4] In 1832, Kay was still a young medical man, newly appointed to the position of senior physician at the Ardwick and Ancoats Dispensary in Manchester. In his autobiography, composed in 1877, Kay (by then Kay-Shuttleworth) described how his experience—and failure—as a medical man led him to recast physiological disorders into more general social and political terms. As a medical attendant on the poor, Kay writes,

I necessarily became familiar with the foulest slums in which this wretched population seemed to be continually perishing. Their habits, wants and sufferings were constantly before my eyes. I came to know how almost useless were the resources of my art to contend with the consequences of formidable social evils. It was clearly something outside scientific skill or charity which was needed for the cure of this social disease. . . .

Parallel, therefore with my scientific reading I gradually began to make myself acquainted with the best works on political and social science, and obtained more and more insight into the grave questions affecting the relations of capital and labour, and the distribution of wealth, as well as the inseparable connection between the mental and moral condition of the people and their physical well-being.[5]

The sequence Kay describes here characterizes the logic of his pamphlet and the social movement he helped inaugurate. Empirical observations of specific instances of working-class distress, gathered and interpreted by a middle-class (white male) expert, constitute the basis for understanding distress not primarily as an individual, physiological problem (bodily infirmity) but as a sign of social disorder that requires collective (legislative) action. So compelling were the investigative method and the descriptive genre of Kay's pamphlet that they provided the paradigm for the work of the Manchester Statistical Society, which was founded, also in response to Kay's work, in 1833. This society, which was a prototype for numerous reform societies, typified both the government commissions that investigated and publicized social problems in the 1830s and 1840s and the extra-parliamentary pressure groups whose influence was so marked during these decades.[6] No doubt to his chagrin, Kay's pamphlet was also extensively quoted by Richard Oastler in the campaign for factory reform.[7]

In order to understand the contribution that the social reform movement made to a national identity, it is necessary to work through both Kay's diagnosis of his society's ills and the historical issues that his analysis explicitly—and sometimes implicitly—addressed. Essentially, Kay's diagnosis highlights three sets of symptoms: the chronic social and moral woes that afflicted the laboring population—their lack of education, their poverty, and their lax morality (which Kay calls *pauperism*); the "popular tumults" that had racked the country since 1811; and Asiatic cholera, which first struck Manchester in June of 1832.[8] While Kay insists that these apparently unrelated symptoms are inextricably bound up with one another, he assigns cholera the most prominent role, both socially and rhetorically. Socially, cholera functions as an "unerring guide," which leads the medical man to "the very heart of society." There, the doctor sees exactly what he expected to find.

> He whose duty it is to follow the steps of this messenger of death, must descend to the abodes of poverty, must frequent the close alleys, the crowded courts, the overpeopled habitations of wretchedness, where pauperism and disease congregate round the source of social discontent and political disorder in the centre of our large towns, and behold with alarm, in the hot-bed of pestilence, ills that fester in secret, at the very heart of society. (p. 8)

Rhetorically, as this passage suggests, cholera provides the metaphor that draws all of society's problems into a single conceptual cluster, which Kay designates *ills* or *maladies*.[9] This metaphorical use of cholera enables Kay to convince his middle- and upper-class readers that the fate of the poor has implications for the wealthy too—or, in other words, that everyone belongs to one "social body."

> The ingression of a disease, which threatens, with a stealthy step, to invade the sanctity of the domestic circle; which may be unconsciously conveyed from those haunts of beggary where it is rife, into the most still and secluded retreat of refinement—whose entrance, wealth cannot absolutely bar, and luxury invites, this is an event which, in the secret pang that it awakens, at the heart of all those who are bound to any others by sympathies which it may harshly rend, ensures that the anxious attention of every order of society shall be directed to that, in which social ills abound. (p. 12)

If the various maladies that afflict England's social body are like the symptoms of cholera, then their origin is (like cholera again) "remote and accidental" (p. 15). By the same analogous logic, the cure for these disorders must be to purge the body of whatever interferes with its natural condition.[10] Kay initially identifies the interfering agent as "injudicious legislation"—a poor law that "operat[es] as a direct bounty on the increase of an indigent population" (pp. 15–16), a beer tax that increases "the haunts of intemperance" (p. 16), the threat of factory legislation, and, most ruinous of all, a Corn Law that restricts free trade. Thus—by the metaphorical logic that assimilates poverty to cholera and turns trade restrictions into the "poisoned chalice" of the poor (p. 15)—Kay manages to offer as an antidote to both cholera and poverty the repeal of the Corn Laws.

Representing England's social problems as a kind of disease also enables Kay to present the unruly poor as victims in need of aid rather than agents who should be punished. This is especially important to Kay's argument because class conflict—and class consciousness—would undermine his image of a single, harmonious body, which, in turn, underwrites his argument for mutual interests and therefore for repeal. It is also important because, as the following passage suggests, "popular violence" has proved to be one of the chronic symptoms of the social body's ills:

> Between the manufacturers of the country, staggering under the burdens of an enormous taxation and a restricted commerce; between them and the labouring classes subjects of controversy have arisen, and consequent animosity too generally exists. The burdens of trade diminish the profits of capital, and the wages of labour: but bitter debate arises between the manufacturers and those in their employ, concerning the proper division of that fund, from which these are derived. The bargain for the wages of labour develops organized associations of the working classes, for the purpose of carrying on the contest with the capitalist: large funds are subscribed: frequent meetings are held, at which inflammatory harangues are delivered, and committees and delegates are chosen;—a gloomy spirit of discontent is engendered, and the public are not infrequently alarmed, by the wild out-break of popular violence, when mobs of machine breakers defy the armed guardians of the peace. In these contests personal animosity and party rancour have sometimes indulged in the most flagrant excesses; the characters of individuals have been most grossly maligned, their property destroyed, and such severe personal assaults have been made on those of the labouring classes, who did not unite in the general league, that they have occasionally produced the loss of life, and, more than once, a master has been sacrificed by an assassin. (pp. 9–10)

Kay never specifies the setting of this violence, but his references to machine-breaking would have called to readers' minds the Luddite activities of 1811–17, when cotton weavers and framework knitters protested declining wages by vandalizing machines and goods. Similarly, his picture of "mobs . . . defy[ing] the armed guardians of the peace" would have summoned up Peterloo, when the peaceful protest of an enormous crowd provoked the retaliation of government troops. In the wake of the 1819 Peterloo Massacre, Parliament passed the repressive Six Acts in the government's most determined effort to curtail working-class organization.

Kay's reliance on abstract nouns and passive constructions obscures the responsibility for these actions, just as his use of the continuous present effaces, even as it alludes to, the identity of these riots. Such rhetoric helps assimilate the politicized violence of laborers and trade unionists to the violence of cholera, thereby displacing arguments such as those offered by Robert Owen and John Bray that the root of the problem was the inequitable distribution of economic resources.[11] The assimilation of riots to cholera opposes to an economic analysis a vision in which what others call class conflict appears as a function of ignorance: the workers do not know enough to assess the consequences of their "desperate deeds" (p. 16); the manufacturers do not know enough about how their operatives live. If this is the problem, then education is the cure—"religious and moral instruction" for the poor, and empirical education for the middle classes, which will be advanced both by the personal excursions of benevolent inspectors into the homes of the poor and by pamphlets such as Kay's, which will vicariously transport mill owners into working-class neighborhoods. From such education, the proper model of government will emerge—a paternalism in which those who know best rule: "The lives, the fortunes, and the liberties of the people will henceforth we may hope be entrusted to those who know their wants, sympathize with their distresses, and in whose experience, ability, and integrity, they can repose the trust of devising means for their relief" (p. 13).

The logic of Kay's argument, in which working-class protests are superseded by middle-class action via the *agent provocateur* of cholera, also entails another substitution: the substitution of middle-class *social* reform for political reform by any class. Even if it is not explicit, however, the theme of political reform constitutes an important subtext of this pamphlet. The popular violence closest to Kay's composition of *The Moral and Physical Conditions of the Working Classes*, after all, was not that of the Luddites or Peterloo but the "days of May" disorders of 1831. This violence was sparked by the campaign for political—that is, parliamentary—reform. Following the repeal of the Test and Corporations Act (1828) and the passage of the Catholic Emancipation Act (1829), some Whig and even Tory leaders had come to view moderate parliamentary reform as a possible—even desirable—goal, but when the new Whig ministry failed to get a reform bill passed, the country erupted into violence. From early 1831 until May 1832, there were successive crises, marked by meetings of workers, torchlight processions, and outright riots. So many disparate hopes had been pinned to reform, according to one M.P., that defeat brought the country to the brink of revolution.

> The whole country took fire at once. The working people expected that they were to change places with their employers. The middle classes believed that by breaking down the parliamentary influence of the peers, they should get the governing power of the State into their own hands.

And the ministers, the contrivers of the design, persuaded themselves that the people, out of sheer gratitude, would make the rule of the Whigs perpetual. If, to all these interested hopes, we add the jealousy of the vulgar at all privileges not shared by themselves,—the resentment of the majority of the nation at the disregard of their sentiments respecting the Roman Catholic Bill—and the superficial notion that the direct representation of numbers is the principle of the elective franchise,—we shall have a tolerably correct conception of the motives of a revolution.[12]

I will return in a moment to the issue of Catholic Emancipation and to the reform bill that was finally adopted in June, 1832. Here I simply want to underscore the fact that Kay does not specifically mention this political ferment, which had not only a working-class dimension but a middle-class component as well. This silence is striking, even though reform riots did not take place in Manchester itself, not only because the riots were so widespread and severe, but also because, by 1830, most manufacturers in Lancashire and the West Riding supported parliamentary reform as necessary to their continued prosperity. In 1831, Kay himself had supported reform in a pamphlet entitled *Letter to the People of Lancashire Concerning the Future Representation of the Commercial Interest*. Kay's failure to reiterate his support here and his repeated references to "popular tumult" point to a second displacement in his 1832 pamphlet: the displacement of the socialists' economic analysis of working-class discontent by a medical formulation centered on cholera has its counterpart in the displacement of an explicit discussion of the political interests of middle-class manufacturers by a discussion of the social components of unrest, the "moral and physical condition of the working classes."[13]

Both of these displacements are instrumental in generating the terms by which the social body—and with it, national character—were to be conceptualized by successive Whig governments in the 1830s and 1840s. Kay's formulation proved successful partly because it drew upon fantasies and fears already shared by many of his middle- and upper-class contemporaries. These fears, which were also addressed in the texts of social and political science with which Kay supplemented his medical studies, had first been named by Thomas Malthus in 1798. Malthus's dire prediction about the tendency of population growth to outstrip food production is imported into Kay's argument by his organizing metaphor, for to call society a body in the wake of Malthus's thesis necessarily focused attention on the body's most unruly capacities—its appetites and, more specifically, its sexuality.[14] We see this in *The Moral and Physical Condition of the Working Classes*, when the word *morality* repeatedly devolves into the "moral check" on sexual intercourse that was Malthus's (reconsidered) solution to the "problem" of population. Arguing against the position that increased wages will remedy society's ills, for example, Kay explicitly alludes to Malthus's grim admonition.

> The fruits of external prosperity may speedily be blighted by the absence of internal virtue. . . . In vain may the intellect of man be tortured to devise expedients by which the supply of the necessaries of life may undergo an increase equivalent to that of population, if the moral check be overthrown. Crime, diseases, pestilence, intestine discord, famine, or foreign war—those agencies which repress the rank overgrowth of a meagre and reckless race—will, by a natural law, desolate a people devoid of prudence and principle, whose members constantly press on the limits of the means of subsistence. We therefore regard with alarm the state of those vast masses of our operative population which are acted upon by all other incentives, rather than those of virtue; and are visited by the emissaries of every faction, rather than by the ministers of an ennobling faith. (p. 65)

While Kay rejects the formulaic approach to social problems associated with classical political economists like Ricardo, Malthusian political economy provides him with both a supplement to the threat of cholera and a further rationale for focusing his analysis not on economic or political relations but on the site of the workers' most intimate relations—the domestic sphere. Just as the image of a social body conjures up the Malthusian nightmare, so the figure of a "people devoid of prudence" introduces what were soon to become commonplaces about working-class licentiousness. "There is . . . a licentiousness capable of corrupting the whole body of society, like an insidious disease, which eludes observation, yet is equally fatal in its effects." . . . Sensuality has no record, and the relaxation of social obligations may coexist with a half dormant, half restless impulse to rebel against all the preservative principles of society" (p. 62). A footnote, which makes it clear that Kay has sexual promiscuity in mind, provides a bridge to a sustained analysis of working-class domesticity. According to Kay, the home ought to be the center for that penetralium of nervelike connections that link individuals and, in so doing, make one social body—one nation—from disparate localities and interests. Instead of playing this crucial role, Kay complains, the working-class household is not a home at all. In it, the "bonds of domestic sympathy" have been severed because women and children leave the home to work for pay. From this transgression, a series of interconnected problems follows: "Too frequently the father, enjoying perfect health and with ample opportunities of employment, is supported in idleness on the earnings of his oppressed children" (p. 64); "the early age at which girls are admitted into the factories, prevents their acquiring much knowledge of domestic economy"; "the infant is the victim of the system; it has not lived long, ere it is abandoned to the care of a hireling or a neighbour, while its mother pursues her accustomed toil" (p. 69). Most pernicious of all, too many infants perish for want of proper care: "the child is ill-fed, dirty, ill-clothed, exposed to cold and neglect; and in consequence, more than one-half of the offspring of the poor . . . die before they have completed their fifth year" (p. 70).

Kay's analysis of the destructive role that "abnormal" domestic relations play in vitiating the health of the social body was to influence not only fellow bureaucrats like Edwin Chadwick and Hector Gavin but also aristocratic M.P.s like Viscount Ashley, Seventh Earl of Shaftesbury, who spent much of his rhetorical capital supporting factory legislation by melodramatizing the plight of unmothered infants.[15] Whereas similar analyses of the condition of England written only a few years later tended to emphasize the class-specific nature of domestic impropriety, Kay reads domestic disorder not primarily in the context of class (which could exacerbate social conflict) but in relation to his foundational metaphor (which emphasized harmony or health). Like other maladies of the social body, that is, domestic disorder could be cured if noxious elements, of "accidental and remote origin," were removed from working-class neighborhoods. Kay's brief history of England's cotton industry makes it perfectly clear that although injudicious legislation now retards his country's recovery, the ills that afflict England originated in another country—Ireland.

> The rapid growth of the cotton manufacture has attracted hither operatives from every part of the kingdom, and Ireland has poured forth the most destitute of her hordes to supply the constantly increasing demand for labour. This immigration has been, in one important respect, a serious evil. The Irish have taught the labouring classes of this country a pernicious lesson. The system of cottier farming, the demoralization and barbarism of the people, and the general use of the potato as the chief article of food, have encouraged the population in Ireland more rapidly than the *available* means of subsistence have been increased. Debased alike by ignorance and pauperism, they have discovered, with the savage, what is the minimum of the means of life, upon which existence may be prolonged. The paucity of the amount of means and comforts *necessary for the mere support of life,* is not known by a more civilized population, and this secret has been taught the labourers of this country by the Irish. As competi-

tion and the restrictions and burdens of trade diminished the profits of capital, and consequently reduced the price of labour, the contagious example of ignorance and a barbarous disregard of forethought and economy, exhibited by the Irish, spread. The colonization of savage tribes has ever been attended with effects on civilizations as fatal as those which have marked the progress of the sand flood over the fertile plains of Egypt. Instructed in the fatal secret of subsisting on what is barely necessary to life—yielding partly to necessity, and partly to example,—the labouring classes have ceased to entertain a laudable pride in furnishing their houses, and in multiplying the decent comforts which minister to happiness. What is superfluous to the mere exigencies of nature, is too often expended at the tavern; and for the provision of old age and infirmity, they too frequently trust either to charity, to the support of their children, or to the protection of the poor laws. (pp. 20–22)

The domestic theme in this passage is both manifest and latent. If one explicit effect of the Irish invasion has been the loss of English "pride in furnishing their houses," then this failure of English pride has implicitly been caused by the increase in the Irish population, which drives the Irish to subsist on the potato and to cultivate other "barbarous" habits. The sexual profligacy behind this population explosion is elided in Kay's description, although the awkward syntax of his allusion to it suggests what is missing ("The system of cottier farming, the demoralization and barbarism of the people, and the general use of the potato as the chief article of food, have encouraged the population in Ireland [to reproduce] more rapidly than the *available* means of subsistence have been increased"). Because of this Irish profligacy, Kay suggests, the English working classes now fail to multiply the decent comforts of domesticity and threaten instead to multiply indecently, like the Irish—to bear more children than they, or the nation as a whole, can feed.

As this passage makes clear, Kay's image of a healthy social body cannot accommodate the Irish, because—especially in their domestic habits—they are not human. In his climactic description of the Irish, Kay explicitly presents them as a cross between matter and beast: the Irish are a "mass of animal organization" whose "savage habits" counteract any short-term gain they might bring to the unwitting employer.

The introduction of an uncivilized race does not tend even primarily to increase the power of producing wealth, in a ratio by any means commensurate with the cheapness of its labour, and may ultimately retard the increase of the fund for the maintenance of that labour. Such a race is useful only as a mass of animal organization, which consumes the smallest amount of wages. The low price of the labour of such people depends, however, on the paucity of their wants, and their savage habits. When they assist the production of wealth, therefore, their barbarous habits and consequent moral depression must form a part of the equation. They are only necessary to a state of commerce *inconsistent* with such a reward for labour as is calculated to maintain the standard of civilization. A few years pass, and they become burdens to a community whose morals and physical power they have depressed; and dissipate wealth which they did not accumulate. (pp. 82–83)

Throughout his pamphlet, Kay associates every English problem with the Irish. The poverty and ignorance from which the English workers suffer, for example, is typified by the condition of Irish houses (pp. 32, 34–35, 38). He depicts the poor laws, which "pauperize" the English poor and oppress the respectable classes, as disproportionately devoted to relieving Irish immigrants (pp. 53, 55, 56), and this is true partly because the Irish, more than any other group, have suffered from the introduction of machinery, especially the power loom (p. 44). Taverns, which Kay connects explicitly to intemperance and crime, he implicitly associates with the Irish (p. 22). Kay does not specify the Irish when he laments the working class's lack of religion, but Catholicism, which was practiced by most Irish immigrants after 1810, was thought by many of the English to be worse than no religion at all. Finally, Kay depicts the strikes and trade unionism that he holds responsible for so much of the English problem as exacerbated by the Irish—both because, according to Kay, English strikes necessitated the importation of these workers (p. 110) and because, once in England, Irish workers have driven wages down, thereby increasing English workers' discontent (p. 80).

Kay's denigration of the Irish obviously draws upon a long tradition of English prejudice against them, which by the 1830s could target both the "racial" difference between the two peoples[16] and their religious differences.[17] Such prejudices were not always articulated in the same terms, however, nor were they always more prominent than the concern for national well-being.[18] In Kay's treatment of the Irish, we see a particularly complex example of the way that a proponent of one set of issues—in this case, social reform at the national level—mobilized prejudices against a particular group of people by constructing an image of the nation that excluded this group. The complexities in Kay's treatment arise from the fact that, even though the Irish could be so vilified in 1832 because they did occupy slum dwellings in Manchester, they were also necessary to the prosperity and security of England. Indeed, by 1832, the Irish were the beneficiaries of three decades of legislation that had explicitly included them in the kingdom of Great Britain. For James Kay, then, the Irish were available *both* as a scapegoat for national woes and as a resource to be exploited when needed. To trace the intricacies of Kay's representation, we must review briefly some aspects of the turbulent relationship between England and Ireland.

What most of the English in the early nineteenth century saw as the self-evident racial differences between the Anglo-Saxons and the Celts seemed to coincide with and be reinforced by the difference between the Protestant and Catholic religions. The latter was mapped onto national identity when England broke from Rome in the sixteenth century; it was reinscribed in the early eighteenth century when England levied the repressive penal codes against Irish Catholics as punishment for the 1641 Ulster uprising, the Catholic rebellion against Protestant incursions during the first decades of the century. Paradoxically, however, the penal codes, which, among other restrictions, denied Catholics the right to own land, served to drive Irish Catholics into trade and therefore eventually into increased prosperity. By the late eighteenth century, Irish Catholics as a whole constituted a creditor class, in stark contrast to the debtor class of Irish Protestants. Meanwhile, the relationship between the two countries, which had been one of colonial occupation, had also become more complex. By the late 1770s, it had become clear to many English legislators that it was more important to forestall an Irish move toward independence and to consolidate Great Britain by securing its Celtic fringes than to enforce the penal code. As the conflict between England and France persisted, then, restrictions against the Catholics' right to own property were eased. In 1793, Irish Catholic forty-shilling freeholders were enfranchised in a further move to keep Ireland part of Great Britain and to counteract Ireland's susceptibility to France. In 1800, Ireland was drawn even closer to England by the Act of Union, which established the United Kingdom of Great Britain and Ireland. The Act of Union was passed for security reasons on both sides: international security was at stake for England; domestic security was the concern of the Protestant Anglo-Irish Ascendancy, which, while politically dominant, constituted a distinct and embattled minority within Ireland. By this time, of course, the identity of England had been further complicated by the 1707 amalgamation of Scotland. Within the resulting Great Britain, differences of "race," religion, diet, habit, and even time (before the railways managed to standardize Greenwich mean time in the 1840s) continued to render the representation of the nation problematic and highly various, depending on where one lived, one's party alliance, and the importance of local concerns in relation to national interests.[19]

If the 1801 Union promised to solve the problem of Ireland, however, it actually exacerbated both the religious and political differences that still divided the two parts of the kingdom. Because Irish representatives constituted an unassimilated minority in Parliament, their very presence and political isolation there kept the issue of Catholic emancipation alive. By the 1820s, in the midst of widespread agrarian violence, the issue of emancipation had become so pressing that the Duke of Wellington capitulated to the cause. Without emancipation, Wellington argued, Ireland was rushing headlong toward civil war. Equally frightening, of course, were the possibilities that, without some remedy for the uneasy alliance of Ireland and England, either Ireland would secede from the Union or else the British people would urge more sweeping parliamentary reforms.[20] Wellington and Peel therefore supported the Catholic Emancipation Act of 1829—with its freehold wing that raised the Catholic voting qualification from forty shillings to ten pounds.[21] Their support split the Tory party and, to compound the paradox, helped pave the way for the very parliamentary reforms Wellington and Peel sought to foreclose.

The complex series of concessions and alliances that culminated in Catholic Emancipation in 1829 and the qualified triumph of the Whigs in 1830 constitute the backdrop to Kay's pamphlet. Equally important, however, is the extent to which his pamphlet repeats—and therefore exposes—the tensions that characterized these events. Just as various groups of English legislators with their own (often party) interests in mind had alternately invoked the innate differences between the Irish and the English to authorize keeping the Catholics subordinate (the official Tory position) and emphasized the two peoples' commonalities to advocate legislative programs of social reform (the Whig position), so Kay alternately insists that the Irish are unlike the English *and* suggests that the two populations have become alike, because of the "contagious example" of the Irish. This textual alternation does not simply reflect the contentious context of party politics, however, with Kay taking first one position, then the other. Instead, Kay's representation constitutes an attempt to advance the basic program of the Whigs without allowing it to be taken—as popular agitation and some Whig radicals were trying to do—to its logical extreme. As part of his effacement of any specifically *political* formulation of a cure, that is, Kay's contradictory representation of the relation between the English and the Irish functions to advance social reform while keeping parliamentary representation out of working-class hands.

Kay's insistence that the Irish are different from the English is explicit and adamant. The Irish are not only "debased," according to Kay; they are "savage." As such, they cannot be reformed, but must be sent back to Ireland, where Kay is apparently unconcerned about their fate. Indeed, in contrast to his multifaceted program for curing English maladies, his only suggestion for alleviating Irish distress is to levy "an impost on the rental of Ireland"—a suggestion that obscures what was, in many ways, *the* problem of Ireland, the problem of the land.[22]

Kay's blurring of the distinctions between the two populations is less explicit but no less pervasive. Partly, the difference between the two groups dissolves through the metaphor with which he repeatedly characterizes their relationship. If the Irish constitute a "contagious example," after all, the differences between the original carrier of the disease and its victims soon disappear. More striking, perhaps, is the way that Kay's discursive treatments of the Irish so often simply evolve, without transition, into descriptions of English workers. So, for example, Kay's primary diagnosis of the Irish problem, which begins on page 21, blends into his discussions of the domestic chaos generated by women working and the demoralizing effects of long hours, poor diet, and domestic overcrowding. These last problems are clearly shared by English and Irish workers, and Kay's use of generic nouns and pronouns conflates the two groups into a single "population." Only when this section culminates six pages later does the difference between the two groups surface again.

If English politicians' anxieties about party and revolution led even some Tory stalwarts like Wellington to shift positions on Catholic emancipation in 1829, then Kay's repetition of this alternation addresses the political results *of* emancipation. That is, prior to the Emancipation Act, the identity of the English could be more securely tied to the differences that the Tories represented as paramount: the innate differences between a tolerant Protestant Anglo-Saxon Establishment and a tyrannical Catholic Celtic fringe. Never mind that these oppositions were already blurred by the existence of the Anglo-Irish Ascendancy and by a small Catholic minority in England, or that both radicals and Foxite Whigs were beginning to say that the English government could be a tyrant too. Before 1829, the Tory position seemed less like a party position than simple common sense, and distrust of the Catholic French fueled widespread suspicion that all Catholics were enemies. With Emancipation, however, the traditional bases of the English identity clearly demanded reformulation. After 1829, the decisive diacritical mark that separated "us" from "them" was no longer race or religion, nor could "us" mean simply the English. Instead, with the appending of the freehold wing to the Emancipation Act, the diacritical mark of Britishness (not Englishness) became a certain level of property ownership. If a man met the £10 qualification, even if he was a Catholic, he belonged to the kingdom of Great Britain in a way that he did not if he failed to meet it.

The foundation for reformulating British identity had already been laid by the time cholera invaded Manchester in June of 1832. Kay's insistence that because the Irish epitomize and cause the English problem, they should be sent home, to their own country, is clearly one response to this situation; Kay's program is to reinforce the health of the English workers and the autonomy of the English nation by getting rid of foreign agents. When he also blurs the boundary between the Irish and the English, however, Kay simultaneously acknowledges that a new mark of difference has been instigated by Emancipation and suggests that it must be reinforced if it is to work as effectively as the old. That is, only if English workers are in some way *like* the Irish workers is it clear why the former (who are, by nature, human) should be denied political representation when all of the latter (who are, by nature, animals) are not.

In order to ground property ownership in some legitimating discourse, so that it can seem as unobjectionable a basis for British identity as religion and race had seemed for Englishness, Kay links certain *attitudes* toward property with certain domestic behaviors, which he has already linked to the Irish. By implication, of course, this grounds British respectability not in class but in "nature"—the natural morality of sexual self-control, cleanliness, forethought, and health—all of which are implicitly the domain of women. Kay, however, is less interested in assigning women the responsibility for upholding this ideal than in arguing that the "contagious example" of the Irish has infected English workers with domestic (especially reproductive) improvidence. In his climactic description of a Malthusian degeneration of the race of workers, Kay elides the difference between the English and the Irish once more.

Want of cleanliness, of forethought, and economy, are found in almost invariable alliance with dissipation, reckless habits, and disease. The population gradually becomes physically less efficient as the producers of wealth—morally so from idleness—politically *worthless* as having few desires to satisfy, and *noxious* as dissipators of capital accumulated. Were such manners to prevail, the horrors of pauperism would accumulate. A debilitated race would be rapidly multiplied. Morality would afford no check to the increase of the population: crime and disease would be its only obstacles—the licentiousness which indulges its capricious appetite, till it exhausts its power—and the disease which, at the same moment, punishes crime, and sweeps away a hecatomb of its victims. A dense mass, impotent alike of great moral or physical efforts, would accumulate. . . . They would drag on an unhappy existence, vibrating between the pangs of hunger and the delirium of dissipation. . . . Destitution would now prey on their strength, and then the short madness of debauchery would consummate its ruin. (pp. 81–82)

Because the entire working population exhibits a "want of cleanliness, of forethought, and economy," English workers are more like Irish workers than they are like their English betters, who are immune to the "contagious example" the Irish present because they do embody these virtues.

Such passages function not just to secure the likeness among all workers, but also to consolidate that group to which they are opposed—the class of (male) British property owners, which is characterized not by birth or by the kind of property they own but by their *attitude toward* property and the domestic sphere. In arguing that the working class is "politically *worthless*" because their domestic improvidence leaves them responsive to "emissaries of every faction," Kay is also arguing, by extension, that those who incarnate domestic virtues are politically *valuable* because their material and psychological investment in property makes them impervious to bad influence. Kay does not make this specifically *political* argument in his pamphlet because he wants to efface all traces of the political case being made in 1831 and 1832; he wants to do this because only the most radical Whigs were willing to advocate dramatically extending the franchise.[23] Despite Kay's silence on this issue, however, the *economic* argument that he makes implies this political component, just as his allusions to the economically motivated Peterloo and Swing riots also refer to the reform riots of 1831. Instead of emphasizing a political solution, however, Kay focuses on removing the other accidental interference to English well-being—the Corn Laws.

Repealing the Corn Laws, Kay promises his readers, will bring England both economic and moral reform. "Unrestricted commerce," Kay explains, ". . . would rapidly promote the advance of civilization, by cultivating the physical and mental power of individuals and nations to multiply the amount of natural products, and to create those artificial staple commodities, by the barter of which they acquire the riches of other regions" (pp. 85–86). This economic improvement will foster individual improvement because it will increase the time available for education: "Were an unlimited exchange permitted to commerce, the hours of labour might be reduced, and more afforded for the education and religious and moral instruction of the people" (p. 88). Free trade will also purge England of the Irish, for once English workers work without costly trade unions, English manufacturing will no longer require cheap Irish labor.

In 1832, it could hardly have seemed plausible that the Corn Laws, which explicitly protected (upper-class) land owners, not (middle-class) manufacturers, would be repealed unless parliamentary reform gave political representation to at least some segments of the middle classes.[24] When the visitation of cholera interrupted Kay's work on behalf of this reform, then, his attention turned to disease in the context of politics— or, phrased differently, to the kind of political reform that would facilitate the economic power of manufacturers *in the context* of a program of social reform that was acceptable to the newly ascendant Whigs.[25] Cholera proved the perfect vehicle for Kay's position because it enabled him to harness one kind of "remote and accidental" affliction (the Corn Laws) to another (the Irish) and to propose the removal of both as a cure for all of England's ills, including cholera. What Kay's formulation reveals but does not acknowledge is that in each case the metaphor derived from cholera also provides an interpretation of the way the emergent social domain should be understood. That is, just as the invasion of cholera has enabled Kay to formulate the economic problems of the poor *in bodily and then domestic terms,* so using the metaphor of a foreign disease to describe Irish immigration constitutes as "other" a group once assumed to be essential to both British security and prosperity. Just as the Union was critical in consolidating Britain's immunity to France, in other words, so the existence of Irish labor, investment capital, and uncompetitive markets had been critical to the consolidation of Britain's international superiority. Only because Ireland was also part of Great Britain was English manufacturing now strong enough to profit from free trade.[26]

The cure Kay suggests for the maladies of society therefore reinscribes the contradiction that pervaded England's relationship to Ireland throughout these decades. Just as he alternately insists upon and obscures the characteristics that distinguish the Irish from the English, so too does Kay implicitly argue for both the divorce of the two nations and a continuation of their unhappy marriage. On the one hand, Ireland must remain another country; otherwise, the chronic poverty that continued to cripple Ireland would necessitate much larger expenditures of British poor relief and increase the national debt. On the other hand, however, like a good wife or sister, Ireland must remain sufficiently accessible to the needs of English manufacturers to provide cheap labor when world demand is high, and noncompetitive markets when world demand falls.

Kay's argument that England was a nation sufficiently consolidated to engage in and profit from free trade depended on constituting the Irish economy as neither autonomous nor free and as simultaneously separable from and dependent on the English economy.[27] Emphasizing cholera is part of this argument, because cholera, as Kay described it, was an ill that conflated physical disease with moral failings epitomized by domestic improvidence; as such, cholera, like immorality, could be cured. That Kay's solution implied but did not explicitly include political reform helped restrict the terms in which the maladies of society— and the social domain more generally—were formulated, and at the same time made this reform the necessary basis of Great Britain's health. If the Catholic Emancipation Act had jeopardized the traditional foundation of English identity, Kay's cure promised to give the nation a new foundation—not simply, as disgruntled Tories imagined, by marshalling a majority of newly enfranchised Protestants against Irish Catholics, but by equating national well-being with the economic health of a newly politicized, respectable middle class. This physic, which was liberally administered in England during the next two decades, did at least temporarily enshrine domestic virtues as distinctively English at the same time that it authorized the government apparatus epitomized by the New Poor Law and the Board of Health. In Ireland, of course, Kay's cure proved bitter medicine indeed. Appropriately, perhaps, its legacy was not an embrace of English respectability but the growth of an increasingly militant Irish nationalism.

Four

ANATOMICAL REALISM AND SOCIAL INVESTIGATION IN EARLY NINETEENTH-CENTURY MANCHESTER

"Our age is pre-eminently the age of great cities," Robert Vaughan proclaimed in 1843.[1] If by *great* Vaughan meant "populous," he was merely echoing what by 1840 had become a commonplace: the three censuses published since 1801 showed a remarkable growth in the population of England and Wales, but the increase in the five largest cities was positively astronomical. "Whilst the increase of population in England and Wales, in 30 years, from 1801 to 1831, has been something more than 47 per cent.," reported the Select Committee on the Health of Towns, "the actual increase in the number of inhabitants of five of our most important provincial towns has very nearly doubled that rate; being . . . almost 98 per cent."[2] While this explosion in the urban population signaled to contemporaries the success of the manufacturing and commercial concerns central to Britain's growing prosperity, it also spelled trouble. Indeed, the very existence of a parliamentary select committee on the health of towns meant that by 1840 the great cities had come to seem problematic to government officials. As the Health of Towns committee described it, the problem epitomized by these cities was the moral impact that urban conditions had on the laboring poor. According to the report issued in 1840, overcrowding, poor sanitation, and dirt were major causes of pauperism, that moral debility that encompassed, but exceeded, poverty.

> Independent of the physical evils to the working classes arising from the
> causes before adverted to, Your Committee are desirous to express the

strong opinion they entertain, that the dirt, damp, and discomfort so frequently found in and about the habitations of the poorer people in these great towns, has a most pernicious effect on their moral feelings, induces habits of recklessness and disregard of cleanliness, and all proper pride in personal appearance, and thereby takes away a strong and useful stimulus to industry and exertion.[3]

Contemporary observers and historians agree that the deplorable physical conditions detailed by the *Report from the Select Committee on the Health of Towns* did exist and that they profoundly affected the health, longevity, and daily experiences of those who lived in densely peopled cities like London and Manchester.[4] While it would be cruel to minimize the material effects of urban living conditions in the early nineteenth century, it would be naive to imagine that the conceptualization of the urban space—especially by those powerful enough to implement solutions—did not affect the way that problems were identified and experienced. In this essay I focus on one of the central metaphors employed by a particular group of middle-class reformers to represent the city and its working-class inhabitants in the decade 1832–1842.[5] The metaphor is the image of the social body.[6] My argument is that, in adapting the age-old analogy between the human body and social organizations to a social situation that was new in the first decades of the nineteenth century, Whig reformers helped forge from inherited representational strategies and epistemological assumptions a genre that made a new version of the city visible in a new way.[7] For the purposes of this essay, I will call this genre *anatomical realism*.[8]

Borrowing from eighteenth-century scientific medicine (especially anatomy), this descriptive and analytic genre produced an image of the urban environment—and the social domain more generally—that privileged minute particulars obtained by eyewitness investigation. Paradoxically, however, this epistemology also located truth in dark recesses, which only theoretical interpretation could illuminate. Ideally, the anatomical approach to the city replaced more traditional ways of representing the city—both the universalized abstractions by which many eighteenth-century analysts had invoked the living conditions of the poor and the slang-ridden guidebooks by which young aristocrats had chronicled their urban adventures in the 1820s.[9] At the same time that it grounded its own authority in scientific disinterestedness, moreover, this mode of representation also reduced its object of analysis to a passive aggregate, whose spatialization rendered it more suitable to minute inspection and quantification. Finally, I suggest that, just as anatomical realism and the metaphor of the social body institutionalized one way of seeing and managing (one version of) the city, so this mode of representation introduced problems that Whig reformers could not solve. On the one hand, because the image of the social body carried with it assumptions about physiological and economic self-regulation, this figure authorized the removal of restrictive measures like tariffs and poor relief. On the other hand, however, because scientific medicine had yet to provide guidelines for when a doctor should intervene in the operations of organs still imperfectly understood, the image of the social body could not help reformers address the issues of when and how to interfere in a social process that seemed increasingly out of control.[10] Indeed, because the epistemology associated with the image of the social body instituted evaluation at the heart of what passed within the scientific community as disinterestedness, anatomical realism could neither guarantee uncontested knowledge nor stabilize the meanings it produced, especially when social analysts sought to apply scientific formulations outside the scientific domain in which they were developed.

I present my argument in two sections. In the first, I use James Phillips Kay's 1832 treatment of cotton operatives in Manchester, *The Moral and Physical Condition of the Working Classes . . . in Manchester,* to illuminate the disciplinary and epistemological issues raised by scientific medicine. Kay's text, which is organized around the image of the social body, is important for several reasons. First, it was the first detailed investigation of the urban space and its inhabitants to combine the representational strategies of eyewitness reports and statistical tables. In so doing, it established some of the most important conventions of the mode of social analysis adapted from anatomy.[11] Second, the *Moral and Physical Condition* directly or indirectly inspired some of the most important investigatory organizations of this period, including the Manchester Statistical Society (founded 1833), of which Kay was a member, the London Statistical Society (1834), the Statistical Section of the British Association for the Advancement of Science (1834), and the National Association for the Promotion of the Social Sciences (1857).[12]

Finally, Kay himself was a critical—and in some respects symptomatic—figure in the historical process by which knowledge about the newly urbanizing and industrializing cities was produced and distributed. The son of a Unitarian cotton manufacturer, Kay studied medicine at Edinburgh University, whose curriculum emphasized the eighteenth-century Scottish amalgamation of "polity, economy and society" and a nerve-centered model of the body.[13] In 1835, Kay assumed the first in a series of administrative posts, which culminated in the position of secretary to the Committee of Council on Education, from which he spearheaded the campaign for a national system of education. In addition to his official activities, Kay was also active in numerous voluntary associations, including the Manchester Statistical Society, the Manchester Provident Society, the Anti-Corn Law League, and the National Association for the Promotion of the Social Sciences. In 1842, Kay solidified his social and financial position by wedding the daughter of the wealthy Robert Shuttleworth, whose surname Kay adopted. In the training and career of James Kay-Shuttleworth, then, we see not only an example of how the so-called new men acquired power and social prestige in a newly bureaucratizing society, but also how Scottish Enlightenment theories—many of which focused on an agricultural society—were infused into the English reform movement, which was preoccupied with urban problems and the administration of the social domain.[14]

In the second section of the essay I turn to the primary guise in which women figured in early representations of the city. As prostitutes, women were considered part of the "moral and physical evils of great towns" by reformers like Kay. Such reformers—exemplified here by an anonymous reviewer of Parent-Duchâtelet's study of French prostitution—addressed the problem of prostitution by assimilating the woman's body to the waste-clogged social body. Both, in theory, could be sanitized once systems of surveillance and waste-management were instituted. In this writer's treatment of prostitution, we begin to see that, implicitly at least, the social body was always gendered, however gender-blind its analysts claimed to be. At the same time, we also see one reason why anatomical realism proved problematic as soon as it was deployed in the social domain. The problem manifested itself most clearly in the notorious elusiveness of prostitution: even the most meticulous social analysts conceded that they could neither identify nor quantify prostitutes. This elusiveness had little to do with the deviousness of women (as analysts charged); instead, it was an effect of transporting a mode of representation developed within a community unique in its tolerance of representational license to a domain still governed in part by theological rationality in the form of evangelical morality. To compensate for the interdiction imposed on anatomical realism in the social domain, and in the arena of sexuality in particular, social analysts developed an elaborate system of connotation which, like anatomy, could bring into visibility things that they could not otherwise examine. Because the theoretical assumptions upon which connotation depended infused what was otherwise unmentionable with ambiguity and doubt, however, the subject of connotation could neither be defined nor controlled, as the subject of anatomy apparently could be. The discourse about prostitution, in other words, that dared not be explicit lest the problem get worse, incited fears that every woman might be a prostitute.

Let me emphasize two further points about the argument that follows. First, although the issues raised in the texts I examine did not apply exclusively to the new urban centers, cities like London and Manchester were focal points for those concerns because the disruptions that industrialization and urbanization caused in traditional living and work arrangements were clearest in urban areas. Just as the new factories crystallized anxieties about class and gender relations because factories challenged the sexual division of labor, so urban neighborhoods focused pervasive worries about the effects of capitalism on social stability and morality because they foretold the end of an agricultural, communal society.

Second, while the concerns I highlight have implications beyond the cities with which they were most frequently associated, I would not generalize the conclusions I draw beyond the decade I examine here. To understand the stakes of the rhetorical contests I describe, it is important to remember that this ten-year period marked a crucial transition in contemporary perceptions of capitalism. The traditional system of paternalism had been in crisis since 1815, and even in 1830 the national economy had yet to recover from its postwar slump. With inadequate provisions for the numerous unemployed, and no consensus about how to negotiate religious, political, or economic demands, neither workers nor manufacturers, landowners nor financiers, theorists nor politicians were quite sure what form social relations would take. In 1832, the viability of the factory system and the utility of machinery were still very much in question;[15] the extent of religious toleration and the nature of political representation had just been fiercely contested; and the viability of class society was a question of considerable debate. Things were by no means settled by 1842, but with over four-fifths of English cotton mills powered by steam and the nation moving to a laissez-faire, rather than protectionist, solution to economic distress, machines and capitalism were clearly in Britain to stay.[16] By 1842, England had instituted limited parliamentary reform and a punitive new poor law, and—even if labor unrest and poor harvests had generated Chartism and economic depression—reformers of both parties had successfully forged a national agenda that placed the administration of the social domain—the improvement, that is, of the morality and health of the poor—before political or economic reform. Between 1832 and 1842, pervasive uncertainty about the nature of social convulsions—much less their outcome—made every metaphor advanced to describe the problems especially promising and especially problematic. In this context, the image of the social body took on special importance—as a defense against treating humans like machines, as a basis for authorizing programs of surveillance and control, and as a license for politically unrepresented groups to claim some of the power that reformers also struggled to seize from each other.

I

To late twentieth-century readers, James Phillips Kay's *Moral and Physical Condition* seems like a disciplinary hodgepodge. Having identified poverty and disease as the primary evils that beset Manchester cotton operatives, Kay designates as the cure an economic solution: repeal of the restrictive Corn Laws—in other words, free trade. The logical displacements in Kay's argument, which get him from cholera to free trade, are underwritten by a metaphor that links literal disease, moral debility, and economic distress.[17] Kay introduces the image of the social body with a discussion that simultaneously hints at how a healthy body governs itself and explains society's failure to achieve this equilibrium. Whereas the animal body is governed by a central faculty that monitors and connects every part of the organism, the social body wants—both lacks and needs—an equivalent "sensorium":

> Society were well preserved, did a similar faculty preside, with an equal sensibility, over its constitution; making every order immediately conscious of the evils affecting any portion of the general mass, and thus rendering their removal equally necessary for the immediate ease, as it is for the ultimate welfare of the whole social system. The mutual dependence of the individual members of society and of its various orders, for the supply of their necessities and the gratification of their desires, is acknowledged, and it imperfectly compensates for the want of a faculty resembling that pervading consciousness which presides over the animal economy.[18]

Kay's overall aim in this pamphlet is to argue that even though the social body is as lawful as the physiological system, its laws are still unknown because no sensorium exists to alert one part of the body to the distresses of the others. As this description suggests, Kay assumes that the nervous system is the most important part of both animal and social bodies because he considers knowledge and sympathy prerequisites to health.

The image of a lawful body unified and superintended by the nervous system was the product of the Edinburgh medical community in which Kay trained in the 1820s.[19] To a certain extent, the elevation of the nervous system was a function of anatomical work conducted in Edinburgh beginning in the middle of the eighteenth century. According to the model of the body elaborated by Robert Whytt and William

Hunter, the function of each part of the body was both highly specialized and precisely correlated to its structure; the body as a whole was unified by the nerves and, more precisely, by a special case of physiological sensibility. Whytt called this function *sympathy*, by which he meant the communication of sensations among bodily organs.[20] Although physiologists disagreed about whether or not sympathetic action was centered in a specific location, those who thought it was often used the term *sensorium* to designate the seat of sensations.[21]

If the image of the body depicted by Scottish anatomists emphasized its unity, then the epistemology by which medical scientists claimed to know this body emphasized a complex relationship between empiricism and theory. Herein lies one of the central features of eighteenth-century anatomy, which was crucial to the kind of truth that medical scientists claimed to produce.[22] On the one hand, anatomists like Whytt and Hunter emphasized that scientists should see what is before them clearly and represent it exactly: "every part is represented just as it was found," Hunter declared of his plates in *The Anatomy of the Human Gravid Uterus* (1774), "not so much as one joint of a finger having been moved."[23] We find this emphasis on empirical observation and transparent representation both in eighteenth-century anatomists' insistence that their anatomical drawings are exact and in the extraordinary detail that characterizes many anatomical figures from this period.[24] On the other hand, however, anatomists tended both to use artificial means to highlight parts of the body that were indistinct and to supplement empirical observations with normative judgments. Thus, Hunter admitted to making his "material" legible by "filling the vascular system with a bright coloured wax." This made thousands of minute vessels visible, "which from their delicacy, and the transparency of their natural content, are otherwise imperceptible."[25] Even more important, because nature presented an infinite variety of bodies to those who sought to standardize knowledge, anatomists produced images of a normative body rather than exact copies of any particular bodies. They justified eliminating the idiosyncrasies of individual cadavers by appeals to a characteristic representative or by admitting the aesthetic attraction of frankly idealized figures.[26]

Far from residing on the surface where it was obvious to the eye, then, the truth of the body was assumed to hide in its interior. Far from being transparent to the messy interior, the models and drawings by which anatomists represented this body's truth cleaned up and clarified organs and tissues that initially appeared hopelessly undifferentiated or obscure. And far from being as particularized as their highly detailed features seem to suggest, the anatomical figures from this period represent the outcome of numerous observations that have been supplemented with theoretical norms. The preference we see in eighteenth-century anatomical representations for normative over mimetic representation suggests that, for these medical scientists, true penetration only begins with sight; its next, decisive phase is abstraction, generalization, or theory, which displaces actual bodies as surely as the knife displaces the obscuring flesh.[27]

The epistemology favored by eighteenth-century anatomists, then, produced a set of theorized norms whose relationship to the empirical world remained unexamined and, for them, unproblematic.[28] The knowledge generated by eighteenth-century anatomists was considered unproblematic because medical scientists claimed that their disinterestedness guaranteed political and religious neutrality. At the same time, laboratory experience and wisdom were assumed to ensure that practitioners identified an ideal that accurately represented the "universal nature of mankind." By and large, the aesthetic and cultural assumptions implicit in such wisdom remained unexamined, precisely because knowledge in general was assumed to be universal and recognizable by disinterested individuals.[29] If the cultural assumptions written into anatomical truth went unremarked, so too did other features of this knowledge. Despite anatomists' claims to illuminate the functions (dynamics) of bodily parts, for example, this characteristic eighteenth-century science could only describe synchronic relations within the organism. This structuralist bias meant that, despite additional insights provided by comparative anatomy, anatomical drawings and models could not self-evidently lead to predictions about bodily processes or medical interventions in the name of cure. Then, too, because anatomists could only work on material that, until the Anatomy Act of 1832, consisted almost exclusively of criminal bodies, eighteenth-century anatomical knowledge was ineluctably linked to what its practitioners never mentioned: the literal violation of socially outcast individuals.[30]

Eighteenth-century anatomical knowledge may have been based on empirical research whose practitioners effaced their cultural and class biases, but its normative component can be traced to the theoretical and social context in which this work was conducted. At both theoretical and practical levels, for example, the highlighting of sensibility enabled medical scientists to accrue social authority by taking on the venerable Cartesian problem about the relationship between body and mind.[31] Emphasizing the nervous system, in other words—a system that supposedly fused physiological structure with emotional affect—lent credibility to the medical scientist's claims to produce disinterested knowledge about the social economy. By midcentury, such claims had to compete with the ethical claims that were being advanced by moral philosophers,[32] but in Scotland the competition between medical scientists and ethical theorists did not erupt into explicit antagonism. For much of the century, conflict was averted because Scottish theories about society were so compatible with the physiological models their colleagues produced that it seemed unnecessary to discriminate rigorously between physiology and the domain where ethical considerations were paramount. Beginning with Francis Hutcheson in the 1740s, Scottish moral philosophers like Adam Ferguson, David Hume, Adam Smith, and Dugald Stewart described society as an organic whole whose specialized units were correlated to their functions and whose unity was guaranteed by the sympathy inherent in every "man." The holistic approach to social problems that resulted from the compatibility of Scottish medicine and moral philosophy was still prominent in Edinburgh in the 1820s, even though in London and elsewhere it was being replaced by the disciplinary division that eventually separated medical from social science.[33]

The Scottish model of the organism also both derived support from and informed the social context in which it was developed. In the first place, the prominence given to the unity of a body differentiated by both structures and functions played well in a society in which one group of university-based intellectuals produced readily accessible knowledge for another group of landowners and noblemen in return for financial support and social prestige.[34] In the second place, the priority given to nerves helped set limits on who could participate in the production of such "universal" knowledge. Because manual labor was thought to militate against the refinement of nerves, because less "civilized" peoples were considered less delicate, and because overly responsive nervous systems were thought to predispose one to hysteria, the working population, "barbarians" like the Highlanders (and colonial subjects), and women were all considered unqualified to contribute to the knowledge about mankind generated by the Edinburgh intelligentsia. Anatomists in particular capitalized on these social discriminations, just as the presence of this hierarchy informed the emphasis they placed on theory. By emphasizing theory, that is, anatomists distanced themselves from lowly surgeons, who were debased by the manual nature of their labor, and aligned themselves with aristocrats, who displayed a special interest in comparative anatomy during this period.[35]

Kay's representation of the Manchester cotton operatives reproduces both the eighteenth-century organicist model of the body and the epistemological assumptions that governed anatomical representations. Like the models produced by eighteenth-century anatomists, Kay's picture of the social body shows a unified whole whose members are specialized according to function. Like eighteenth-century anatomists with their colored wax, moreover, Kay highlights some parts of the system to emphasize their importance. In Kay's social body, the most significant parts are not the most obvious (diseased) parts but the good (normal) parts—that is, the well-to-do who have undertaken errands of mercy into densely populated slums. Note that these members of the social body remain individuals in Kay's representation, even when he is discussing the necessity of their collective effort; by the same token, Kay obscures impoverished individuals by aggregating the poor and assimilating them to the houses and neighborhoods they inhabit. This aggregation tends to spatialize the poor, so that when good individuals explore urban neighborhoods, they also authorize forays into domestic interiors and investigations of bodily processes like eating and sleeping. Personifying houses, as Kay does here, further transfers agency from the aggregated poor to social investigators, even though it remains unclear whether the outstretched arms plead for help or extend a contaminating embrace.

> The dense masses of the habitations of the poor, which stretch out their arms, as though to grasp and enclose the dwellings of the noble and wealthy, in the metropolis, and in our huge provincial cities, have heretofore been regarded as mighty wildernesses of building, in which the incurable ills of society rankled, beyond the reach of sanative interference. The good despaired that by their individual efforts they could relieve the miseries, which, in their errands of mercy, they beheld. . . . One fact alone became prominent, *that the united exertions of the individual members of society were required, to procure a moral and physical change in the community;* and it was evident that some circumstance was wanting, to disturb the apathy which paralyzed their energies. (pp. 11–12)

If this body is to be made healthy, well-to-do individuals must assert themselves and monitor the aggregated mass that infects the organism. The wake-up call Kay reiterates here had actually already been sounded in the spring of 1832, when Asiatic cholera struck Manchester. In anticipation of the cholera epidemic, Manchester had established a Board of Health, of which Kay was a member. If only his readers could see the danger hiding in the urban wilderness, Kay suggests, this institution could provide both the occasion for systematic forays into urban slums and the personnel necessary to implement the anatomical procedures Kay derived from his medical training.

As he explains it in *The Physical and Moral Condition,* Kay's plan is to dissect the diseased parts of the social body. To do so, he proposes minutely subdividing the police districts (which already spatialize people's lives), then assigning officials to "minutely inspect . . . the state of the houses and streets" (p. 19). To discipline their own vision, the inspectors are to be given "tabular queries" so that they can produce uniform "minute returns" (pp. 19, 20). In theory, the effect of such inspection will be new, and more manageable—that is, statistical—knowledge about the actual living conditions of the poor. Like eighteenth-century anatomical atlases, in other words, the statistics generated by the inspectors will simultaneously standardize information about the poor and teach others how to penetrate and interpret the dense masses of urban slums.

The influence of anatomy upon this kind of social survey is even clearer in subsequent examples of the genre, as, for example, in the engravings that depict working-class houses with their external walls peeled back to reveal sparsely furnished interiors, babies crawling on damp-stained floors, and overcrowded beds.[36] Kay's descriptions of working-class interiors are, by contrast, quite abstract; he describes houses as "ill-furnished," for example, "uncleanly, often ill-ventilated— perhaps damp" (p. 25). The very abstraction of Kay's descriptions is in keeping with his anatomical method, however, for it replicates the tendency we have already seen in eighteenth-century anatomical representation to supplement minute particularization with interpretive, theoretical norms. To describe a house as "ill-furnished" or "uncleanly," after all, is to assume some (class-specific) standard of furnishing and hygiene, and to emphasize poor ventilation over other problems is to assume that stagnant air breeds disease, as proponents of the miasmatic theory maintained.[37]

At some points, the need to supplement empirical observation with theoretical norms sits less comfortably with Kay than it did with eighteenth-century anatomists. Whereas William Hunter could simultaneously praise the verisimilitude of his anatomical figures and admit to using wax to enhance features he considered important, Kay occasionally calls attention to the inadequacy of his representational conventions. These passages, however, do not highlight the gap between empirical observation and theory so much as they lament the modes of retrieving information currently available. For Kay, the new discourse of statistics represents both the inadequacy of available information and the possibility of perfect (transparent) representation.

For nearly every one of the statistical tables Kay supplies, he offers some apology for what the figures cannot tell. In his effort to anatomize crime, for example, Kay admits that the tables record only some transgressions:

There is . . . a licentiousness capable of corrupting the whole body of society, like an insidious disease, which eludes observation, yet is equally fatal in its effects. Criminal acts may be statistically classed—the victims of the law may be enumerated—but the number of those affected with the moral leprosy of vice cannot be exhibited with mathematical precision. (p. 62)

Statistics are imperfect because the subject Kay is concerned with here—illegitimacy—leaves no record, partly because social conventions informally police admissions of sexual indiscretion. Here we begin to see one of the limitations anatomical realism manifests when it is mobilized in the social domain: the social investigator cannot measure what people will not allow him to see, especially, as in the case of illegitimacy, when laws are also insufficient to identify every person who commits this crime. Because Kay does not focus exclusively on areas governed by moral decorum, where the inhibitions imposed upon representation are so severe, he can also express confidence that, when information can be gathered, statistics will tell society's truth.

Still, Kay acknowledges that there are limits to what the rationalizing knowledge epitomized by statistics can do. No matter how precise, quantification cannot inspire action, especially in a society whose bonds are forged by sympathy, not mere calculation. When Kay supplements his empirical observations and statistical tables with theoretical assertions, then, he does so not only because he shares eighteenth-century anatomists' belief that true knowledge takes the form of normative universals, but also because he intends his description to initiate action, to incite reform. Because Kay's pamphlet is explicitly polemical, and because it specifically engages in a debate about policy, he cannot simply claim, as early nineteenth-century scientists did, that disinterest guarantees political neutrality. For Kay, achieving neutrality was impossible, precisely because the debate about policy was conducted in politicized terms—that is, in terms that appealed to both party loyalty and interest more generally construed. Thus, Kay's language explicitly calls attention to the class and party positions inherent in his theoretical assumptions, despite the scientific stance he tries to assume. These assertions are drawn from the Whig interpretation of Smithian political economy: that restrictions on trade inhibit profits, wages, education, and social progress; that government poor relief accelerates population growth; and that some form of government interference in the social domain is necessary to counteract the pauperism of the poor.

By discriminating between the kind of knowledge he produces and another kind of knowledge that is even less disinterested, Kay finesses the challenge posed to scientific disinterestedness by transporting anatomical realism into the social domain. His specific target is the purely theoretical work of classical political economists like David Ricardo, who, having narrowed Adam Smith's more capacious social theory to a science of wealth and commerce, seem to have lost sight of the people who produce this wealth. For Kay, the problem with Ricardo's abstract theorizing is epitomized in the latter's claim that society is a machine. Kay rejects this metaphor because thinking of social relations as mechanical ignores the interior life, which is the source of sympathy and therefore of social health.

> The social body cannot be constructed like a machine, on abstract principles which merely include physical motions, and their numerical results in the production of wealth. The mutual relation of men is not merely dynamical, nor can the composition of their forces be subjected to a purely mathematical calculation. Political economy, though its object is to ascertain the means of increasing the wealth of nations, cannot accomplish its design, without at the same time regarding their happiness, and as its largest ingredient the cultivation of religion and morality. (pp. 63–64)

Anyone who visits a poor neighborhood, Kay suggests, will see that the poor are not machines. The abilities to calculate and theorize are insufficient qualifications for producing knowledge about an organism whose truth resides both in the superficial details of everyday life and in the hidden recesses of oppressed souls. The authoritative analyst must see for himself, penetrate the wilderness of buildings, and, most important, learn to sympathize with those he governs. "The lives, the fortunes, and the liberties of the people will henceforth we may hope be entrusted to those who know their wants, sympathize with their distresses, and in whose experience, ability, and integrity, they can repose the trust of devising means for their relief" (p. 13). If Kay's emphasis on firsthand observation and sympathy disqualifies economists like Ricardo, however, it also threatens to undermine the authority Kay wants to claim, for in many towns the slums were already being visited by a group with impeccable qualifications to sympathize—the clergy. It is partly to render the clergy supplemental to the bureaucratic expert that Kay emphasizes the scientific nature of his enterprise.

> It is not sufficient that the sidesmen or churchwardens should give a few hours daily to an examination of all applicants in our enormous townships, but the towns should be minutely subdivided, each district having its local board, which (besides an executive parish overseer resident in the district, and thus possessing every means of becoming minutely acquainted with the character of the inhabitants,) should also be furnished with its board of superior officers. By such means: by adopting the test of desert, at least to determine the *amount* of relief bestowed; by discourag-

ing or even rejecting those whose indigence is the consequence of dissipation, of idleness, and of wilful impudence; and by making the overseers
themselves the means of instructing the poor, that every labourer is the
surest architect of his own fortune—by constituting them the patrons of
virtue and the censors of vice . . . the sources of a powerful moral
agency—much good might be effected. (pp. 50–51)

Identifying personal inspection and scientific method as the qualifications that authorize certain people to interfere in the interior lives of
the poor legitimizes the efforts of medical scientists to participate in social reform. If Kay succeeds in replacing scientific disinterestedness with
a legitimate form of interest, however, his formulation cannot solve one
of the central problems introduced by the image of the social body: How
can one know precisely when and how to interfere? Here, anatomy
could provide no help, for not only did the very nature of anatomical
investigation render the diagnosis of disease too late for prevention or
cure, but medical knowledge about the body was still incomplete. In the
case of some bodily functions—especially the operations of the brain
and its relationship to the nervous system—anatomists were admittedly
in the dark.[38] By the same token, the popular physiology texts that pro-
liferated in the 1830s tended to emphasize not remedies for bodily disorders but the rational state of a system that, once in motion and if
unimpeded, followed a natural course.[39] Then, too, the relationship between scientific medicine and medical practice remained attenuated
even in the 1830s; most doctors practiced by empirical observation and
experience, not by the formally rationalized knowledge supplied by
anatomy texts.[40] Kay, by contrast, who was as interested in cure as in
description, could not leave unattended a social body clearly in distress.
Kay could claim that moral improvement was necessary, and he could
prescribe a board of experts to investigate and determine "desert," but
his anatomical method could not insure that the scientific programs he
advanced would transcend controversy or guarantee cure. Quite the
contrary. His use of such evaluative categories as dissipation, idleness,
and willful impudence virtually guaranteed that his suggestions would
inflame the poor, and his advocacy of state-sponsored education was
certain to irritate both Christian economists and liberal Tories. To many
of Kay's contemporaries, the cure he recommended seemed worse than
the disease he identified.

By and large, Kay does not address the problem that politics introduces into the ideal of scientific disinterestedness. Instead, he displaces
the local issues of when and how to intervene by declaring the source of

England's "maladies" to be of "remote and accidental origin" (p. 15). In a process I have described elsewhere, he can then identify the Irish as the human equivalent to (and carrier of) cholera and equate cure with the elimination of this "evil" from England's social body.[41] A discrimination that anyone can make (between the Irish and the English) thus stands in for a judgment with which only certain experts can be trusted (between the deserving and the undeserving poor), and the class and political assumptions that underwrite Kay's specific recommendations disappear beneath racist assumptions that all (English) men share.

The substitution by which Kay displaces the political controversies that haunt his analysis repeats the combination of empiricism and theory that he carries over from scientific medicine. Other contemporary sources support the claims that Kay based on his own firsthand observation: that Manchester *was* inhabited by large numbers of Irish workers who *did* live in crowded neighborhoods and *were* the first victims of disease. To compare the Irish to savages and barbarians, however (p. 21), and to highlight their criminal propensities and sexual profligacy (pp. 34, 44) was to mobilize stereotypes that had informed English attitudes since the sixteenth century. Kay never fixes the boundary between what he observes and what he assumes, and the concentration of statistical tables in areas that specifically concern the Irish reinforces the impression that this line did not exist or matter.

If Kay's suggestions about the Irish deflect attention from his genuinely controversial recommendations—that the poor should receive state-sponsored education, that the Corn Laws should be repealed— then the necessity for such diversion suggests the strains that appeared in anatomical realism when it was adapted to the social domain. Within the scientific community, these strains were not so obvious: not only did scientific practitioners explicitly exempt themselves from politics while tolerating—indeed, encouraging—considerable representational explicitness, but the limits of their knowledge were less ruinous to the claims they made when exact description, not prediction or cure, was the point of the analysis. The limitations of anatomical realism, in other words, only became troublesome when this mode of analysis was applied in a domain also governed by competing analytic discourses and epistemological objectives. When scientific knowledge was applied to the politicized domain where policy mattered, it no longer seemed disinterested. When it was mobilized in the social domain, which encompassed sexuality, it did not even seem capable of controlling what it implied. As the maladies that Kay consolidated into pauperism were gradually disaggregated into separate ills during the next decade, the contradictory tendencies of anatomical realism emerged into starker relief.

II

Prostitution was a target of sporadic reform initiatives in the 1830s because, like the cities in which it flourished, it focused anxieties associated with industrialization and capitalism more generally. As labor that was neither regularly waged nor taxed, prostitution seemed to epitomize the uncertainty and irrationality of work in this changing world. As women who were neither moral nor irrevocably lost, prostitutes challenged prevailing stereotypes about gendered morality.[42] As victims who were also agents, these women crystallized pervasive concerns about determinism and free will.[43] Most important, for my purposes, as bodies that (sometimes) carried syphilis from man to man, prostitutes provided a literal site where the dirt and disease associated with the poor could be assumed to breed. Manage prostitution, some reformers seemed to believe, and you would simultaneously contain pauperism, control population growth, and reverse the moral debility that vitiated national prosperity.

In 1836, the scattered English campaigns against prostitution received new momentum from the publication of A. J. B. Parent-Duchâtelet's two-volume survey of French prostitution, *De la Prostitution dans la ville de Paris*. This French text focused Kay's general concern about the relationship between urban overcrowding and pauperism into a specific anxiety about this kind of "moral gangrene."[44] A review of Parent-Duchâtelet's work published in the *Foreign Quarterly Review* in July 1837 set the tone for the various treatments of prostitution that appeared in subsequent decades. Entitled "Moral and Physical Evils of Large Towns," this anonymous review borrows the authority established by texts like Kay's to bring a subject hitherto monopolized by theological (and particularly evangelical) discourse into the purview of the emergent social sciences. By claiming the respect accorded the "moral physiologist," this writer explains, he hopes to avoid the charge that he "revel[s] in vice and delight[s] in infamy" (p. 181). This charge, which the writer clearly anticipates, stems from the fact that clergymen had so successfully appropriated the topic of prostitution that the opprobrium associated with it tended to sully anyone who studied it. Invoking both Kay's anatomical method and the acceptance that anatomy had won enables this writer to ridicule such aspersions and to exonerate both his subject and himself. Just as anatomy was once "denounced as an unhallowed and useless violation of decency," he acknowledges, so the study of prostitution is now disparaged. Just as anatomy has been made respectable (or at least legal) because it promotes medical expertise, so must contemporaries grant legitimacy to the study of sexual immorality because it can raise legislation from an empirical (haphazard) practice to a rigorous social science. "If, while anatomy was unknown, physicians prescribed at hazard for organic disease, . . . no less true is it that legislators are mere empirics, when they have not anatomized society, and that laws aggravate the evil they profess to cure when they are based on loose and imperfect analyses" (p. 181).

To counteract loose analyses and loose sexuality, this writer tries to duplicate Kay's anatomical realism. Like Kay, he claims that the treatment of this moral gangrene will require detailed information, which should be obtained by minute inspection and presented in statistical form (p. 182). Like Kay, he also assumes that the truth of prostitution is hidden and that its treatment will require expert analysis and interference. Here, however, the problem of prostitution begins to exceed the anatomical method to which it theoretically should submit. Just as Kay acknowledged that "sensuality has no record" (p. 62), so this author ruefully admits that the "evil" of prostitution defies both anatomical scrutiny and statistical representation. The elusiveness with which this and all subsequent analysts associate prostitution exposes decisively the problems generated when anatomical realism was transported into the social domain. That is, anatomists' assertions that they could generate exact knowledge only remained (relatively) uncontroversial as long as this knowledge was consumed within the community of like-minded experts in which it was produced. Outside that community, this mode of analysis actually produced precisely the uncertainty its practitioners claimed to be able to contain.

Most explicitly, prostitution challenged anatomical analysis because prostitutes were so difficult to count. So perplexing were their numbers, in fact, that exaggeration and underestimation presented equal dangers to the would-be statistician. So many women move in and out of this most occasional of all occupations, this writer complains, that there may actually be far more prostitutes than previous writers have guessed. Yet, because they are "the most restless of all human beings" (p. 188), prostitutes may just as easily be counted more than once as missed altogether. Despite the obvious challenge prostitution posed to quantification, however, the problem of counting dwindles as the writer continues. The problem of counting, after all, was partly a problem of definition: one could not count prostitutes until one defined (described) prostitution. But the problem of definition turned out to be a function of something else—a social inhibition that militated against both counting and describing. The problem, this writer explains, is that enumerating or describing prostitutes would exacerbate the evil the moralist wants to control, because realistic representation incites imitation.[45]

> It is unnecessary to dwell on the evils that would attend publicity . . . ; there are few parents or guardians who do not know the danger to which youth is exposed by the gratification of prurient curiosity; there is no statistician ignorant of the effect of the imitative principle in extending crime. (p. 187)

Anxieties about the imitative principle almost derail this writer's analysis. After all, if moral inhibitions forbid representation, how can one conduct a "moral anatomy" (p. 182)? Since social conventions prohibit even the degree of descriptive specificity Kay enjoyed, this writer abandons empirical analysis and offers instead three alternatives to an eyewitness account. First, he devotes three full pages to the similarities between prostitutes and other women. Then, he turns to Parent-Duchâtelet's statistical tables, which could claim scientific precision because of an 1828 French law that mandated the weekly inspection of prostitutes. Finally, he abandons the subject of prostitution altogether for the other topic Parent-Duchâtelet minutely explored: waste removal from urban streets and waterways. Instead of departing from anatomical realism, however, these three strategies actually elaborate tendencies inherent in anatomical realism. These tendencies expose both the conditions necessary to make anatomical realism comprehensible and the limitations these conditions imposed on the kind of knowledge this genre could produce.

Highlighting the similarities between prostitutes and other women enables this writer to forego explicit definition and detailed description, which, in a domain traditionally governed by evangelical morality, would have seemed dubious at best. In so doing, this writer also seems to affirm the superiority of the anatomical gaze, which locates an essential truth by penetrating deceptive appearances. Yet because this writer's indirect construction of prostitution renders prostitutes both deceptive and elusive, such penetration cannot succeed, because the object of analysis seems alternatively everywhere at once and nowhere to be found. The *Foreign Quarterly* writer tries to counteract this problem by imagining the prostitute a prisoner: once she has been confined, he suggests, the prostitute will be as tractable as the anatomist's corpse.

> Were we to form our estimate indeed from what is seen and heard in the streets, we should at once conclude that the wretches are thoroughly de-

praved, and that all human means must fail to convince them of their guilt, or turn them from the iniquity of their proceedings. But it is in the solitude of prison, and the sufferings of the hospital, that their real character must be studied, when compassion unlocks the secret stores of hidden thought and smothered emotion. (p. 184)

Once the prostitute is confined, it seems, she yields her "secret stores" to the sympathetic analyst. That these secrets simply reproduce what the analyst expected to hear becomes evident when he tells us that the prostitute judges herself more harshly than a virtuous woman would. Our writer makes this assertion even though it contradicts the point he is explicitly pursuing—that the prostitute is just like a virtuous woman. Prostitutes, he writes, "are conscious of their degradation, and are a subject of horror even to themselves; it would almost appear that their contempt and loathing for their abject state is more intense than what is shown to them by the innocent and the virtuous" (p. 184). According to the perverse logic dictated by his inability to define prostitution, the fallen woman becomes more virtuous than the innocent virgin. So virtuous does she become, in fact, that she voluntarily removes herself from prostitution—through repentance, insanity, or suicide (p. 184).

Applying the anatomical gaze to prostitution enables this writer to respect the moral interdiction against explicitness while probing the truth that lies beneath the surface. Yet the truth he perceives has repercussions as devastating as any description could, for if prostitutes who do not go mad or take their lives disappear into the ranks of respectable women, then how can any man tell which women have fallen and which are pure? The possibility of such confusion so alarms our writer that he suddenly demands the kind of interference he has just declared unnecessary.

> If it appears that any considerable portion [of prostitutes] return into the general mass of the population, if we daily run the risk of entrusting to them our dearest interests, there arises a strong argument for subjecting prostitution to some *surveillance,* and counter-acting, as far as possible, its pernicious influence. (p. 187)

Since such surveillance was exactly what the Parisian system of police and medical inspection mandated, Parent-Duchâtelet's tables provide our author with the evidence necessary to justify his fears. Sure enough, out of the 121 prostitute marriages Parent-Duchâtelet records, "5 belonged to an elevated rank of society!" (p. 187). Even more shocking, Parent-Duchâtelet tells of five husbands who stepped forward to remove their new wives' names from the official register; all "five who showed such absence of shame belonged to the higher classes of society!" (p. 187). The problem for this English writer (if not for French husbands) is that the theoretical assumption that converts empirical observation into the anatomical gaze—that all women are alike in being moral—now obscures the very distinction upon which social order and morality depend—that some women are different from others.

This writer's entanglement in the effects of combining anatomical realism with morally mandated indirection might have led to a demand for less sanctimonious silence and more precise record-keeping. This is what his reference to "dearest interests" leads us to believe. Instead of demonstrating the importance of more explicit information, however, the discovery of reformed prostitutes "even . . . in the higher circles" constitutes for him "further proof of the necessity of discretion and secrecy" (p. 187). Beyond the threat posed by the imitative principle, that is, lies the embarrassment that plain speaking might inflict on the well-to-do, the prosperous few who, having frequented the haunts of vice (as he has), now act as if they are not contaminated. The class bias expressed here reinforces the ban on explicitness levied both by the imitative principle and by evangelical decorum in general. To respect the overdetermined interdiction against explicitness, this writer suddenly abandons the subject of prostitution altogether and takes up instead a topic that writers like Parent-Duchâtelet had successfully subjected to anatomical analysis: sanitation.

The turn to sanitation is not actually a turn away from prostitution, of course. As the author of "Moral and Physical Evils" "run[s] lightly" over the "physical disadvantages" of large towns, he also elaborates the subject that decorum forbids him to explore (p. 189). Even though he never makes the connection explicit, juxtaposing a discussion of the immorality spread by prostitutes to an analysis of the diseases spread by contaminated water renders the clogged sewer pipes that he does describe analogous to an infected vagina, which he does not describe.[46] Like contaminated water, this juxtaposition suggests, the prostitute is "unfit for domestic purposes" (p. 189). Like the sewer, which can be regularly opened, illuminated, and flushed, the woman's vagina can be exposed to the medical eye, inspected, and cleaned. This writer's description of sewer work sounds ominously like Dr. Acton's detailed descriptions of how to sanitize a woman's infected vagina. Here is our anonymous author: "A man would pass along this gallery, carrying a safety lamp, to see and remove any obstructions that might accidentally have occurred in the sewer" (p. 190). Here is Acton, who is actually quoting one J. Lane: "An external examination alone is quite insufficient for the discovery of these complaints. . . . The house-surgeon, when the speculum is used, . . . inserts a strip of lint dipped in the lead-lotion, and this is allowed to remain for three or four hours. . . . By these means, discharges proceeding from the vagina may usually be cured in a few days."[47] Juxtaposition even affords our writer greater latitude than an explicit analogy would. Metonymic contiguity allows him to imply both that prostitutes *are* excrementitious matter and that they simply carry it, in the form of venereal disease. This double connotation enables him to condemn prostitution and to suggest that, like contaminated water that can be made to yield *poudrette* (manure), individual prostitutes might actually be turned to society's use: "what now produces disgust and disease might be a source of wealth and growth," in the form of prostitutes turned milliners, field laborers, and washing women (p. 189).

So elaborate are the implied parallels between prostitutes and waste that our writer virtually begs to be charged with the calumny he initially repudiated: that he "find[s] pleasure in the contemplation" of "all that is shameful and loathsome in society" (p. 181). At the very least, this juxtaposition makes explicit the erotic overtones implicit in anatomical investigations. Indeed, the erotic component of scientific medicine, which was implicit in metaphors equating seeing with unveiling and penetrating the feminized body of nature, was especially clear in the anatomical models and engravings I have already discussed.[48] Hunter's lavish engravings of the gravid uterus, for example, convey a vivid impression of the woman's delicate skin, not to mention her carefully delineated sexual organs.[49] Assimilating the sexual organs of prostitutes to city sewers therefore exposes the erotic overtones inherent in both scientific medicine and social analysis, making it perfectly clear that, just as the body of nature was feminized, so too was the body of the city. By the same token, of course, just as the body was feminized and rendered inert, so the investigator's masculinity was enhanced as his aggression intensified. The connotations of engendering analysis become even clearer in W. R. Greg's 1850 review of Parent-Duchâtelet, where the analyst describes himself "prob[ing]" the "lowest dens of filth and pollution . . . with a courageous and unshrinking hand."[50]

As Greg's description suggests, comparing the prostitute's body to the city not only feminized the latter but spatialized the former, turning the woman's body into a neighborhood (or theater) that could be entered and explored at will. Such spatialization also exposes the violence implicit in both scientific medicine and Kay's social analysis. While the violence that rendered anatomical knowledge possible was supposedly subsumed by the importance of this knowledge and by the lifelike nature of the figures, its traces linger in cuts that are clearly extraneous to the subject under discussion, as in Hunter's excision of the woman's external genitals in his picture of the full-term fetus.[51] In Kay's pamphlet, this violence is directed primarily toward the Irish, but it also appears in the nonchalance with which he exposes the interiors of working-class homes. In the "Moral and Physical Evils," it appears both in the figure of moral gangrene with which this author describes prostitutes and in his implicit approval of the women who remove themselves from the "profligate herd" through suicide (p. 187).

Juxtaposing anatomy to the analysis of prostitution and prostitution to human waste clearly cut at least two ways in the 1830s. On the one hand, the analogies established by these juxtapositions seemed to render prostitution as manageable a problem as waste removal, and the prostitute as tractable as the inert corpse. Cesspools, after all, did not defy quantification by perambulating through urban streets, and cadavers never resisted the anatomist's knife; waste-laden water might permeate the city, but its source could be exposed as easily as the diseased organ; and, most important, sanitary measures could be implemented and overseen so as to guarantee the orderly elimination of excrement, just as anatomical models could convert death into useful information.

On the other hand, however, because the system of connotation to which these juxtapositions belonged was not the only determinant of the causes or conceptualization of prostitution in the early nineteenth century, simply equating prostitutes to waste could not guarantee their elimination. Indeed, given prevalent assumptions that national prosperity depended on late marriages and that male sexuality demanded gratification early and often, it is not even clear that it was universally considered desirable *to* eliminate prostitution. The imprecision that governs the *Foreign Quarterly*'s article therefore not only respected evangelical morality; it also preserved assumptions about the asymmetry of sexual desire and the link between male prosperity and the availability of female sexual resources. At the same time that it allowed reformers to retain assumptions crucial to their personal and class well-being, of course, this indirection also meant that, because no definitive definition of prostitution could be given, no plan advanced to treat this moral gangrene could possibly go unchallenged. As men differentiated themselves from women, that is, they set themselves up as rivals to each other.

At first glance, the undecidability of prostitution and the uncontrollable effects that it generated seem simply to be a function of the connotation used to describe it. As every literary critic knows, after all, connotative signs are explicitly insufficient to their referent and to their speaker's intention. As opposed to denotation, which seems to be transparent and exact, connotation can thus raise doubts about what has been said at the same time that it proliferates meanings beyond a writer's intent.[52]

In practice, however, connotation is never employed simply in a linguistic context (that is, in contrast to denotation) but always takes place in a social setting, as part of a communication or conversation. In the situation I am describing, undecidability was actually a function not of connotation per se but of a historically specific clash of conventions (or specific rationalities) that differentiated one cultural subgroup (and domain) from another. As I have already suggested, one rationality obtained within the scientific community, while another—considerably more restrictive—rationality governed public discourse about sexuality. This was true in part at least because the public was assumed to be more sexually and morally heterogenous than was the largely white, male, and middle-class audience for science. Thus, when anatomical realism was transported outside of the scientific community to this more capacious audience, the clash between the two sets of conventions created uncertainty, because the connotations used to circumvent evangelical morality mobilized precisely those innuendoes that evangelical morality supposedly policed. The confrontation between scientific conventions of representation and public conventions also bred uncertainty for a second reason: the protocols and rationality that stabilized connotation within the scientific community did not obtain in the world at large. Within the scientific community, that is, the assumption that hidden truths were available to men who were properly trained limited contests over the nature of those truths and underwrote the concept of political neutrality that scientists called disinterestedness. In the variously defined and intensely interested communities that made up society at large, by contrast, connotation produced not consent but controversy and rivalry because, far from sharing a common goal, these groups competed for both resources and social authority.

This clash of conventions exposes not only the historically specific source of connotation's undecidability but also the limitation on the kind of knowledge that anatomical realism could produce. In one sense, the connotation that was apparently added to anatomical analysis to circumvent social interdictions simply extended the epistemology of anatomical realism. Like anatomy, that is, connotation brought into representation something hitherto unspeakable (invisible) by evading a barrier that forbade speech (obstructed vision). In another sense, however, in enabling the application of anatomical realism in a new domain, connotation also exposed its repressive *and* undecidable potential. As long as the producers and consumers of knowledge were both governed by the same rationality and protocols, as they were within the scientific community, a single set of assumptions passed as truth—even though this truth repressed competing views and voices. As soon as knowledge was consumed outside of the community that produced it, however, the producers could not control the meanings inferred by the members of other communities. Because the city and its problems constituted a new terrain that was fiercely contested by competing political interests and rival forms of expertise, no stable conventions could govern interpretation or disguise the self-serving interests that informed every program advanced to solve urban problems or cure the social body.

Without a community of like-minded experts to stabilize knowledge and establish social authority, analysts of the city were forced to authorize themselves. Such self-authorization appears in Kay's pamphlet when he distinguishes between himself and both classical economists and the clergy. It appears in the 1837 essay on prostitution when the author borrows the prestige of the moral physiologist to ennoble his subject and exonerate himself. It also appears in the appeals of eighteenth-century anatomists to the truth of nature and the ideals they supposedly saw in the welter of messy details. This last claim could hold sway, however, only as long as like-minded medical practitioners agreed that there was a normative body and that truth was normative too; efforts to authorize one's self and one's interpretation of what one saw were less effective when no community of interests or common protocols obtained. Thus, Kay worries that others will see in English workers the propensities everyone sees in the Irish, and the reviewer of Parent-Duchâtelet fears that his interest in prostitution will be taken for a prurient interest in sex.

The clash of rationalities I have been describing constitutes a chapter in the epistemological disaggregation by which new disciplines were formalized in relation to the emergence of new objects of analysis and the consolidation of new domains. The eventual outcome of this process was the institutionalization of an entire range of social sciences, each with its own protocol, system of credentialization, and foundational assumptions. At this early stage—before anthropology, sociology, and psychology attained disciplinary identity and before the subjects they eventually claimed were fully differentiated—anatomy proved attractive to social analysts because it offered a model by which they could compare the new urban environment to something familiar and (relatively) clear as well as an epistemology that explicitly valorized supplementing empirical observation with theoretical assumptions. The metaphor of the social body enabled Kay and other Whigs who supported certain laissez-faire policies to embed their theoretical-cum-political assumptions in what they claimed empirical evidence revealed: that society was an entity that would run itself if sympathy ruled. By the same token, however, anatomical analysis installed a problem at the heart of social analysis. This is the problem that connotation makes clear: As soon as the supplementation of firsthand observation with theory was transferred *to a community that disagreed about those theoretical assumptions,* the disinterest that authorized scientific knowledge was exposed as the interest it had always been.

If the attempt by some writers to adapt anatomical realism to social analysis exposed the biases within this mode of representation, then this exposure was soon foreclosed by two developments. On the one hand, the protodisciplines adumbrated in Kay's pamphlet and in the review of Parent-Duchâtelet rapidly attained a relative degree of autonomy. The social sciences that resulted rejected the metaphor of the social body and sought their legitimacy instead in the figure of the machine. In 1857, the National Association for the Promotion of the Social Sciences provided a community of like-minded reformers capable of stabilizing social scientific knowledge; this organization rendered even prostitution an acceptable subject for social scientific research.[53] On the other hand, the practice of scientific medicine turned away from the explicit combination of empiricism and theory that characterized anatomical realism. After 1850, practitioners of scientific medicine continued to probe the body's interior, but they explicitly aspired to eliminate all traces of the analyst's theoretical assumptions. Like social scientists, who even more assiduously imitated the methods of natural scientists, medical practitioners also tried to become like the machines they increasingly used.[54] When Herbert Spencer tried to resuscitate the figure of the social body in 1860, then, he did so not in the name of an anatomical practice that infused theory into empirical observation, but according to the rules and technical procedures by which a newly "objective" scientific medicine constructed *its* truth as immune to the contaminating assumptions that engendered the social body and exposed the anatomist's violence in the 1830s.[55]

Five

THOMAS CHALMERS, EDWIN CHADWICK, AND THE SUBLIME REVOLUTION IN NINETEENTH-CENTURY GOVERNMENT

In this essay I want to engage—albeit obliquely—with the historiographical debate about the so-called revolution in nineteenth-century English government. As this debate is typically formulated, it raises the twin questions of causation and agency. Following A. C. Dicey, S. E. Finer and his supporters have attributed the ramification of the English administrative apparatus to the influence of Jeremy Bentham and his disciples.[1] Disputing the role of any individual or set of ideas, Oliver MacDonagh has argued that the growth of English government was an autonomous process initiated as a series of responses to intolerable social problems and then sustained by its own momentum.[2]

Instead of taking sides in this debate, I propose that the controversy illuminates a paradox that was also implicit in the dynamics by which Britain's government grew in the 1830s. For the purposes of this essay, I can best exemplify this paradox (which I will describe more explicitly in a moment) by two paradigmatic scenes taken from this decade. The first scene is the tableau of Thomas Chalmers preaching. The second is the much less picturesque spectacle of Edwin Chadwick rhetorically managing the New Poor Law of 1834.

What fuses these two scenes into an exemplary version of the paradox I want to examine is the work of another modern analyst. Max Weber has argued that modernity is characterized by bureaucratic forms of social organization, an early example of which was the Poor Law Amendment Act of 1834. Weber also argued, however, that because bureaucratic institutions tend primarily to replicate themselves, some kind of initiative is typically necessary to provoke institutional change, including the kind of change that introduced bureaucracy in the first place. Weber identified charisma as one force capable of inaugurating change.[3] As innumerable contemporary accounts attest, Thomas Chalmers epitomized charisma to those people lucky enough to hear him preach between 1816 and 1838, just as Edwin Chadwick personified the form of government that has come to be called bureaucracy. By juxtaposing Chalmers and Chadwick, I want to reexamine the historians' debate about the Victorian revolution in government in the context of the relationship between charisma and bureaucracy. I will not be arguing that Chalmers or Chadwick contributed directly to the nineteenth-century revolution in government. Instead, I will argue that Chalmers and Chadwick helped consolidate a mode of individuality compatible with—indeed, necessary to—the modern form of liberal government instituted by the nineteenth-century changes in administrative procedure and authority. Chalmers and Chadwick, in other words, helped normalize what Michel Foucault has called *disciplinary individualism,* that paradoxical configuration of agency whereby freedom is constituted as "voluntary" compliance with a rationalized order, which is (not incidentally) as capable of producing irrationality as embodying rationality. I will also argue that, just as recognizing the historical consolidation of disciplinary individualism dissolves Weber's distinction between bureaucracy and charisma, so reviewing the historians' debate in the light of this consolidation reveals this contest of interpretations to be a repetition of the paradoxical form of individualism historians are just beginning to recognize.

"A SOLAR MAN"

Thomas Chalmers, the influential Scottish divine, enjoyed unprecedented popularity as a preacher from 1815, when he began his lectures on astronomy, through 1838, when he preached on Church extension in London.[4] Before I turn to contemporary accounts of Chalmers's preaching, let me briefly outline the critical role that preaching played in his multifaceted career. Chalmers's eloquence, which Oxford University cited as one of the four grounds for conferring upon him an honorary doctorate in 1835, was a primary reason for the early fame that gained him an appointment to the Edinburgh parish of Tron in 1815. This appointment, in turn, prompted Chalmers to develop a more systematic approach to poor relief, the theory of which he put into practice in the famous St. John's experiment in 1819.[5] Chalmers publicized this experiment in the three-volume *Christian and Civic Economy of Large Towns*

(1821–26), the definitive statement of his ideas about social reform.[6] The administrative success Chalmers described in this influential work, along with the prominence his preaching had given him in the evangelical wing of the Scottish Church, led church leaders to elect him Moderator of the Church Assembly in 1832, then Convener of the Church Accommodation Committee in 1834. As convener of this committee (renamed the Church Extension Committee), Chalmers spearheaded the most ambitious project of his career—the campaign to extend the Established Church throughout Scotland. Chalmers's committee was the most powerful permanent committee ever founded by the Church; as its leader, he directly oversaw 130 members and indirectly supervised dozens of local societies throughout Scotland.[7] When the English government failed to support the Church Extension movement, Chalmers delivered his celebrated *Lectures on the Establishment and Extension of National Churches* (1838). The continued resistance of the English government to church extension—indeed, the intrusion of the government into what Chalmers declared to be church matters—eventually led to his secession from the Established Church in the 1843 split known as the Disruption.[8]

Chalmers's preaching was thus the springboard to both his experiments in social reform and his (disruptive) campaign to extend the influence of the Established Church. Beyond the role it played in his career, moreover, preaching also enjoyed pride of place in his theory of social improvement. As he set out this theory in *The Christian and Civic Economy*, religion—the critical bulwark for morality—was not always experienced as a necessity by those who needed it most; unlike food, for which demand was sufficient to ensure supply, religion was a good for which the demand had to be created. The two primary means for doing so were clerical visitation to the homes of the poor and public preaching, which could engage middle-class individuals who were otherwise distracted by more worldly concerns. By 1836, Chalmers could argue that for the latter audience, the platform had replaced the press as the most effective forum for arousing and satisfying "a certain impetuous demand for mental excitement."[9]

Just as preaching made Chalmers famous, it also transformed the audience that crowded into the arenas where he spoke. By his own and his auditors' accounts, Chalmers's preaching not only awakened desire where demand was previously dormant, it also transformed desire from a bodily appetite focused on material gratification into a social hunger inflamed (and assuaged) by less tangible sustenance. This transformation begins to illuminate the paradox exemplified by the scene of

Chalmers preaching. In order to appreciate this paradox, we need first to return to this scene, as eyewitnesses attempted to convey it. Most of the accounts we have of Chalmers preaching emphasize two things: the unprepossessing nature of the preacher and the mesmerizing effect of the preaching. Henry Cockburn, for example, dutifully noted the "external disadvantages" Chalmers suffered: "He is awkward and has a low rough husky voice, a guttural articulation, a whitish eye, and a large dingy countenance. In point of mere feature, it would not be difficult to think him ugly." But Cockburn went on to acknowledge the "magic" that occurred when the ugly man began to speak: "I have often hung upon his words with a beating heart and a tearful eye," Cockburn admitted.[10] Struggling to comprehend the same discrepancy, a young Oxford student reported being "surprised and perplexed" by his first glimpse of Chalmers's "coarse" face, his "rude and awkward" gestures. "His voice is neither strong nor melodious," the student continued; ". . . his pronunciation is not only broadly national, but broadly provincial, distorting every word he utters into some barbarous novelty, which, had his hearer leisure to think of such things, might be productive of an effect at once ludicrous and offensive." No such leisure exists when Chalmers's eloquence "shine[s] forth," however; "swaying all around him with its imperial rule," Chalmers's "heated spirit" thrills the "mighty mingled congregation" gathered to hear him preach.[11]

The mesmerizing effect of Chalmers's preaching is conveyed even more clearly by the Rev. Wardlaw's account of a sermon Chalmers preached at Tron in 1817.

Suppose the congregation . . . assembled—pews filled with sitters, and aisles, to a great extent, with standers. They wait in eager expectation. The preacher appears. . . . The entire assembly set themselves for the *treat*, with feelings very diverse in kind, but all eager and intent. There is a hush of dead silence. The text is announced, and he begins. Every countenance is up—every eye bent, with fixed intentness, on the speaker. As he kindles the interest grows. Every breath is held—every cough is suppressed—every fidgety movement is settled—every one, riveted himself by the spell of the impassioned and entrancing eloquence, knows how sensitively his neighbor will resent the very slightest disturbance. Then, by-and-by, there is a pause. The speaker stops—to gather breath—to wipe his forehead—to adjust his gown, and purposely, too, and wisely, to give the audience, as well as himself, a moment or two of relaxation. The moment is embraced—there is a free breathing—suppressed coughs get vent—postures are changed—there is a universal stir, as of persons who could not have endured the constraint much longer—the preacher bends forward—his hand is raised—all is again hushed. The same stillness and strain of unrelaxed attention is repeated, more intent still, it may be, than before, as the interest of the subject and of the speaker advance. And so, for perhaps four or five times in the course of a sermon, there is the *relaxation* and the *'at it again'* till the final winding up.[12]

The "novel and strange sight" Wardlaw describes here is a scene of discipline. In it, the bodies of more than 1400 people are disciplined not merely to the bodily rhythms of a single man but also into a single body, which breathes and coughs and fidgets as one. In it, "feelings very diverse in kind" become "a universal stir," a collective alternation between two states: "the *relaxation* and the *'at it again.'*" The scene at the Tron Church is all the more remarkable, to Wardlaw at least, because of the time of the sermon and the composition of the audience. Held on a *"Thursday forenoon,* during the busiest hours of the day," this sermon drew from their businesses people "in all descriptions of professional occupation, the busiest as well as those who had most leisure on their hands."[13] The discipline of Chalmers's sermon, in other words, created one body from precisely those individuals most accustomed to independent, even competitive, activities. His preaching created a single social body from the competitive individualism that supposedly guaranteed and signified freedom and autonomy in a market society.

The magic of this transformation was repeated in Chalmers's reorganization of the St. John's parish. The social experiment that Chalmers launched at St. John's depended on generating in the poor a desire for religion as keen as that displayed by the affluent who flocked to hear him preach. Because he assumed that this desire had to be created in the poor by home visitation, and because the parish was too large for one man to cover, Chalmers delegated laymen to visit those homes he could not reach. The eagerness with which local merchants and professionals filled his deaconry was aptly captured by the essayist John Brown in his posthumous description of Chalmers: "You felt a power in him, and going from him, drawing you to him in spite of yourself. He was in this respect a *solar man,* he drew after him his own firmament of planets. They, like all free agents, had their centrifugal forces acting ever towards an independent, solitary course, but the centripetal also was there, and they moved with and around their imperial sun—gracefully or not, willingly or not, as the case might be, but there was no breaking loose."[14] The dynamics by which Chalmers's disciplinary influence was imagined to act is even clearer in Brown's description. Here, the discrete bodies remain "free agents"—indeed, each individual retains his own "attendant moons"—yet all bodies are rendered parts of one solar system as they orbit, "willingly or not," about the luminous star.

The paradox staged in Chalmers's preaching and in the charismatic influence he exercised at St. John's is the paradox that Stewart Brown calls "evangelical individualism" and Michel Foucault calls "disciplinary individualism."[15] While the specific corollaries of these variants of modern subjectivity—the nature of responsibilities, for example, and the kinds of rewards—differed according to whether one's subject-status was articulated in relation to the church or civil society, both evangelical and disciplinary individualism promised freedom in exchange for voluntary submission to those laws by which liberty was defined.[16] According to this model of individualism, freedom *is* voluntary compliance with laws, which are understood to be regular and therefore predictable; whatever measures exist to enforce the laws typically incite conformity through tutelage and example rather than coercing obedience by punishment or fear. An eventual effect of this ensemble was the normalization of what has variously been called *analytic* or *species* equality—that condition in which individuals become interchangeable because they appear as instances of the same abstract entity.[17] In St. John's parish, these features of disciplinary individualism are clear in the activities of the professionals and businessmen, who expressed their devotion and sense of responsibility by voluntarily relinquishing their own "solitary course" to orbit the "solar" Chalmers. The scenes of Chalmers preaching make the paradoxical nature of this form of individualism even more obvious, for at the same time that descriptions of Chalmers's eloquence insist on his uniqueness, they do so in order to guarantee every individual the possibility of being unique, too. Precisely at the moment when the power of the charismatic individual dissolves all other individuals into a single sighing body, the individuality of every man is affirmed by his voluntary submission to the greater whole.

The paradox of disciplinary individualism informed all of Chalmers's evangelical projects. In both his home visitations to the poor and his sermons to the well-to-do, Chalmers sought to instill a *collective* sense of *individual* responsibility. Government intervention, whether in the form of poor relief or trade laws, would not be necessary, he reasoned, if every individual voluntarily disciplined immediate desires so that some greater law could work through them. This paradox also lay at the heart of Chalmers's political economy. As he explained it most schematically in *On Political Economy* (1832), his economic theory yoked Malthus's warnings about population to the theory that unlimited production would eventually outstrip demand.[18] As with his pedagogical overtures to his two audiences, Chalmers's approach to the crisis these tendencies foretold took two parallel paths that diverged at the issue of class. For poor and working men and women, the stick so generously wielded by Providence was hunger; the carrot was the spiritual reward that would accompany poor men's "elevating their minds above their passionate flesh."[19] For middle-class business and commercial men, the providential carrot was a natural growth of personal and national prosperity; the stick consisted of bankruptcies at the individual level and general busts in the economy as a whole. Both of these, according to Chalmers, operated (like famine) as "positive checks" that disciplined desire without curtailing free will.[20]

Just as Chalmers's visits to the homes of the poor promoted "amended habits, . . . moralised characters, and . . . exalted principles" as a "counteraction" to excessive population, so his discourses on commerce recommended to a business and professional audience the self-restraint that would limit production and thus forestall a general glut.[21] Both of these paradigms of self-regulation propose a voluntary sacrifice of immediate, personal, bodily gratification for rewards that are deferred, social, and spiritual. Both, that is, solicit the same kind of abandonment of self to the social that Chalmers's eloquence also commanded.

The elaborate system of home visitation Chalmers established at St. John's and the twenty-six volumes of his collected works suggest that the voluntary self-restraint Chalmers recommended required constant encouragement and oversight. As Chalmers never tired of reiterating, there is no "natural appetite" for Christian instruction: "it is just as necessary to create a spiritual hunger, as it is to afford a spiritual refreshment."[22] Chalmers's most ambitious campaign to create both hunger and refreshment, the Church Extension initiative that absorbed him during the 1830s, lays out another version of the paradox inherent in his charismatic career. The object of this campaign was to raise enough money to build churches in impoverished working-class neighborhoods where neither local demand nor resources currently supported the established church.

At the local level, Chalmers's plan for accommodating the poor was based on the St. John's experiment; at this level, he mapped out plans for poor relief and education financed by the philanthropy that "internal Voluntaryism" would naturally call forth.[23] In Scotland as a whole, this "principle of locality" was supported by "a wise general superintendence" exercised by a central committee. The Church Extension Committee raised money by mandating subscriptions to subsidize the local parishes and to defray administrative costs. By 1835, subscriptions to the Central Committee alone totaled £15,000, and £50,000 had been pledged to local parishes. Sixty-four churches had already been built or were by then under construction.[24]

Despite tensions within the Church Extension movement, Chalmers's organization continued to grow. By 1836, he had established a hierarchy of committees as well as a Church Extension press; he also employed twenty agents to address public meetings throughout Scotland. In May 1838, Chalmers delivered his celebrated *Lectures on the Establishment and Extension of National Churches,* and in August he embarked on a national lecture tour of Scotland. Given the Scottish Church's history of defying the civil government and the aggressive nature of Chalmers's campaign, it is not surprising that the English government refused to support extension. After a series of devastating setbacks dealt by the English prime minister and the Scottish civil courts, the Church Extension campaign collapsed in 1841.[25]

The point I want to make about Chalmers's involvement in church extension has less to do with the collision course he ran with the English Parliament than with the similarities between his organization and the state apparatus he fought. Despite their diametrically opposed positions on the critical details of poor relief and the proper relationship between church and state, Chalmers's Church Extension Committee and the central government that oversaw social welfare in England shared an elaborate administrative apparatus that combined local implementation with central oversight.[26] Both the New Poor Law of 1834, which was extended to Ireland in 1838, and Chalmers's Church Extension campaign rationalized government in the sense that they sought both to render uniform and manageable all the localities under their jurisdiction and to administer those localities by uniform rules and local commissions that reported to and were overseen by a central board.

This example of charisma being harnessed to a rationalized administrative machinery takes us further into the paradox of disciplinary individualism, for it shows the interdependence between the success of a charismatic individual and a mode of administration characterized by routine procedures and the wherewithal to replicate itself. Ultimately, Chalmers's charisma depended upon some form of bureaucracy, because the latter created the institutional conditions in which devotion could be generalized. In Chalmers's case, charismatic influence was generalized both by the incitement of emulation, as exemplified in the tableaux of Chalmers preaching, and through the more coercive imperialism of direct intervention, as when the Church Extension Committee imposed tithes even in the remote regions of the Highlands.[27] In both cases, the effect of Chalmers's charisma—which was also the source of its power—resembled the effect of the bureaucracy he opposed and re-created: the encouragement of a universal and voluntary surrender of self to the larger whole.

"A Despot and a Bureaucrat"

The dynamic by which Chalmers's increasingly bureaucratized efforts to seize the souls of Scotsmen redefined the individuality he also sought to preserve was repeated—albeit in inverted form—in Edwin Chadwick's attempts to eradicate all traces of individual agency from the adminis-tration of poor relief.[28] The apparatus of the New Poor Law exposes decisively the coercive face of disciplinary individualism. Beyond this, however, the machinery by which poor individuals were forcibly sub-sumed into a single social body also reveals the tendency of this bureau-cratic machine to violate its own rationality—and thus to replicate some of the features we generally associate with charisma.

Although they do not use this language, Sidney and Beatrice Webb come closest to identifying the New Poor Law's contribution to disci-plinary individualism.[29] The Webbs point out that the act sought to eliminate the need to make individual judgments about which individ-uals were deserving and which the undeserving poor. For the poor recip-ients of relief, the act instituted anti-individualistic aggregation both outside the workhouse, where the "large class of cases" that uniform reporting could assemble was intended to undercut the importance pre-viously granted to individual cases, and inside the workhouse, where the system of pauper classification was intended to override idiosyncra-tic needs.[30] The principle that Chadwick designated "aggregation for the purposes of segregation" belonged, according to this interpretation, to a program designed to erase all of the bases of charismatic engage-ment—sympathy, identification, judgment, and desire—from both dis-pensers and recipients of poor relief.

The New Poor Law was also designed to establish an apparatus for gathering information about the cost of poverty and machinery capable of addressing this poverty uniformly, efficiently, and disinterestedly. By replacing the 15,000 poor-law authorities with 600 boards of identical constitution and power, the framers of the act established a single instru-ment designed to do both: by means of elaborate, standardized systems of accounting, all local boards were to generate the same kind of infor-mation on a regular basis; by means of the "self-acting" workhouse test and the "principle of less eligibility," all local boards were intended to compel the poor to administer themselves—a task that was taken over by workhouse officials only if the poor elected not to do so.[31]

As this last point makes clear—and as Chadwick's insistence on amending the laws of settlement confirms—the ultimate object of this elaborate machinery was not to deprive poor individuals of their agency, but to ensure that they would act freely—according, that is, to the laws of the market. In a mirror image of Chalmers's charismatic preaching, the New Poor Law forcibly aggregated and disciplined the social body expressly to set individuals on their own, competitive feet.[32] In theory not an imposition of government at all, the ramified and imposing edifice of the New Poor Law forced the poor to discipline themselves so that they could rise from an impoverished and dehumanized aggregate to a state of free—that is, self-disciplined—market agency. At the same time that it imposed agency on the poor, however, the New Poor Law also *relieved* the well-to-do of the necessity to act as autonomous agents. In an important supplement to the Webbs' interpretation, Peter Mandler has identified this class asymmetry at the heart of disciplinary individualism: the "vast majority" of local landlords, Mandler argues, embraced the law because the national and uniform laws it established relieved landlords of the necessity of making difficult decisions about impoverished dependents and strangers.[33]

Mandler quite properly alerts us to the limits that landlords voluntarily placed on their own autonomy under the new law, but this should not lead us to forget the limitations the law imposed upon the poor—even upon their ability to act as the market agents they supposedly now were. Here we begin to see the ways in which the New Poor Law generated alongside its own rationality instances of what—in terms of its own criteria—can only be called irrationality. In general, these instances of irrationality appeared because both the framers and the enforcers of the law retained vestiges of traditional attitudes toward charity, morality, and justice, even as they superimposed a new rationality upon them. Thus, for example, the framers of the law recognized that it could not be uniformly enforced immediately or throughout England because of local resistance and established patterns of social interaction. In order to accommodate these prejudices, the framers of the law staggered its implementation, but in order to curtail old habits of dispensing relief as charity, they declared that outdoor relief should only be given as bread, not money.[34] Since bread was not a counter of exchange in a money economy, this tactic undermined the professed aim of the law to integrate the poor into the market economy. The imperfect rationality we see here is even clearer in the case of the bastardy clauses, for, as early as 1835, it had become clear that they were not being applied to reduce expenditures on out-of-wedlock births, as they were intended to be, but were being adapted to punish recreant fathers.

By 1836, Chadwick found it necessary to reiterate the basic principles of the New Poor Law to a public that remained unconvinced of its merits. Reviewing (anonymously) all of the Commission's publications for the *Edinburgh Review,* Chadwick enumerated what he saw as the three cardinal virtues of the New Poor Law: uniformity, efficiency, and impersonality. According to Chadwick, the apparatus of the law was designed to replace the fallible (because individualistic) instruments of traditional relief (sympathy, ignorance, passion, and interest) with an impartial (because machinelike) apparatus that embodied and enforced *"Reason."*[35] Chadwick presents Reason as the outcome of extensive inquiry; as the inductive fruit of a "mass of facts," Reason stands opposed to the deductive—and therefore "interested"—theories of Malthus and Chalmers, which consist of "general principles" deduced from erroneous assumptions.[36] Having empirically identified the problems of traditional poor relief as variability, inefficiency, and individual interest, Reason has dictated a rational solution: a "new machinery," capable of implementing a "uniform principle of administration," epitomized by the "self-acting" workhouse and less-eligibility tests.[37] "Pass[ing] over" the fact that the framers decided to make this machinery a central board (the most controversial part of the act), Chadwick triumphantly presents three tables that document the "almost magical" results of the New Poor Law.[38] The first shows a dramatic decrease in the number of paupers in the four unions of Kent; the second and third document in various ways the savings that the act had produced.[39]

Once Chadwick has demonstrated the success of the New Poor Law with these (theoretically) indisputable numbers, he can afford to include a few testimonials from local officials. These subjective accounts, however, begin to suggest that another logic was also operating through the machinery of the law. The testimonial of Mr. G. Smyth of Bradford and the anecdote about Thomas Pocock of Maple-Durham show the extent to which character, which the New Poor Law eliminated as a criterion for receiving relief, was being reimported as a criterion for receiving employment. "Now character is of great importance," Mr. Smyth explains—as Thomas Pocock learns when trips to the public house earn threats of dismissal from his employer.[40]

Chadwick might have explained this reappearance of a value-laden term in the supposedly value-free system of poor relief as a sign that the new law had created something like a free market in character. Another way to read it, however, is to say that the supposedly rational and impersonal principles of the law were smuggling in a set of assumptions every bit as interested and ideological as were the old criteria for dispensing relief. To the extent that (middle-class) assumptions about what constitutes character got produced as a valuable commodity in the labor market, the New Poor Law did not simply implement self-evident or universally accepted values. Instead, it produced these values *as* self-evident and universal by elevating to abstractions the social arrangements that facilitated market productivity. Thus Marriage, Property, Order, and Science were produced as universally desirable virtues, even though Chadwick presented them as being valuable because their contribution to society could be quantified and assigned a monetary value.

Given the general prosperity of the *Edinburgh* readership, it was undoubtedly less difficult for Chadwick to defend the universality of these values than to sell the Central Board as their trustworthy guarantor. Even though the Central Board spoke to landlords' desire to absolve themselves of the responsibility for making individual decisions, it also threatened to impinge on a principle every bit as precious to the well-to-do as was their right to own property. This principle, which was inextricably linked to property rights, was the liberty guaranteed the free-born English man. In the potential conflict between the right to own property and the right to be free, we see another paradox of the disciplinary individualism that was being written into classical liberalism: a man (and I use the gendered noun advisedly) could only be free if he owned enough property to participate in the market economy, but he could only participate freely in this economy if normative rules dictated who could participate and how. Chadwick addressed the paradox of such rule-bound freedom by opposing one kind of power (the disinterested power incarnate in the Central Board) to another (the interested power wielded by "local oligarchies"): "The power of the Central Board is in fact the immediate power of the Legislature," Chadwick assured his readers, "and indirectly (inasmuch as the Commissioners are payable by an annual vote from the Commons representatives) it is the power of the public at large, the power of an instructed democracy, as against all local oligarchies or petty and adverse interests."[41] The key to the opposition Chadwick is establishing here is the link between disinterest and abstraction: abstractions like "the public at large" and "an instructed democracy" can be presented as disinterested because the commonalities that underwrite the abstractions override the presumed interests of discrete individuals. Equating such abstractions with a specific (and controversial) government agency, then, theoretically confers the disinterest of the whole on its (supposed) representative. The effect of these equations is the creation of a new version of liberty—the freedom to be part of a social aggregate, which defends the right to own property (unequally) by representing every man as an instance of the same abstract entity: "in the strength of the distant, well-instructed, and comparatively disinterested central authority, will the industrious many . . . find their protection from the active and peculating, but most powerful few."[42]

The abstraction and disinterest with which Chadwick credits the Central Board constitute the prototypes for modern bureaucracy. By the last third of the nineteenth century, this apparatus had been institutionalized as the permanent English civil service. In many respects, of course, the New Poor Law machinery did not conform to what Kitson Clark has identified as the essence of civil service; neither political neutrality nor personal anonymity was a goal to which Chadwick aspired, and, in terms of organization, the Poor Law Board was excluded from the hierarchy of government, for it lacked a clear means of reporting to the Commons.[43] Indeed, as Anthony Brundage has argued, bureaucratic routine "emerged partly as a response to Chadwick's excesses"—his tendency to court public support through the press, his desire to pack Royal Commissions so as to monopolize power, and his attempts to control local organizations both inside and outside of government.[44] If the first half of Brundage's statement rings true, however, then so does the second half: "bureaucratic routine . . . was also a natural outgrowth of the Benthamism [Chadwick] espoused and the reforms he instigated. Ironically, both his triumphs and his reverses helped insure there would be no more Chadwicks."[45]

In what Clark called "the heroic age of the civil servant who was also a social reformer," it was certainly possible to act out the kind of Prussian despotism of which Chadwick's critics accused him while advocating an administrative machinery dedicated to making the individual both obsolete and free.[46] This is, of course, the mirror image of Chalmers's program to enhance individual responsibility by subsuming everyone into a single social body. Indeed, it is at this symbolic level, where Chalmers's and Chadwick's projects appear as complementary articulations of disciplinary individualism, that both Chadwick and the New Poor Law can be said to have been most effective. Even though the Central Board—and Chadwick—remained sources of fierce controversy, and even though the law was never implemented or enforced uniformly, the equation of pauperism with the loss of liberty epitomized by incarceration in the workhouse "bastilles" created the widespread impression that transgressing the norms supported by the law would result in a life less "eligible" than starvation. To the extent that it did achieve its framers' goals, the New Poor Law succeeded because it incited in the poor the fear that all freedoms would be abrogated if one acknowledged the need for relief. To the extent that it failed, the New Poor Law exposed the dynamic by which nineteenth-century English government had already begun to grow.

Despite Chadwick's claims about the machinelike application of Reason, this dynamic of government growth had as much to do with the irrationality that resulted from imposing a new order upon traditional ways of life as with rational planning. Given Chadwick's insistence on demonstrating rationality with quantifiable results, it seems fitting that the first signs of this irrationality were financial. By 1838, when the Poor Law Commissioners issued their *Fourth Annual Report,* it had become clear that the New Poor Law was not actually producing the savings that Chadwick had so recently trumpeted. One problem was that the act, which was conceptualized primarily according to conditions affecting agricultural labor, had not anticipated the effects of epidemics and infectious diseases, which were most visible in urban centers. To cover the expenses caused by disease (and made visible by the apparatus of the New Poor Law itself), the commissioners petitioned to be able to use the poor rates to pay for the removal of contagion-breeding "nuisances."[47] A second unforeseen expense emanated from the enforcement of the very restrictions that the *First Report* wanted unions to implement. If deserting fathers were allowed to abscond, as the bastardy clauses mandated, then the New Poor Law, far from inspiring greater familial loyalty (as Chadwick had claimed in 1836), was making more bastards chargeable to the state. Thus the commissioners requested that poor rates be applied to cover all costs incurred in recovering the offenders.[48] A third expense hinted at an even more grievous oversight by the act's framers. It seems that attacks upon poor-law officials had become so extensive and severe that the commissioners had to petition for the right to use the rates to finance their administrators' protection.[49]

These petitions approach an admission that, far from implementing a system that simply reflected the universal wishes of the public at large, the 1834 act had imposed a normalizing system of values on a population whose heterogeneity and attachment to traditional forms of morality, justice, and relief resisted such rationalization. The bastardy clauses neither reflected the naturalness of the family unit nor encouraged poor men and women to marry before they bred. The assaults on Poor Law administrators proved that the principle of laissez-faire that underwrote the original act did not guarantee that individual interests were—or could be—identical.[50] Most telling of all, the law's provisions were inadequate to conditions that already existed in 1834 (in urban areas in particular), which meant that the law could not reduce pauperism simply by forcing the poor to seek employment. If poor men and women were not able-bodied, as typhus and cholera guaranteed they would not be, then the freedom to work meant nothing at all. Paradoxically, of course, even though the increased attention paid to urban centers in the 1830s—partly as a result of the New Poor Law—revealed an incidence of disease for which the act was utterly unprepared, this revelation did not simply undermine the New Poor Law or the centralized bureaucracy Chadwick aspired to create. Instead, in demonstrating the inadequacy of this protobureaucratic machine to deal with the hitherto incalculable cost of disease, the information gathered for the *Fourth Annual Report* laid the groundwork for an expansion of the bureaucratic state apparatus. Largely as a consequence of the revelations Chadwick published in his *Sanitary Report* of 1842, public health became the next great object of public concern and the next site of government growth. Partly as a result of the resistance that the centralized Poor Law Board continued to provoke, however, the Public Health Act of 1848 limited the central government's authority to compel compliance with national sanitary standards. Voluntary compliance, not national uniformity, characterized the administration of public health, but this, along with self-help measures like savings banks and friendly societies, simply generalized the disciplinary form of individualism to which the New Poor Law had already contributed.

The point of juxtaposing Chalmers's preaching with the New Poor Law has been to argue that both the incitement of the former and the coercion of the latter installed disciplinary individualism as the normative model of agency for most British subjects for most of the nineteenth century. As I have suggested, disciplinary individualism took different forms for different segments of the population: paradoxically, both Chalmers's paradigm of tutelary reform and the workhouse test demanded a peculiar form of self-government from the poor, while Chalmers's preaching and the Central Board freed the well-to-do (especially landlords) from the exercise of personal judgment by referring individual action to a higher spiritual authority or to a national system of uniform rules.[51] Identifying such variations within the paradigm of disciplinary individualism is critical to our understanding of this historical phenomenon, both because these variations reveal the internal irrationalities of this cornerstone of modernity and because such irrationalities constitute sites where resistances most easily form.

This juxtaposition also suggests that when we direct our attention to the symbolic horizon where disciplinary individualism operates, the opposition that Weber identified between charisma and bureaucracy seems less like an opposition than an interdependent structure. In the case of Chalmers, charisma, which seems like a form of agency, contributed to a redefinition of agency that was wholly compatible with the anti-individualistic apparatus of bureaucracy. In the case of the New Poor Law, bureaucracy, which seeks to replace individual judgment with impersonal and universally applicable rationality, proves capable of generating provisions that—by its own criteria of efficiency, universality, and economy—appear as irrationalities that are every bit as idiosyncratic as the most anarchic form of individualism. Thus, charisma and bureaucracy turn out to contribute to the same paradoxical logic of disciplinary individualism—the first because it inspires individuals to discipline their desires; the second because it both depends on and produces irrationalities as the very condition of its possibility.

But what of the debate between historians, with which I began this essay? Once we recover the historical consolidation of disciplinary individualism, do the differences between the so-called Benthamites and the anti-Benthamites dissolve as well? My sense is that they do not, but recovering the role played in the 1830s by what Peter Mandler has called "a redefinition of individual responsibility" renders the historians' debate less central to our understanding of this decade.[52] To see why this is true, we must recapitulate briefly the appeal of each of the two historical interpretations. As Jennifer Hart makes perfectly clear, Finer's position, which argues for the importance of Bentham's ideas, is attractive to modern historians because it assigns moral responsibility for historical events to particular individuals. In so doing, the Benthamite paradigm of intention and influence makes activism both possible and meaningful.[53] Oliver MacDonagh's position, the anti-Benthamite position, which privileges contingency and identifies an independent historical process as the agent of change, seems attractive on two grounds: first, it accommodates the mixed allegiances of the supporters of legislation like the New Poor Law (who manifestly did not share a single intention); second, it takes into account the historical specificity of particular circumstances and thus is able to respond to the venerable historical question: Why now?[54]

It should be obvious from this summary that the Benthamite and anti-Benthamite positions replicate, respectively, the individualism implicit in the concept of charisma and the impersonality implicit in bureaucracy. To a large extent, however, both of these interpretations are actually devoted to identifying agency—in the sense of causal responsibility; they fail to recognize that the events typified by the nineteenth-century revolution in government constituted a redefinition *of* agency, which was the necessary counterpart to the redefinition of administration that *was* the Victorian revolution in government. This is true even of MacDonagh's anti-Benthamite position, which seems to call agency into question. By attributing causation to an independent historical process, MacDonagh simply widens the definition of agency by rendering the causal agent abstract. The proximity of this abstraction to agency becomes clear in its susceptibility to personification. When David Roberts—who supports MacDonagh—calls this abstract process "humanitarianism," or when Jennifer Hart—who opposes MacDonagh—calls it "Tory," we see the ease with which a process can be conceptualized as a cause that is every bit as unitary as ideas and intentions are generally thought to be.[55]

To recognize that Benthamites and Scottish preachers, English landlords and Scottish philosophers all contributed to a redefinition of individualism in the early nineteenth century is to identify the opposition that historians make between individual intention and historical process as a repetition of the paradoxical form of disciplinary individualism, which Chalmers and Chadwick helped to normalize. As the example of Chalmers suggests, it would be nonsense to say that these men intended to consolidate disciplinary individualism. As the example of the New Poor Law makes clear, it would be wrong to say that a simple and noncontradictory process was at work in the law. Instead of designating either intentions or a process as the motor of a revolution assumed to enact some deeper rationale, it might be more productive to describe nineteenth-century government growth as irrational in the sense that it realized no ulterior logic, whether individual or deep-structural. To say that the growth of nineteenth-century government was irrational, of course, is not to say that it did not contribute to coherent or identifiable effects. As my discussion of disciplinary individualism should suggest, one effect of the changes in nineteenth-century government was a further consolidation of the form of subjectivity that both facilitated and depended on the administrative routines institutionalized *by* these changes. Once we identify the interdependence of the modern forms of individualism and administration, it seems necessary to devise a new narrative to describe—and account for—change.

Six

DOMESTICITY AND CLASS FORMATION: CHADWICK'S 1842 *SANITARY REPORT*

This essay is about the "sanitary idea," which, along with the "statistical idea" and the "educational idea," has been credited with "energiz[ing] the system of national improvement that was state formation" in the early nineteenth century.[1] In the 1840s, in other words, the sanitary idea constituted one of the crucial links between the regulation of the individual body and the consolidation of those apparatuses we associate with the modern state. In order to grasp the implications of this argument, of course, we have to understand that the sanitary idea encompassed a number of related theories, technologies, and policies. Among the theories it implied, for example, was the medical thesis that disease was spread by miasma, the noxious fumes generated by decaying matter. Among the technologies associated with the sanitary idea were the house-by-house surveys of working-class neighborhoods, which were first conducted in the 1830s, and the compilation of data about these houses through statistics, that modern version of political arithmetic that was first institutionalized in 1833. The policies related to the sanitary idea, finally, constituted an arena of intense political debate in the 1840s. Such projects as laying sewers and ensuring continuous supplies of uncontaminated water sparked fierce battles between, in the first case, the newly consolidated central government and those local agencies that had traditionally governed England and, in the second case, the private water companies, which sought to keep prices high, and the urban public, who needed water but were at the mercy of the companies that piped it in. My argument, then, is that in the 1830s and 1840s, this dense network of interdependent theories, technologies, and political disputes about policy simultaneously reorganized individuals' relations to their own and their neighbors' bodies *and* constituted the conditions of possibility for the formation both of the social domain and of the professionalized, bureaucratized apparatuses of inspection, regulation, and enforcement that we call the modern state.[2]

My purpose in racing through some of the components of the sanitary idea is to gesture toward the tentacular complexity of the subject I'm about to address. I also want to remind you what is at stake in such an analysis. My specific subject in this essay is merely a modest part of this larger network. In fact, by most historians' accounts, it is a pretty modest subject altogether: my subject is domesticity and ideas about the home. I will argue, however, that ideas about domesticity played a crucial role in the sanitary idea, in the constitution of the social domain, and, through these, in the process of state formation whose outlines I have sketched. My specific argument is that Edwin Chadwick, author of what was probably the most widely read government document of the Victorian period, deployed assumptions about domesticity that both brought the laboring class into the newly forming social domain and set limits to the role that (what we call) class could play in the government of the English nation.[3]

In 1839, at the time he began the *Report on the Sanitary Condition of the Labouring Population of Great Britain,* Edwin Chadwick occupied the relatively subordinate position of secretary to the Poor Law Commission, which had been formed in 1834 as part of the New Poor Law Amendment Act.[4] The three poor-law commissioners, who disliked Chadwick intensely, assigned him the sanitary inquiry partly in order to ease him out of the office of secretary, and partly to get rid of this apparently trivial subject, which, on the face of things, had only a tangential relation to the New Poor Law or pauperism, the problem that the New Poor Law was intended to address. When he was appointed to this task in 1839, Chadwick had no particular interest in or knowledge about public health or sanitation. With characteristic determination, however, and with the help of the fact-gathering apparatus of the New Poor Law, the bureaucrat-par-excellence transformed his ignorance into expertise and his drudge-work into professional gold. Despite the obstacles created by his own unpopularity and the fall of the Whig government in 1841 (over widespread hatred of the New Poor Law), Chadwick pushed his investigation to a conclusion, and in July 1842, the government published the *Sanitary Report.* Even though it was an official document, the *Report* was signed only by Chadwick, because the poor-law commissioners were unwilling to take responsibility for it. Even though it was originally a House of Lords paper (thus expensive, cumbersome, and published in small numbers), the *Report* gained an enormous readership because Chadwick, ever the entrepreneur, arranged for a simultaneous printing in quarto size and large numbers at the same time that he sent proof copies to luminaries such as Carlyle, John Stuart Mill, and Dickens, not to mention all the newspapers and quarterlies likely to run a review.

The formal features of Chadwick's *Report*—its statistical tables, eyewitness reports, and summary of policy recommendations—were soon codified as *the* protocol for government reports. The familiarity of this kind of writing should not blind us, however, to the constitutive role such early documents actually played in shaping what counted as authoritative and official in government reports. At the same time, of course, such documents also helped constitute social norms, about, for example, what counted as an improved population or an overcrowded apartment. As part of the establishment of social norms, documents like Chadwick's *Sanitary Report* also contributed to the consolidation of class identities during the period in which the economic basis of wealth (the definition of property) and the political basis of citizenship (the franchise) were both undergoing revision. In his depictions of the laboring population, Chadwick reveals one of the most important paradoxes of this process, for he simultaneously condemns members of the working class for failing to live up to middle-class standards (thereby implying that the classes could be alike) and suggests that the poor are—and will remain—fundamentally different from those who write about them. One effect of this paradoxical relation is to establish the "naturalness" of middle-class living habits by proclaiming their superiority in terms of health and longevity. Another is specifically to deny to members of the laboring population the opportunity of establishing the kind of relationships with each other that facilitated the consolidation of the middle class as a political entity. Central to both of these effects is Chadwick's representation of domesticity.

The importance Chadwick assigns to the domestic sphere is clear not only from the fact that his sanitary reforms begin in the home and move outward,[5] but also from one of the biases evident in his use of statistics. The most prominent example of this bias occurs in chapter 4, which contains the widely cited discussion of "comparative chances of life in different classes of the community."[6] In this section, Chadwick is intent on correlating life expectancy to the location in which one resides. His first task is to clear away material that might challenge his thesis. This involves dismissing insurance tables that show the mean chances of life, because they do not support the correlation he wants to prove, and discounting figures that indicate the prevalence of migrant labor, because migrant labor complicates the idea of a fixed residence. Next, Chadwick breaks down his information by place and class. According to Chadwick's divisions, an individual's "class" is determined partly by the kind of work he does (that is, professional, trade, or labor) and partly by how and where he resides. (The conditions of one's birth or family do not figure here.) Even though Chadwick acknowledges occupation, however, he assumes that one's place of residence is more important than how (or even where) one works. Chadwick cites reporters from Aberdeen, for example, who were asked to mark maps first for the fever rates of various neighborhoods, then for the class affiliations of neighborhoods. "They returned a map so marked as to disease, but stated that it had been thought unnecessary to distinguish the streets inhabited by the different orders of society, as that was done with a sufficient accuracy by the different tints representing the degrees of intensity of the prevalence of fever" (pp. 225–26). This statement assumes a strict correlation between place of residence, class, and susceptibility to disease. While class and neighborhood might well have been correlated, however, especially given the gradual subdivision of cities into suburbs and working-class areas, the transmission of disease could be tied to one's place of residence only if individuals spent all their time where they lived—or if the air where one worked could not carry miasmas.

Chadwick's elaborate tables, in other words, assume that *locality* means "place of residence." This becomes clear when he elects to divide his statistical findings according to gender. Acknowledging that a man "is subject to the influence of his place of occupation," Chadwick dismisses the death rates among men from his figures and asserts that women's mortality provides the most accurate index to general mortality because women spend most of their time in the home: "the mortality prevalent amongst the females is given separately, as probably indicating most correctly the operation of the noxious influences connected with the place of residence" (p. 231). In so organizing his data, Chadwick dismisses all occupational factors (such as hazards posed by machinery or toxic by-products); he takes all women out of the nondomestic workplace; and he effaces all of the time a man or woman might spend outside the home as not contributing significantly to his or her health.

Several factors help account for Chadwick's focus on the homes of workers. In the first place, as Chadwick acknowledges early in the report, many of the earliest surveys of the poor, upon which the *Sanitary Report* is partially modeled, were based on house-by-house, neighborhood-by-neighborhood visitations by local medical men. This tendency to cor-

relate neighborhood of residence with susceptibility to disease was reinforced by the cholera epidemic of 1831–32, for the progress of the
disease could be (and was) graphically charted by residential neighborhood. The fact that infant mortality accounted for such a large percent-
age of deaths also justified Chadwick's equation of "location" with
"place of residence," as did the fact that, even in industrial cities like
Manchester, so much work was still performed in homes, whether the
work was "slop" (or piece) work or work requiring modest equipment,
like spinning or weaving.

When Chadwick instructed his informants to begin their surveys by
going to schools and asking the most sickly children where they lived,
then, he was simply responding to the fact that many members of the
laboring population got sick and died where they slept.[7] Representing
the working-class life as primarily domestic, however, did not simply reflect the realities of Chadwick's contemporaries; it also produced ideological effects that had a strong moralizing—and, ideally, regulative—
component. One example of the moralizing dimension of Chadwick's
representation is the image implied by the recurrent word *overcrowding,* which conjures up its converse as well—a home that is *not* overcrowded but "normally" occupied—that is, occupied exclusively by
members of the same family (and their servants), who are appropriately
segregated within the home by age, sex, and class.[8] The moralizing assumptions that accompany the word *overcrowding* leap into relief in the
section of the *Report* that immediately follows Chadwick's decision to
focus exclusively on women's mortality. Along with three and one-half
pages of tables, this section includes some of the most explicitly moralizing passages in the *Report,* which Chadwick characteristically presents
through quotations from his informants. Here, for example, is the Rev.
Whitwell Elwin, writing about Bath:

> Whatever influence occupation and other circumstances may have upon
> mortality, no one can inspect the registers without being struck by the de-
> teriorated value of life in inferior localities. . . . The deaths from fevers
> and contagious diseases I found to be almost exclusively confined to the
> worst parts of the town. . . . Everything vile and offensive is congregated
> there [in Avon-street and its offsets]. All the scum of Bath—its low pros-
> titutes, its thieves, its beggars—are piled up in the dens rather than houses
> of which the street consists. Its population is the most disproportionate to
> the accommodation of any I have ever heard; and to aggravate the mis-
> chief, the refuse is commonly thrown under the staircase. . . . A promi-
> nent feature in the midst of this mass of physical and moral evils is the

extraordinary number of illegitimate children; the off-spring of persons who in all respects live together as man and wife. Without the slightest objection to the legal obligation, the moral degradation is such that marriage is accounted a superfluous ceremony. . . . And thus it invariably happens in crowded haunts of sin and filth, where principle is obliterated, and where public opinion, which so often operates in the place of principle, is never heard; where, to say truth, virtue is treated with the scorn which in better society is accorded to vice. (pp. 235–36)

The correlation that Elwin assumes between the filthy and overcrowded "dens" where the poor live and the "physical and moral evils" he associates with illegitimacy and extramarital cohabitation was made absolutely explicit by Chadwick's contemporary Horace Mann, who wanted the 1841 census to include information about religious affiliation. In trying to explain why the poor were alienated from organized religion, Mann pointed to the "vice and filth" of their "degraded homes." To these he contrasted the "religious character by which the English middle classes are distinguished [which] is the consequence of their peculiar isolation in distinct and separate homes."[9]

Chadwick's emphasis on the "overcrowded" working-class residence as the primary site of disease not only normalizes a "proper" form of domesticity, which is moral and sanitary (or moral *because* sanitary), it also produces the impression that working-class life not only ought to be but *is* centered in the home—however "degraded" these homes may be. At several points in his *Report,* Chadwick contradicts this impression, as, for example, when he refers to the "migratory character of the population," which makes it impossible for him to construct tables accurate enough to prove his thesis (p. 243), or when he complains that the lack of domestic comforts in such homes drives working men into public houses for relief (p. 195). Such passing references to life outside the place of residence are echoed much more centrally in nearly all the eyewitness accounts of the 1840s and 1850s, which, by the same token, depict the insides of houses as almost completely devoid of human occupation. When Hector Gavin takes the reader into the homes of the poor in his *Sanitary Ramblings* (1848), for example, most of the houses are empty, depicted as places where people sleep, not live. Henry Mayhew's accounts of London in his *Morning Chronicle* reports, collected as *London Labour and the London Poor* (1849–50), similarly show the streets teeming with people hawking their wares, while pubs and pantomimes fairly burst with the young and old. By contrast, the residences Mayhew visits are most often occupied only by his guide or the person he goes to see.[10]

Chadwick's 1842 *Sanitary Report* does contain a few extensive descriptions of working-class individuals who do not reside in anything remotely resembling a middle-class "home." Significantly, these passages constitute the most graphic and emotionally charged descriptions in the entire document. Their narrative vigor—especially when read in the light of other writers' reports that nondomestic activities prevailed within the working population—suggests that Chadwick's emphasis on domesticity may actually have a defensive and regulative purpose. We first glimpse the logic of Chadwick's emphasis in his depiction of French *chiffonniers,* men who earn their living by scavenging and selling bits of rubbish from city streets. Distinguished from other members of the laboring poor by their extremely "degraded and savage" living conditions, the chiffonniers, according to Chadwick, are "outcasts from other classes of workmen; they sleep amidst their collections of refuse, and they are idle during the day; they are like all men who live under such circumstances, prone to indulgence in ardent spirits; being degraded and savage, they are ready to throw away their wretched lives on every occasion" (p. 163).

Perverse in every sense, these men not only hoard up refuse like treasure and squander their lives like garbage, but they also threaten both social stability and public health. As "conspicuous actors in the revolution of 1830," the chiffonniers are explicitly associated with political turmoil, and this revolutionary activity had recently been linked to the panic inspired by cholera. According to Chadwick's account of the relevant incident, the insanitary accumulation of refuse that was exacerbating the epidemic prompted the French government to commission special garbage collectors to haul rubbish from Paris streets with their own carts. The chiffonniers, who opposed all sanitary improvements as threats to their livelihood, took this as a declaration of war. They

> rose in revolt, attacked and drove away the conductors, broke to pieces the new carts, threw the fragments into the river, or made bonfires with them. . . . The mobs of chiffonniers which collected on the following days were swollen by other crowds of ignorant, terrified, and savage people, who were persuaded that the deaths from the strange plague were occasioned by poison. "My agents," says the then prefect of police, in an account of this revolt, "could not be at all points at once, to oppose the fury of these crowds of men with naked arms and haggard figures, and sinister looks, who are never seen in ordinary times, and who seemed on this day to have arisen out of the earth. Wishing to judge myself of the foundation for the alarming reports that were brought to me, I went out alone and on foot. I had great difficulty in getting through these dense masses, scarcely

covered with filthy rags; no description could convey their hideous aspect, or the sensation of terror which the hoarse and ferocious cries created. Although I am not easily moved, I at one time feared for the safety of Paris—of honest people and their property." (p. 163)

The contrasts in this passage—between the mobs of savage, ignorant, and barely clothed rioters and the prefect of police, who is the vulnerable yet brave champion of the "honest people" and their property—refer English readers most explicitly to the contrast between France, where two violent revolutions had already occurred, and the more civilized Britain, where revolution continued (narrowly) to be averted. Chadwick does not underscore this nationalistic contrast, however. Instead, he insists that a subhuman population also inhabits Great Britain. Significantly, what distinguishes these people from the rest of the British population is that neither of the two groups that make up the subhuman population inhabits proper houses.

The first group, which Chadwick explicitly compares to the French chiffonniers, are the "bone-pickers," the lowliest occupants of the workhouse "bastilles" created by Chadwick's other major administrative innovation, the New Poor Law. "The bone-pickers are the dirtiest of all the inmates of our workhouse," Chadwick quotes an eyewitness as reporting.

> I have seen them take a bone from a dung-heap, and gnaw it while reeking hot with the fermentation of decay. Bones, from which the meat had been cut raw, and which had still thin strips of flesh adhering to them, they scraped carefully with their knives, and put the bits, no matter how befouled with dirt, into a wallet or pocket appropriated to the purpose. They have told me, that whether in broth or grilled, they were the most savoury dishes that could be imagined. I have not observed that these creatures were savage, but they were thoroughly debased. Often hardly human in appearance, they had neither human tastes nor sympathies, nor even human sensations, for they revelled in the filth which is grateful to dogs, and other lower animals, and which to our apprehension is redolent only of nausea and abomination. (pp. 164–65)

The second group that arouses Chadwick's voyeuristic disgust had also been constituted, in part, at least, by the New Poor Law. This group includes members of the "vagrant population" who inhabit "common lodging-houses."[11] Chadwick devotes an entire chapter (chapter 8) and some of his most aggressive polemics to these itinerant poor. Here, for example, is Chadwick quoting Dr. Baron Howard on lodging houses in Manchester:

In some of these houses as many as six or eight beds are contained in a single room; in others, where the rooms are smaller, the number is necessarily less; but it seems to be the invariable practice in these "keepers of fever beds," as the proprietors were styled by Dr. Ferriar, to cram as many beds into each room as it can possibly be made to hold; and they are often placed so close to each other that there is scarcely room to pass between them. The scene which these places present at night is one of the most lamentable description; the crowded state of the beds, filled promiscuously with men, women, and children; the floor covered over with the filthy and ragged clothes they have just put off, and with their various bundles and packages, containing all the property they possess, mark the depraved and blunted state of their feelings, and the moral and social disorder which exists. (p. 413)

Chadwick devotes so much attention to lodging houses because he believes that they incarnate the "most serious and extensive" of all residential "evils." Like Dr. Howard, Chadwick maintains that the effluvia exhaled by "depraved" human beings is more poisonous than the miasma created by decomposing organic matter. Thus, having too many bodies in a small room is even more unhealthy than sleeping in rubbish. "It is my decided opinion," Chadwick quotes Howard as writing, "that the vitiation of the atmosphere by the living is much more injurious to the constitution than its impregnation with the effluvia from dead organic matter . . . the 'human miasmas' generated in over-crowded and ill-ventilated rooms [are] a far more frequent and efficient cause of fever than the malaria arising from collections of refuse and want of drainage" (pp. 413–14).

Whatever medical explanation underwrites his criticism of the irregular living habits of workhouse bone-pickers and the itinerant poor, his singling them out for particular notice suggests that Chadwick's reforms were directed most pointedly toward exactly those all-male, nondomestic associations represented so horrifically by the French chiffonniers. Chadwick's tendency to associate such groups with "moral and social disorder" was also manifested in the temperance movement and in the chronic concern voiced by middle-class commentators about the working-class use of public space. Pubs, after all, were associated—in fact and in fantasy—not only with alcoholism and disorderly conduct, but with radical working-class organizations and with trade unionism in particular.[12] By the same token, the vibrant street life Mayhew describes in his series on the poor appeared as a kind of Pandemonium where all kinds of boundaries and taboos were violated: children posed as adults, the poor mocked the rich, and boys lounged together on street corners or formed homosocial gangs led by a father-thief.[13] Such "irregular" associations—especially when they were exclusively male—smacked of those unspeakable parodies of the "regular" domestic relation, the homosexual "marriages" that were rumored to form in prisons, among sailors, or even in the boy-gangs.

In specific contrast to these nondomestic males, Chadwick presents numerous portraits of "improved" members of the laboring population. The improvement of these men, not surprisingly, is figured in their domestic habits. Here is a description from Bedford, for example:

> I have much pleasure in saying that some cases of the kind have come under my own observation, and I consider that the improvement has arisen a good deal from the parties feeling that they are somewhat raised in the scale of society. The man sees his wife and family more comfortable than formerly; he has a better cottage and garden: he is stimulated to industry, and as he rises in respectability of station, he *becomes aware* that he has a character to lose. Thus an important point is gained. Having acquired certain advantages, he is anxious to retain and improve them; he strives more to preserve his independence, and becomes a member of benefit, medical, and clothing societies; and frequently, besides this, lays up a certain sum, quarterly or half-yearly, in the savings' bank. Almost always attendant upon these advantages, we find the man sending his children to be regularly instructed in a Sunday, and, where possible, in a day-school, and himself and his family more constant in their attendance at some place of worship on the Lord's day. . . .
>
> A man who comes home to a poor, comfortless hovel after his day's labour, and sees all miserable around him, has his spirits more often depressed than excited by it. He feels that, do his best, he shall be miserable still, and is too apt to fly for a temporary refuge to the alehouse or beer-shop. But give him the means of making himself comfortable by his own industry, and I am convinced by experience that, in many cases, he will avail himself of it. (pp. 323–24)

The model of improvement contained in this description implicitly presents gender as the bedrock of domesticity. Gender, moreover, is constructed as a strict binary opposition, which entails a complex set of assumptions about women, and female nature in particular. Among these are the assumptions that a woman's reproductive capacity is her most salient feature, that this biological capacity makes her naturally self-sacrificing and domestic, and that her more delicate nervous and physiological constitution makes her more susceptible both to her own emotions and to the influence of others. Because of this peculiar combination of self-denial and susceptibility, which women of all classes presumably shared, working-class women could be counted on to transport middle-class values into the working-class home. At the same time, because all women (ideally) reflected the labor of their husbands (rather than manifesting or profiting from their own waged work), working-class women could function as the sign of and incentive to the working-class man's successful performance as a disciplined, productive, respectable wage-earner.[14]

At the same time that they depended on and reinforced this definition of women's nature, descriptions of improvement like the one I have quoted also represented the man's primary relation as his monogamous, legally sanctioned marriage to his wife. Beyond this, moreover, they also ensured that a man's most significant same-sex relationship would be formed *through* his wife to *himself*—to his "character." This relation, of course, was also the basis for a man's participation and investment in those institutions developed to promote the working man's "independence"—friendly societies, savings banks, religious organizations, and educational programs.

Despite the collective nature of such organizations, the form of independence they facilitated supported the model of domesticity I have just described. Both working-class societies and respectable domesticity, in other words, tended to link the individualized identity of the working man to his family *instead of* to any all-male association. The significance of this becomes clear when we remember two things: the process by which men of the middle-class consolidated and politicized *their* class identity, and the forms of all-male association that were available to the working class in the 1830s.

During the eighteenth century, men of the middling ranks began to consolidate their identity as a class through a number of related activities, both economic and social.[15] Two of the most important of these were the constitution of social and economic alliances through networks of kin and the formation of same-sex relationships in such public meeting-places as coffee-houses.[16] For the kin networks, the extension of a man's family through marriage was critical. As Leonore Davidoff and Catherine Hall have argued, the "hidden investment" a woman contributed to her marriage constituted a crucial addition to the family's worth both because her relations expanded the pool of potential economic resources and partners for her husband and because her judicious management of household resources could decrease unnecessary expenditures.[17] By contrast, the formation of nonfamilial alliances entailed the exclusion of women. In the public but informal meeting places provided by coffee houses, men—but not women—discussed ideas and news, founded the characteristic organizations of the middle class (including the stock exchange), and developed shared standards for appropriate and effective behaviors.[18]

For both psychological and material reasons, then, men of the middle-class tended to represent their social superiority partly in terms of their domesticity. The middle-class man was recognizably different from both the licentious, spendthrift aristocrat and the promiscuous and improvident working man, because he faithfully maintained an orderly family. By the same token, however, the self-proclaimed domesticity of middle-class men was accompanied—especially after the turn of the century—by an increasingly formalized segregation of the sexes. Restrictions on property ownership, political representation, and legal rights limited all (married) women's participation in social activities outside the home, just as increasingly rigid standards of decorum and modesty limited the literal mobility of middle-class women in particular. Thus, while the politicization of middle-class men went hand-in-hand with the domestication of middle-class life, this process had a dramatically asymmetrical effect on the historical men and women who occupied the middle-class home.

When Chadwick generalizes the domestic values of the middle class to society as a whole, he does so in such a way as to deny specifically to working-class men the opportunity for those same-sex alliances that constituted one critical component of the politicization of the middle-class. This denial, in fact, had a very precise historical referent—although it is mentioned nowhere in the *Sanitary Report*. Chadwick's normalization of domesticity was composed during a period of intense political activity on the part of the very group he sought to individualize and domesticate. This activity was a response to a number of factors, from bitter disappointment at the inadequacies of the 1832 Parliamentary Reform, to the anguish inflicted by the 1834 New Poor Law, to the hardships that accompanied the poor harvests of 1836 and 1837.[19] In 1836, a group of working men under the leadership of William Lovett formed the London Working Men's Association. Two years later, Lovett and Frances Place published the People's Charter. Demanding universal male suffrage among other things, the Charter became a rallying point for the poor and wretched as well as the disenfranchised laboring population. By the end of 1838, Feargus O'Connor had founded the radical *Northern Star,* and torchlight meetings and marches were being held throughout England. In February 1839, the Convention of the Industrious Classes was held in London. On May 6, a petition bearing 1,200,000 signatures supporting the Charter was presented to Parliament, and the leaders of the convention threatened a general strike. In July and again in November, riots broke out; in the latter, fourteen

Chartists were killed. Thus, despite the dissolution of the convention, the arrests of Lovett and O'Connor, and the failure of the general strike, the Chartist movement had proved by 1842 that working men could and would organize in favor of political enfranchisement.

These politicized activities by working men constitute the implicit referent of the savagery of Chadwick's bone-pickers and itinerant poor. Just as he used the French chiffonniers to incarnate (and displace) this barbarism, however, so Chadwick uses another nationalistic argument to further obliterate the class implications of his sanitary reforms. That is, just as he insists that the classes could (and should) be the same because women are the same, so he insists that England, Wales, Scotland, and Ireland could (and should) form one unified nation—a nation strong enough to resist the example and military force of the French. This rhetorical consolidation of "Great Britain," like the normalization of domesticity, serves to depoliticize difference and to authorize the precise form of "improvement" Chadwick wanted to substitute for political change.[20]

Chadwick's determination to consolidate "Great Britain" on the foundation of public health is clear from his initial response to the assignment he was given in 1839. Although he was charged with surveying only England and Wales, one of his first acts was to visit Edinburgh. There he urged sympathetic friends to petition that Scotland be included in the final report, and when this petition succeeded, Chadwick busied himself with obtaining the requisite information. In the *Sanitary Report* itself, Chadwick simply treats Great Britain as a single nation: he juxtaposes reports from Edinburgh to those from Manchester, and he draws figures about mortality from all parts of the United Kingdom. Only in the final paragraphs of the *Report* does he acknowledge arguments that have insisted on regional differences in the treatment of "British" health, and he specifically equates the nationalistic arguments of Scotland with the localist arguments of such towns as Carlisle. We see in this passage how Chadwick's claim that a common interest unites all British people is an argument for administrative "uniformity": as human beings, all Britons need the same protection; giving every individual the same protection will undermine the divisive "independence and separation" of discrete areas; making "Great Britain" one administrative unit will guarantee efficiency and economy of rule. Here is the final paragraph of the *Sanitary Report*:

> The advantages of uniformity in legislation and in the executive machinery, and of doing the same things in the same way (choosing the best), and calling the same officers, proceedings, and things by the same names, will

only be appreciated by those who have observed the extensive public loss occasioned by the legislation for towns which makes them independent of beneficent, as of what perhaps might have been deemed formerly aggressive legislation. There are various sanitary regulations, and especially those for cleansing, directed to be observed in "every town except Berwick and Carlisle"; a course of legislation which, had it been efficient for England, would have left Berwick and Carlisle distinguished by the oppression of common evils intended to be remedied. It was the subject of public complaint, at Glascow and in other parts of Scotland, that independence and separation in the form of general legislation separated the people from their share of the greatest amount of legislative attention, or excluded them from common interest and from the common advantages of protective measures. It was, for example, the subject of particular complaint, that whilst the labouring population of England and Ireland had received the advantages of public legislative provision for a general vaccination, the labouring classes in Scotland were still left exposed to the ravages of the small-pox. It was also complained by Dr. Cowan and other members of the medical profession, that Scotland had not been included in the provisions for the registration of the causes of death which they considered might, with improvements, be made highly conducive to the advancement of medical science and the means of protecting the public health. (p. 425)

Chadwick's concern with sameness shows its other face in his treatment of the Irish. On the one hand, Chadwick adamantly rejects the notion that the Irish are by nature different from the English or the Scots. On the other hand, however, he admits that in some instances at least, sanitary experiments implemented in Ireland have failed. Rather than present these failures as proof of Irish incompetence, however, he uses them to drive home one of his central principles: that administrative uniformity, fiscal responsibility, and executive efficiency can only be guaranteed by a system that combines administrative and technical expertise. What Chadwick has in mind is the consolidation of the areas to be governed and the centralization of the governing apparatus in a body of professional administrators whose technical knowledge ensures the efficiency and quality of their work. Chadwick's insistence on the national and class consolidation of Great Britain, in other words, is inextricably bound to the centralized government by experts that he imagines ought to exist.

In order to appreciate the role played by a centralized, professionalized administrative unit in Chadwick's scheme, we must return once more to the other end of his plan—the individual working-class man. I have already argued that Chadwick's emphasis on the domesticity of the working class (ideally) works against those nondomestic, same-sex relationships that working-class men had already begun to form, and that the elevation of sexual difference underwrites this emphasis on domesticity. Even though Chadwick's focus on domesticity gives considerable power to women, however, it is important to recognize how limited this power really is. Specifically, women's power over men is limited to women's power over the domestic environment, and this power is limited by the enormity of the housekeeping task. Here is the example Chadwick offers to prove the limitations of women's power—or, as he phrases it, to show the "effect of the dwelling itself on the condition of a female servant." Before she married, Chadwick begins, this young woman "had been taught the habits of neatness, order, and cleanliness most thoroughly as regards household work." Such respectable domestic habits, not surprisingly, are also reflected in the woman's appearance, as Chadwick's lady informant reports:

> Her attention to personal neatness . . . was very great; her face seemed always as if it were just washed, and with her bright hair neatly combed underneath her snow-white cap, a smooth white apron, and her gown and handkerchief neatly put on, she used to look very comely. After a year or two, she married the serving man, who, as he was retained in his situation, was obliged to take a house as near his place as possible. The cottages in the neighbourhood were of the most wretched kind, mere hovels built of rough stones and covered with ragged thatch. . . . After they had been married about two years, I happened to be walking past one of these miserable cottages, and as the door was open, I had the curiosity to enter. I found it was the home of the servant I have been describing. But what a change had come over her! Her face was dirty, and her tangled hair hung over her eyes. Her cap, though of good materials, was ill washed and slovenly put on. Her whole dress, though apparently good and serviceable, was very untidy, and looked dirty and slatternly; everything indeed about her seemed wretched and neglected, (except her little child,) and she appeared very discontented. She seemed aware of the change there must be in her appearance since I had last seen her, for she immediately began to complain of her house. The wet came in at the door of the *only room,* and when it rained, through every part of the roof also, except just over the hearth-stone; large drops fell upon her as she lay in bed, or as she was working at the window: in short, she had found it impossible to keep things in order, so had gradually ceased to make any exertions. Her condition had been borne down by the condition of the house. (p. 195)

This vignette sets out another of Chadwick's central tenets: that "circumstances that are governable govern the habits of the population, and in some instances appear almost to breed the species of the population."

Circumstances therefore limit women's power to improve men (just as, in this description, circumstances displace women as breeders of the human species). Significantly, of course, as Chadwick's formulations repeatedly emphasize, the circumstances that govern women are themselves governable—not by political reform, but by the very army of bureaucratic experts who facilitated and were required by a centralized government scheme such as Chadwick's plan to improve public health.

The twin effects of every component of Chadwick's sanitary plan were, on the one hand, to limit the ability of working-class men to organize themselves into collective political or economic associations and, on the other, to empower the kind of professionalized bureaucrat that Chadwick himself represented. The role women were assigned in this plan was strictly auxiliary, although it was crucial to the domestication, individualization, and (by extension) depoliticization of working-class men. Chadwick's plan therefore drew the working class into the social domain but not, as for social analysts like James Kay, as an aggregate. In fact, of course, the roles Chadwick assigned the individualized members of the working class (both female and male) were extremely limited. This is true for two reasons: first, because these roles remained firmly within the organizing framework of patriarchal relations and, second, because Chadwick conceptualized the problem of the social body on such a gigantic scale. Beyond the protective legislation of the poor law lay the preventive legislation about public health—a scheme that figured the problem posed by the human body at such remove from literal bodies that individual reform efforts, while necessary, could never be enough. Chadwick's tendency to translate the problem of the people into a condition of the environment therefore necessitated the very centralized and preventive measures that also finally set limits to what the people could do for themselves.

Historians of this period have tended to divide on the issue of whether the demise of working-class political action after 1848 was a function of the kind of incorporation I've been describing here or a function of the working class's development of class-specific forms of collective organizations. This essay is intended to be a contribution to that debate—in the sense of arguing that when historians of both sides have ignored the role played by ideas about domesticity in the making of the working class, they have overlooked one of the pivotal points of social organization and change. I am not going to take a position here on whether—and to what extent and in what locales—Chadwick's model of domesticity triumphed in the 1850s among members of the working class, for that would take me too far afield. I do want to pose the question, however, of what difference it would make if we revised our understanding of this period in terms of the bond forged among certain ideas about domesticity, the social domain, the nation, and public health. By 1854, after all, even though Chadwick's beloved board had been dissolved, and the regulation of public health had largely been returned to local government, the politicized working-class movement of Chartism was effectively dead, and working-class men had joined middle-class reformers in demanding the regulation of women's work for the sake of the "family wage." By 1848, political contests between the classes had been largely displaced by struggles among men of all classes for the opportunity to achieve the domestic life normalized by Chadwick's *Report*. The divisive issues of the 1850s were not about the right of the working class to vote but about the rights of women to own property, to divorce, and to enter the waged labor force—especially such professionalized occupations as Chadwick's own had become by midcentury.

Seven

Homosociality and the Psychological: Disraeli, Gaskell, and the Condition-of-England Debate

When novelists began to address the condition-of-England question in the 1840s, they did so in the context of the success with which political economists and social analysts had established their authority to represent and make decisions about the social domain. According to some contemporaries, however, Carlyle's phrase implied more than the dirt, disease, and debility implied by the word *pauperism*. To the Chartists, for example, the "condition of England" signaled the political inequality that years of protests had failed to rectify; to trade unionists and Owenite socialists like William Thompson it summoned up the economic inequities that rendered England "two nations," in Disraeli's striking phrase; to Christian political economists like Thomas Chalmers, it suggested a state of nearly universal spiritual impoverishment, made worse by the legalization of poor relief and the concomitant decay of inspiriting charity and gratitude.

Despite the fact that political economists and social analysts (who were often called social economists) had successfully established their authority to diagnose contemporary problems, then, neither group had monopolized the right either to specify or to treat the range of woes suggested by Carlyle's phrase. Indeed, each group of "economists" was divided among itself; followers of Malthus continued to conceptualize society as a body whose maladies could be cured by removing legislative impediments to health, and disciples of Ricardo insisted that society was a machine whose temporary breakdowns could be fixed by additional "regulators" and "governors." Whatever their preferred metaphor, however, and despite competing formulations of the condition-of-England problem, political and social economists *had* generally succeeded in establishing the authority of a mode of analysis for representing these problems. This mode of representation privileged normative abstractions and calculations about aggregates, both of which were (supposedly) derived from empirical observation. The assertion that this mode of representation was authoritative—more than the specific conclusions reached by political or social economists—was the target of novelists like Charles Dickens, Benjamin Disraeli, and Elizabeth Gaskell. According to these writers, the mode of representation epitomized by political economy may have rendered aspects of the social domain visible as never before, but in so doing it also effaced other facets of contemporary life. According to these novelists, paramount among the subjects that political economy obscured were the "romance" of everyday life and those "feelings and passions" that animated even the most downtrodden human being.[1]

As an explicit alternative to the abstract aggregations with which political economists appealed to readers' rational judgment, novelists deployed a mode of representation that individualized characters and elaborated feelings in order to engage their readers' sympathy. The implication of this difference in protocols was underscored by another difference, which further distinguished novelistic from political and economic discourse in the 1840s. Largely because of the eighteenth-century disaggregation of moral philosophy into political economy and aesthetics, the ways of knowing epitomized by these discourses had become gendered by the early nineteenth century: the abstract reasoning of political economy was considered a masculine epistemology, while the aesthetic appreciation of concrete particulars and imaginative excursions was considered feminine.[2] This did not mean that all imaginative literature was written by women, of course, or even that political economy was exclusively composed by men. It did mean that men who wrote poetry and novels struggled to acquire the dignity generally attributed to masculine pursuits—whether by asserting, as Percy Shelley did, that poets were the "unacknowledged legislators of the world" or by taking serious historical events as their subject, as did Sir Walter Scott. It also meant that women who addressed political and economic subjects, like Mary Wollstonecraft and Harriet Martineau, had to contend with the charge that they were "masculine" or "unsexed" females.

When novelists entered the condition-of-England debate in the 1840s, then, they were implicitly arguing that a feminized genre that individualized distress and aroused sympathy was more appropriate to the delineation of contemporary problems than were the rationalizing abstractions of a masculine genre like political economy. In this essay I will examine the contributions that two so-called social-problem novelists made to the debate about representation and therefore to the specification of the social domain in this period. Predictably, the precise relationship each novelist established to the emergent social domain was influenced by the author's own position within the field of gendered meanings, which bisected the social—and every other—domain in Victorian England. In Benjamin Disraeli's *Coningsby* (1845), for example, we see Disraeli introduce the condition-of-England debate only to dismiss not only political and social economists' analyses of it, but also the social and economic problems generally associated with this phrase. For Disraeli, the condition of England could only be improved by a political reform that consisted of reestablishing the paternalism of the aristocracy and restoring dignity to the monarch. In order to promote his political program through novelistic conventions, Disraeli dramatized political life as a romance. Because this romance was set in the homosocial worlds of the public schools and the political hustings, however, Disraeli risked mobilizing alongside an imaginative engagement with politics an altogether more dubious identification with homoeroticism. In *Coningsby*, this dangerous homoeroticism emerges as the price one pays for shifting discussions about reform from the social domain, where an appropriative or voyeuristic heteroeroticism obtained, to the political domain, where there could be no heteroeroticism because there were no women.

In Elizabeth Gaskell's *Mary Barton* (1848), by contrast, the social domain lies squarely at the center of narrative attention. In this novel, moreover, the social domain expands to encompass not only politics and economics but also a form of interiority that Freud would specify as the psychological. In Gaskell's account, the feminized mode of representation epitomized by the novel is perfectly appropriate to analyzing domesticity, which is the heart of the social domain, but her depiction of (proto)psychology suggests both that psychological complexity may be an effect of the violation of domesticity by the masculine worlds of work and politics and that the eruption of (what would eventually become) the psychological is ruinous to the feminized discourse of the novel. In *Mary Barton*, then, we see one example of the contribution made by nineteenth-century novelists to the constitution of the psychological. Paradoxically, in Gaskell's account, this most private of all domains turns out to be resolutely social, at the same time that its relationship to the social domain is nothing if not problematic.

CONINGSBY

Coningsby, Benjamin Disraeli's eighth novel, is the first of what has come to be called the Young England trilogy, after the youth-worshipping politics Disraeli and his friends espoused. In 1870, Disraeli explained that his ambition in the early 1840s was to explore what he held to be the primary issues of the day: "the derivation and character of political parties; the condition of the people which had been the consequence of them; the duties of the Church as a main remedial agency in our present state."[3] While each of these topics is highlighted by one of the novels in the trilogy (with *Sybil, or the Two Nations* [1845] focusing on the "condition of the people," and *Tancred, or the New Crusade* [1847] taking up the place of the Jews in the founding of the Christian Church), *Coningsby* comes closest to capturing Disraeli's sense of the relationships among politics, the people, and the church. In *Coningsby*, it becomes clear not only that Disraeli held the "character of political parties" responsible for the "condition of the people," but also that he believed that reform in the political domain would simultaneously alleviate social distress and revivify the modern church. Thus, at least as a topic of explicit attention, Disraeli turns away from the social domain in *Coningsby* and attempts to transfer the fascination with which his contemporaries contemplated the social body to activities in the political domain. Disraeli attempts to arouse his readers' interest in the political domain by figuring the initiation into politics as falling in love.

Like the depictions of love that had become a staple of novelistic discourse by 1840, *Coningsby* uses a narrative of personal maturation to plot the trajectory of love.[4] In *Coningsby*, this personal saga begins with the first confrontation between the eponymous hero and his grandfather, the wealthy Marquess of Monmouth. As with so many eighteenth-century novels, the boy's hopes center on his inheritance; in this case, Coningsby wants not only to become the old man's heir but also to win from his grandfather the love that Monmouth denied to both of Coningsby's now-deceased parents. The decisive moment of Coningsby's maturation, which occurs some eight years later, also involves his grandfather and threatens to foreclose both of these legacies. Eager to use Coningsby as a "brilliant tool" for advancing his own campaign for a dukedom, Monmouth commands Coningsby to stand as Tory candidate for Darlford against Monmouth's old enemy, the wealthy manufacturer Millbrook. Coningsby refuses to obey Monmouth, however, both because he loves Millbrook's daughter and because the principles he has come to hold are not those of the Tory party. In Coningsby's refusal, then, Disraeli conjoins love and politics. At the same time, he confers upon Coningsby the status of "hero," which, unlike its eighteenth-century counterpart, derives from achieving independence from people, party, and the past. "Great minds," the narrator announces early in the novel, "must trust to great truths and great talents for their rise, and nothing else."[5]

Such Carlylean celebrations of the individualistic basis of heroism punctuate *Coningsby,* but they are complicated by the narrator's equally adamant insistence that his hero is not a self-made man. Not only does Coningsby not initiate meritorious projects (or any projects at all), but the principles he comes to embody all originate with other characters. Coningsby's maturation, in fact, is figured as a series of conversations rather than actions, in all but the last of which Coningsby is a silent vessel into which other men pour their ideas. As a schoolboy at Eton, Coningsby listens to Oswald Millbrook expound his father's theories; his first "adventure" after Eton is a chance meeting with the erudite Jew Sidonia, who lectures the boy on the "influence of individual character" (pp. 140–47); at the family seat of his friend Lord Sydney, Coningsby learns the significance of ancient ceremonies from the Catholic Eustace Lyle; at Millbrook's home outside of Manchester, Coningsby hears first-hand the manufacturer's thoughts about class and merit; and from Sidonia again, first at Coningsby Castle and then in Paris, the youth learns that "national character" and a strong monarchy more adequately represent the "people" than can an elected House of Commons. As this catalogue of conversations suggests, there is almost no conflict at this level of the plot, not only because the significant events are conversations (or monologues), but also because Coningsby is so passive, so unformed. At most, the young man admits to confusion or voices criticism of the Whig party, but until he finally expounds the principles of Young England in book 7, Coningsby's own ideas are presented as sketchily as is his appearance.

The peculiar amorphousness of young Coningsby does not undermine his heroic potential, however. Disraeli represents Coningsby's influence as immediate, irresistible, and self-evident; it is the effect of "genius" and not of effort or accomplishment. At Eton, for example, the boy attains "over his intimates the ascendant power, which is the destiny of genius" (p. 130); and when he finally stands for Darlford after Millbrook voluntarily steps aside, Coningsby is received "as if he were a prophet" by supporters of every party (p. 491). Coningsby's initial lack of character is, in fact, his primary qualification for inaugurating the reform that Disraeli envisions, for by absorbing the ideas of various men, Coningsby is able to incarnate what Sidonia describes as "national character." "A character is an assemblage of qualities," Sidonia explains; "the character of England should be an assemblage of great qualities" (p. 260).

In the course of the novel, then, Coningsby becomes an assemblage that reconciles the interests of a Whig millowner, an apolitical Catholic, and a Jewish financier. As an assemblage, Coningsby resembles neither the "social body," which is an aggregate that effaces the individuality and agency of poor people, nor Parliament, which Disraeli depicts as having degenerated into gossip and self-serving intrigue. Instead, the aggregate-Coningsby functions as a mouthpiece for the interests of "national opinion," which, in a better world, would be expressed by a "free and intellectual press" (p. 374). As the representative of this enunciative function (which is not unlike the role of the novelist himself), Coningsby is capable of rectifying what the narrator calls the "sectional anomalies of our country"—a phrase that neatly conveys the fact that problems exist in England without specifying their nature. Here is Coningsby's formulation of the constellation of remedies that will correct the condition of England: "a free monarchy, established on the fundamental laws . . . ruling an educated people, represented by a free and intellectual press. Before such a royal authority, supported by such a national opinion, the sectional anomalies of our country would disappear" (p. 375).

Like the principles of Young England in general, Disraeli's image of national opinion as a bulwark for fundamental laws and a free monarchy is frankly idealized. Such idealization, in fact, serves as an explicit counter to what Disraeli and his companions considered the morally bankrupt and spiritually deadening specificity that characterized the contemporary debate about the condition of England, dominated as it was by medical men, utilitarians, political economists, and Whiggish politicians. As a counter to anatomical realism, Disraeli's idealization also offers an acceptable version of reform, which would improve the overall "organization" of the political domain, not incidental details like the composition of the electorate or insanitary living conditions.

The political reform Disraeli proposes in Coningsby was therefore an explicit repudiation of the social reforms advocated by men like James Phillips Kay and Edwin Chadwick, just as the idealized generalizations in which Disraeli formulated his program were rejections of the minute particularization from which economists derived their abstractions. Even though Disraeli's suggestions take the form of generalizations, that is, his idealizations are markedly different from the modern abstractions epitomized by the work of David Ricardo. Whereas modern abstraction exemplifies formal rationality, in the sense that it abstracts from empirically observed particulars laws that facilitate calculation, Disraeli's idealization both resembles and deploys rituals, which theoretically embody the spirit or substance of community. The latter is neither subject to nor productive of calculation, and, in so far as it is rule-governed, its conventions reanimate the essence of relationships whose meaning has been lost in their modern, rationalized forms. Thus Coningsby celebrates not specific measures to improve the living conditions of the poor or the nature of political representation but a return to the aristocratic paternalism Disraeli associated with the age of chivalry. In Disraeli's ideal world, government would be conducted by enlightened landowners; ritualized celebrations of the nation would reinvigorate the spirituality of the people; judiciously administered alms would restore the deference of the poor; and belief in the monarchy and the Church would sustain everyone in hard times.

At some points in *Coningsby,* Disraeli mocks the more "obsolete" and aestheticized versions of the reforms he advocates, as when he reduces Henry Sydney's lofty ideas to the absurd suggestion "that the people are to be fed by dancing round a May-pole" (p. 159). Nevertheless, like most other novelists who took up social issues, Disraeli clearly longed for a more spiritual alternative to political economy and for a mode of representing contemporary problems more imaginatively engaging than either the abstractions or the minute particularization used by theorists of the social body. Devising such an alternative and giving it social authority are the principle tasks of the conversations that make Coningsby what he comes to be. At one point in the novel, when Coningsby first visits Manchester, Disraeli even suggests that industrial machines will inspire the imagination, thereby not only reanimating but literally incorporating the people. "A machine is a slave that neither brings nor bears degradation; it is a being endowed with the greatest degree of energy, and acting under the greatest degree of excitement, yet free at the same time from all passion and emotion. . . . And why should one say that the machine does not live? . . . It moves with more regularity than a man. And has it not a voice? Does not the spindle sing like a merry girl at her work, and the steam-engine roar in jolly chorus, like a strong artisan handling his lusty tools, and gaining a fair day's wages for a fair day's toil?" (pp. 179–80).

While Disraeli rapidly abandons the image of the happy machine, this figure does reveal two significant tendencies inherent in his novel. First, the trope of the happy machine converts the fact of an impoverished laboring class into an aestheticized image—the picture of singing workers—and then it displaces these imaginary workers (and the entire economic problem of unemployment) with another aestheticized image—the vision of the melodious automaton. Like the idea that the "peasantry" will be content with May-day celebrations instead of food, in other words, the image of the singing machine acknowledges class concerns but subordinates them to an idealized resolution whose only application is in the domain of aesthetics. This displacement, which can also be read as an incorporation, suggests one of the contributions that aesthetic genres like the novel made to the constitution of modern culture. By providing an imaginative context for the presentation of problems that contemporaries were beginning to assign to separate domains, novels provided the possibility that the gaps *between* domains could be healed—in the domain of the aesthetic. As topics or episodes in a novel, in other words, issues that seemed to belong to the social *or* the economic *or* the political domain could be represented as belonging to a single whole.[6]

The second tendency revealed by the image of the happy machine also derives its momentum from Disraeli's dissatisfaction with the contemporary discussion of the condition-of-England question. The machine that infatuates Coningsby is better than a body (social or otherwise), for not only is it immune to "degradation," to passion, and to emotion, but it also embodies both the virtues of a man and the enthusiasm of a woman. The happy machine, in other words, allows Disraeli to introduce both gender and eroticism into his hero's career. At the same time, however, in the context of a heterosexual world, this image produces eroticism as a "misplaced" affect. In the image itself, the erotic affect is misplaced in the sense that it is directed toward and assigned to the machine rather than to any body: the *steam-engine* is excited; and the workman's *tools* are lusty. In the novel as a whole, the erotic affect is misplaced in the sense that it is generated in a world composed exclusively of men.

What I am calling the misplacement of eroticism provides the narrative momentum that is otherwise absent from *Coningsby.* If the primary plot of the novel is a relatively static account of the conversations that fill Coningsby with ideas, then the two subplots that provide the requisite incitement and impediments to closure focus on the hero's affective engagements, which Disraeli also presents as crucial to Coningsby's maturation. Disraeli's representation of his hero's interiority resembles the invocation, by gothic novelists like Ann Radcliffe, of the aesthetic of the sublime to figure the presence of something unspeakable or unknowable in the otherwise surveyable mental landscape. In Coningsby's case, this sublime mystery first materializes in relation to a portrait that hangs in Millbrook's house (which we are eventually told depicts Coningsby's mother). When Coningsby meets Millbrook's daughter, Edith, in Paris, the spell cast by the portrait swells to encompass the influence exercised by this young girl. In Coningsby's mind, the image of the (deceased) mother fuses with a likeness of Edith's face to generate a spectral image with inexplicable power. After Coningsby meets Edith, the narrator tells us, "a beautiful countenance that was alternately the face in the mysterious picture [namely, his mother], and then that of Edith, haunted [Coningsby] under all circumstances" (p. 339).

Presumably, no physical resemblance connects the two women, since the mystery of the portrait's presence in Millbrook's house turns out to involve only the fact that Millbrook once loved Coningsby's mother, not the even more devastating possibility that she was Edith's mother too. Even though the mystery of the portrait's placement is eventually solved, of course, the fact that Edith's face alternates with his mother's (even if only in Coningsby's imagination) holds open the possibility that the erotic affect that Disraeli associates with this haunting image will be misdirected in the sense of being incestuous. Because Edith and his mother constitute two faces of a single image, in other words, Coningsby's love could be incestuous either because it is directed toward his sister or because it is directed, through her, to his mother, who the narrator tells us was the young Coningsby's "only link to human society" (p. 39).

For much of the novel, Coningsby's attempts to realize his "secret joy" (p. 339) through marriage to Edith are baffled by the presence of the secret that lies behind the secret of the portrait. This originary secret proves more decisive for Coningsby than the (illusory) resemblance between Edith and his mother, and its prominence in the plot highlights the fact that Disraeli is less interested in (what we would call) psychology than in the emotional component of men's relations with each other. This originary secret signals the most telling misplacement of eroticism in the novel, for it involves not some inappropriate variant of heterosexual passion but a love (turned hatred) between men.[7] When Coningsby tells Millbrook that he loves Edith, Millbrook reveals that the "vindictive feud" that binds and separates Millbrook and Monmouth originated in their shared hatred for Coningsby's father. Millbrook hated Coningsby's father because he stole Coningsby's mother from Millbrook, who was engaged to marry her, and Monmouth hated his son because, in marrying Coningsby's mother, the young man defied his father's wishes (p. 38). To express this common—but divisive—hatred, Monmouth has driven the widow from his family; and, in retaliation for the sins of the father and the son, Millbrook now persecutes Monmouth, first by purchasing an estate the old man coveted and then by winning the parliamentary seat Monmouth intended for his functionary Rigby.

This originary relationship among men makes another appearance in *Coningsby*, once more in connection with the hero but this time in the form of passionate love, not hate. Disraeli introduces this "frantic sensibility" in the guise of schoolboy friendship. "At school," the narrator explains,

> friendship is a passion. It entrances the being; it tears the soul. All loves of after-life can never bring its rapture, or its wretchedness; no bliss so ab-

sorbing, no pangs of jealousy or despair so crushing and so keen! What tenderness and devotion; what illimitable confidence; infinite revelations of inmost thoughts; what ecstatic present and romantic future; what bitter estrangements and what melting reconciliations; what scenes of wild recrimination, agitating explanations, passionate correspondence; what insane sensitiveness, and what frantic sensibility; what earthquakes of the heart and whirlwinds of the soul are confined in that simple phrase, a schoolboy's friendship! (p. 72)

Predictably, the unformed Coningsby is not the bearer but the object of this "passionate admiration" (p. 72). When Coningsby saves his young admirer from drowning, Oswald Millbrook pours out his feelings to his hero in what can only be called a love letter. "I want . . . that we may be friends," the besotted Millbrook writes, "and that you will always know that there is nothing I will not do for you, and that I like you better than any fellow at Eton. . . . Not because you saved my life; though that is a great thing, but because before that I would have done anything for you" (p. 83).

It takes some time for Coningsby to replicate Oswald's outburst and even longer for Oswald to fulfill his promise. Along with the feud between their elders, however, this passionate homosocial attachment provides the motor of the romantic plot and the terms by which Disraeli idealizes and eroticizes politics. It is because Coningsby saved young Millbrook that he first visits the Millbrook home, where he sees the spellbinding portrait and Edith; it is because he loves Edith that he defies his grandfather; and it is because Oswald loves Coningsby that the former eventually persuades his father to relinquish his parliamentary seat to Coningsby. Even more important, it is because Coningsby returns Oswald's passionate affection that his grandfather disinherits him, which event first reduces Coningsby to dependence on Millbrook and then permits Oswald to fulfill his vow. Disraeli presents Coningsby's "impassioned" advances to Oswald as a metaphorical seduction, advanced by a man made desperate by the frustration of his heterosexual desires. After Mr. Millbrook reveals the secret of his feud with Monmouth, Coningsby realizes that, for reasons that are political rather than psychological, he cannot marry Edith. In despair, Coningsby "flings" himself into Oswald's arms and hurries his friend toward Coningsby Castle, which Oswald has been forbidden to enter. Despite Oswald's hesitation, a thunderstorm drives the young men inside, just as another storm had sequestered Coningsby and Edith the day before. "Hurried on by Coningsby," Oswald "[can] make no resistance" (p. 407). Once inside the castle, and professing himself as "reckless as the tempest,"

Coningsby orders the servants away "and for a moment [feels] a degree of wild satisfaction in the company of the brother of Edith" (p. 408).

That Coningsby's "wild satisfaction" is transgressive not only to social convention but to the proprieties of the novel is made clear both by the abrupt termination that Mr. Rigby's entrance brings to the midnight supper (and the chapter) and by Monmouth's irate response to Rigby's representation of "the younger Millbrook quite domiciled at the Castle" (p. 440). Disraeli will elaborate no such misplacement of eroticism, in other words, even if it does provide the momentum for his narrative. Thus, alongside the scenes that explicitly depict homoerotic engagements, Disraeli provides numerous correctives to the erotic affect these scenes generate. When Coningsby goes up to Cambridge, for example, he is represented as thinking with "disgust of the impending dissipation of an University, which could only be an exaggeration of their coarse frolics at school" (p. 278). The eventual substitution of Edith for Oswald in Coningsby's embrace signals the narrative's decisive dismissal of the disruptive homoeroticism that provides the source of imaginative engagement for much of the novel.

The homoeroticism that erupts most explicitly between Oswald and Coningsby cannot be so easily dismissed from the world of Disraeli's novel, however, for it is one effect of Disraeli's turn to the political from the social domain (and the heterosexualized relations that form around the social body). That the political domain is shot through with homoerotic connotations is clear in the "keen relish" and "excited intelligence" with which the schoolboys follow the exploits of their political heroes (pp. 132, 133). The erotic potential of political work also surfaces in the image of male political canvassers donning dresses to round up voters (p. 303), and it announces itself clearly when Coningsby is reunited with Oswald at Oxford. Their "congress of friendship" unbroken, each man "pour[s] forth his mind without stint." The narrator blesses their union even as he dismisses the sexual overtones of the word *congress* by describing the conversation as if one man—not two—were present. "Man is never so manly as when he feels deeply, acts boldly, and expresses himself with frankness and with fervour" (p. 371).

The homoerotics of manly conversation constitute Disraeli's version of a reformed political domain. Because politics has been eroticized, it can be plotted in a novel, the nineteenth-century conventions of which demanded characters with whom readers could identify and in whose romances they could imaginatively participate. Yet the very association of the novel with the (French) romance dovetailed with the heterosexism of Victorian culture to dictate Disraeli's insistence that the homoeroticism of politics *not* be understood as sexual. The novel could not be an appropriate vehicle for reforming the political domain if it carried the taint of sexuality (as some contemporaries still feared). Thus Disraeli rewrites schoolboy sentiments and political alliances and the homosocial world of men sharing power as good clean "fun," as an aestheticized adventure, and as patriotism. At the conclusion of *Coningsby,* the two charismatic boys-turned-men stand side-by-side at the head of their country, their infatuation with each other having been converted into an infatuation with England. "Men must have been at school together," the narrator approvingly notes, "to enjoy the real fun of meeting thus, and realising their boyish dreams. . . . Life was a pantomime; the wand was waved, and it seemed that the schoolfellows had of a sudden become elements of power, springs of the great machine" (p. 490).

The great machine of which Coningsby and Millbrook are the springs thus replaces the singing machines of Manchester. In the process, of course, both sexuality and women simply disappear. Eroticism lingers as a volatile effect of the masculine domain of politics, but in *Coningsby* women are, for all intents and purposes, irrelevant. Neither the object of the narrative gaze nor (finally) the site of (proto)psychological complexity, women seem to have vanished along with the social body that also carried the mark of femininity in the 1840s.[8]

MARY BARTON

If Disraeli dismisses the social domain as peripheral to his concerns, Elizabeth Gaskell seeks the social body's most intimate recesses and its most private language. And if Disraeli counters the feminization of the novel by larding his work with "manly conversations" and didactic asides, Gaskell uses the gendered genre to place sexual difference in the foreground as both social symptom and cure. For Gaskell, the crisis of the "hungry forties" should be addressed not by reforming politics or politicizing the novel, but by using the genre's conventional focus on individual characters to engage readers imaginatively with the problems of the poor. According to Gaskell, the capacious mode of knowing associated with the novel and with women can bridge the gulf between England's "two nations" by feminizing both masters and workers—that is, by teaching them to identify with each other, as women (and novelists) already do. For Gaskell, the novel is a mode of representation superior to classical political economy because only the former can transport middle-class readers into the homes and minds of the poor.

As we have seen, Disraeli also relies on imaginative identification to promote a program of (political) reform. Whereas Disraeli ultimately directs his reader's attention to public matters, however, Gaskell explores issues that we (like the Victorians) call private. When the secret of the mysteriously arresting portrait turns out to involve a rivalry between men that is political as well as personal, Disraeli serves notice that the primary site of his drama will not be the dark continent of his hero's mind. In *Mary Barton,* by contrast, this dark continent surfaces as the location of a conflict even more formative than contests in the political domain. Along with several other novels published in this decade (*Jane Eyre, Wuthering Heights,* and *Dombey and Son*), *Mary Barton* begins to specify the relationship between the emergent social domain, which was subject to a new form of government administration, and an even less clearly articulated domain, which seemed to require its own administrative apparatus, not to mention a mode of representation suited to its unique dynamics. In *Mary Barton,* the psychological domain does not assume its modern (Freudian) form, however, for Gaskell presents psychological complexity, in the first instance at least, as an effect of the very problems that constitute the social domain.

Most obviously, of course, *Mary Barton* is not a study of individual psychology but an exploration of the "agony of suffering" endured by the Manchester poor. In this sense, the novel should be read alongside other early attempts to represent the details of working-class life. The affinity between *Mary Barton* and James Phillips Kay's text on Manchester cotton operatives, or even Chadwick's *Sanitary Report,* is clearest in the novel's opening chapters, which contain several graphic descriptions like the following:

> You went down one step even from the foul area into the cellar in which a family of human beings lived. It was very dark inside. The window-panes many of them were broken and stuffed with rags, which was reason enough for the dusky light that pervaded the place even at mid-day. . . . On going into the cellar inhabited by Davenport, the smell was so foetid as almost to knock the two men down. Quickly recovering themselves, as those inured to such things do, they began to penetrate the thick darkness of the place, and to see three or four little children rolling on the damp, nay wet brick floor, through which the stagnant, filthy moisture of the street oozed up; the fireplace was empty and black; the wife sat on her husband's lair, and cried in the dark loneliness. (p. 54)

This passage resembles the descriptions of squalor contained in Chadwick's *Report* both in Gaskell's focus on insanitary details and in her insistence that the house is pervaded—or rather, infiltrated—by the insalubrious environment. The oozing "moisture" is a sign that, for Gaskell as for Chadwick, the homes of the poor can never be private in the sense that they cannot exclude the literal refuse from the streets. The solution that Gaskell recommends for the condition-of-England problem is not Chadwick's centralized system of government regulation, however, but a liberal application of the sympathy that Kay hoped to incite through education. As the millowner Carson summarizes the novel's "wish," it is "that a perfect understanding, and complete confidence and love, might exist between masters and men; that the truth might be recognised that the interests of one were the interests of all, and, as such, required the consideration and deliberation of all; that hence it was most desirable to have educated workers, capable of judging, not mere machines of ignorant men; and to have them bound to their employers by the ties of respect and affection, not by mere money bargains alone; in short, to acknowledge the Spirit of Christ as the regulating law between both parties" (pp. 375–76).

Mary Barton may resemble the writing of social analysts in the ways I have mentioned, but Gaskell's use of novelistic conventions gives her treatment of these problems a very different emphasis. In the description of John Barton and George Wilson's descent into the Davenport home, for example, Gaskell first solicits her reader's imaginative participation with the pronoun *you*, and then distinguishes between the middle-class reader and the working-class characters by noting that the latter have become inured to the noxious smells that would overwhelm her (and her reader). Gaskell's use of point of view does not encourage scientific detachment or (simply) normative disgust, but forges a sympathetic relationship between the reader and the characters that turns on their shared humanity: some people may have become indifferent to fetid smells, this passage suggests, but noting their coarser senses should make those of us whom smells offend want to improve the conditions that have obliterated delicacy in the poor.

Gaskell's use of novelistic conventions also reinforces her emphasis on domesticity. Like Kay and Chadwick, Gaskell treats domesticity as the heart of the social body. Whereas both Kay and Chadwick use discussions of domesticity to punctuate or support sustained theoretical arguments, however, Gaskell dramatizes the centrality of domesticity both by setting the action of her novel in several working-class homes and by treating the controversial topics of the day—poor relief, factory legislation, Chartist politics—as impediments to the "plan of living" that every individual must devise (p. 68). Gaskell's novelistic focus on characters' daily lives also leads her to employ simple, domestic images to signify poverty. Whereas Kay and Chadwick calculated poverty through tables of whitewashed buildings and diminished life expectancies, Gaskell captures want through citing an insufficiency of teacups and a meal made solely of raw oatmeal.[9]

Gaskell's emphasis on the narratives of individual lives thus dove-tails with her use of mundane details to engage the reader imaginatively in a quest for what all people (theoretically) want: domestic security. So prominent is domesticity in Gaskell's novel that her representation of political events, like the workers' presentation of the People's Charter to Parliament, stresses only the domestic repercussions of the petition's failure, not its political significance. In *Mary Barton,* in fact, this event is not even narrated. Instead, at the moment when John Barton might comment on the political implication of his trip to London, he refuses to speak, and Gaskell offers as an explicit substitute for Barton's political story the narrative of another journey to London—the journey on which Job Leigh learned to care for his daughter's newborn child. Gas-kell's treatment of the politically and economically significant subject of imperialism repeats this pattern of displacement. While we discover in passing that Will Wilson has traded in Africa, China, Madeira, and both Americas, his foreign adventures figure most prominently as contribu-tions to the domestic scene to which he returns. Thus, Gaskell registers his trips merely as absences for his aunt Alice, and she immediately do-mesticates the only exotica Will brings back: his dried flying fish be-comes a specimen in Job Leigh's naturalist collection, and his tale about a mermaid is first debunked, then supplanted by a domestic enchant-ress, as Job's granddaughter Margaret "enthralls" Will with her lovely singing.

Just as Gaskell's use of novelistic conventions informs her approach to the condition-of-England question, so her attention to domesticity in the context of this debate informs her adaptation of the novel as a genre. As the example of *Coningsby* suggests, the novel was not conceptualized as a precisely defined, rule-governed genre in this (or any other) decade. Although certain features, like a focus on individual characters, the sub-ordination of "digressions" to closure, and the use of a more-or-less sta-ble point of view had become conventional by this period, individual novels continued to betray the genre's heterogeneous lineage in a variety of ways, including the range of plots that coexisted promiscuously in their pages. *Mary Barton* becomes a domestic novel, for example, which culminates in marriage, by introducing and setting aside a number of competing narratives, any one of which might have governed another contemporary novel.[10] Thus, in the first half of the novel, the presence of Harry Carson holds open the possibility of a sentimental story that fo-cuses on seduction, while Sally Ledbitter threatens to give this narrative a farcical twist; Mary's aunt Esther, with her mysterious appearances and her uncanny resemblance to Mary's mother, threatens a gothic em-phasis; John Barton's fall mimics tragedy; and the (momentary) uncertainty over who killed Carson promises a murder mystery. By the end of *Mary Barton*, these competing plots have been absorbed into the marriage plot that focuses on Mary and Jem, but for most of the novel, it is the rivalry between the domestic plot and these other contenders that gives the narrative its momentum.

This contest among plots produces not just narrative conflict but also another effect that decisively distinguishes between *Mary Barton* and contemporary nonfictional treatments of the condition of England. As Gaskell discriminates a normative narrative of domesticity by specifying its similarities to—and differences from—sentimental, gothic, and tragic stories of love, she begins to delineate a domain that does not precisely coincide with the social domain her domestic narrative supposedly illuminates. Many of the characteristics of this emergent psychological domain bear distinct affinities to features of the narrative plots that compete so ostentatiously in *Mary Barton*. As Freud was to describe the psychological domain, its dynamics are characterized by a sublimity that simultaneously baffles representation and insists on being known (like the specters in gothic mysteries); the conflicts of this domain center around sexuality and frustrated, often transgressive desire (like gothic and sentimental conflicts); and its indomitable narcissism rages in vain against an indifferent world (as does a tragic hero). Without suggesting that Elizabeth Gaskell single-handedly created modern psychologized subjectivity, or even that the competing narratives in *Mary Barton* are its only discursive ancestors, I do want to argue that, along with other nineteenth-century novels, *Mary Barton* helped delineate the psychological in a way that facilitated its disaggregation as an autonomous domain, whose operations are governed by a rationality specific to it, not to social relations more generally understood.

Two characters in *Mary Barton* are cursed with (what we would call) psychological complexity: John Barton and his daughter Mary. Because his is the simpler and, in many ways, more revealing case, I will return to John Barton in a moment. In her characterization of Mary, Gaskell begins to construct psychological complexity when she broaches the subject of Mary's feelings for Jem Wilson. Initially, Mary thinks she does not love Jem, largely because, as the narrator tells us, she has become possessed by "the simple, foolish, unworldly" idea that she is "as good as engaged" to Harry Carson (pp. 121, 120). Mary has derived this idea not simply from Harry's attention but from the interpretation she has been led to place on his flirtation by reading romances.

At this point in the novel, Gaskell represents Mary's "contrariness" as a universal condition—that is, as not peculiar to Mary and as amenable to a traditional, theological analytic: "Such is the contrariness of the human heart, from Eve downwards, that we all, in our old Adam-state, fancy things forbidden sweetest" (p. 121). As the love masked by Mary's "contrariness" begins to make itself known, we see even more clearly the premodern nature of Gaskell's conceptualization of interiority. In chapter 11, when Jem proposes to Mary, Gaskell depicts Mary's emotional response as a process of "unveiling." In this scene, Mary's authentic feelings, which Gaskell signifies by the words *heart* and *soul,* seem to lie beneath those delusive impressions that she has internalized from romances. Mary only gradually sees her hidden but genuine love for Jem, through a process that Gaskell initially describes as a conversation between two "selves":

> It was as if two people were arguing the matter; that mournful, desponding communion between her former self and her present self. Herself, a day, an hour ago; and herself now. For we have every one of us felt how a very few minutes of the months and years called life, will sometimes suffice to place all time past and future in an entirely new light; will make us see the vanity or the criminality of the bye-gone, and so change the aspect of the coming time, that we will look with loathing on the very thing we have most desired. (p. 176)

In Gaskell's representation, the discovery of interior complexity is only momentarily a conflict between two "selves" that occupy the same mental landscape. After the first sentence of this description, Gaskell shifts her emphasis to time. In so doing, she depicts the interior argument as a transition, a passage from one emotional state to another. In keeping with this depiction, Gaskell represents Mary as acquiring immunity to Harry Carson's attractions as soon as she recognizes the "passionate secret of her soul"—that she loves Jem: "In the clear revelation of that past hour, she saw her danger, and turned away, resolutely, and for ever" (p. 177).

It is important to note that, even though it occupies the place of a modern scene of psychic conflict, this description is very unlike Freud's representation of the dynamics of such conflict. In the first place, Mary's self-delusion is not really an *internal* conflict, since the animating force of one of the two "selves"—the "unworldly" idea that she loves Harry Carson—originates in and is sustained by influences external to Mary: her reading of romances and the example of her aunt Esther. The extent to which this delusion is separable from Mary is signaled by Gaskell's use of Sally Ledbitter to confront Mary with ever-more-unwelcome, ever-more-overtly-stylized visions of the spectacle Mary once entertained. In the second place, Gaskell's representation of Mary's "contrariness" is not really a *conflict* between two persistent inclinations. As

a transition (from delusion to self-knowledge), Mary's "unveiling" does not fix her in a dynamic she will forever repeat but frees her from a false impression she temporarily held. The real challenge Mary faces in regard to her feelings for Jem is not resolving psychological ambivalence but finding a socially acceptable way to express her love.

If Gaskell's depiction of Mary's recognition of love is distinctively prepsychological, however, her representation of the conflict that arises when Mary discovers that her father is a murderer more closely resembles our modern notion of psychology. Unlike the earlier confusion over what her true feelings are, the turmoil over her father consists of two sets of feelings, neither of which will go away, and the mutual contradiction of which necessitates a compensatory imaginative gesture from Mary. To accommodate both her love for her father and the dread of him that she now feels, Mary generates two images of John Barton: "Among the mingled feelings she had revealed in her delirium, ay, mingled even with the most tender expressions of love for her father, was a sort of horror of him; a dread of him as a blood-shedder, which seemed to separate him into two persons,—one, the father who had dandled her on his knee and loved her all her life long; the other, the assassin, the cause of all her trouble and woe" (p. 413).

Mary's response to her father, which would be termed *splitting* in modern psychological discourse, originates in Mary's "delirium." This delirium manifests itself most dramatically at Jem's trial when Mary, desperate to tell one truth (that Jem is innocent) without revealing another (that her father is guilty), falls into convulsions (p. 394). The "madness," "hysteria," or "delirium" that results effectively blocks Mary's speech. Even if Mary's contradictory feelings about her father are not resolved by her illness, the impermissible half of those feelings is censored by her breakdown.

The dramatic courtroom scene is a repetition of the episode in which Mary experienced in relation to Jem the same conflict she now feels about her father. In chapter 20, fearing that Jem has murdered Harry, Mary is first possessed by the two contradictory thoughts that Jem is guilty and that he is good; then she is overwhelmed by the equally intolerable thought that if Jem is guilty, then she, who has rejected him, is guilty too (p. 285). At this point, Gaskell depicts her as going "mad," as afflicted with visions of the gallows while "pulses career[. . .] through her head with wild vehemence" (p. 286). Immediately, however, Mary falls from this agitation into a state of "strange forgetfulness of the present" that culminates in "blessed" unconsciousness. The ensuing description is essential to Gaskell's conceptualization of (proto)psychology. "And then came a strange forgetfulness of the present, in thought of the

long-past times;—of those days when she hid her face on her mother's pitying, loving bosom, and heard tender words of comfort. . . . And then Heaven blessed her unaware, and she sank from remembering, to wandering, unconnected thought, and thence to sleep . . . and she dreamt of the happy times of long ago, and her mother came to her, and kissed her as she lay" (p. 286). From this dream, Mary wakes to what she momentarily believes to be her mother's voice, as Esther arrives with the paper that ultimately incriminates John Barton.

The fact that memories and then dreams of Mary's mother soothe the interior conflict that Gaskell calls "madness" suggests that, even in these most modern of all her psychological scenes, Gaskell still does not imagine the psychological as an autonomous domain. In Freud's (reconsidered) conceptualization, the psyche is a domain of originary drives, and the inevitable conflicts among these drives both generate the conditions of not-knowing (the unconscious) and foster an alternative mode of knowledge-production (the symptom). For Gaskell, by contrast, no knowledge is unknown; instead, hysteria and delirium function to block speech—the social communication of knowledge that is intolerable because harmful to the self *and to others*. By the same token, Mary's vision of her mother functions not as a mode of representing something about Mary that she otherwise could not know but as a symbolic consolation for a dilemma she cannot resolve. For Gaskell, then, what would eventually become the psychological domain is social in every sense: its dynamics protect others (not the self), and its conflicts are healed by the mother (not expressed as symptoms).

If we turn for a moment to Gaskell's depiction of John Barton, we can see even more clearly the link Gaskell forges between the social, the economic, the political, *and* the (emergent) psychological domains. Gaskell devotes much less attention to John Barton's interior conflicts than to those of his daughter, and in her most extended treatment of this subject (chapter 15), it is not even clear whether she is suggesting that his "diseased thoughts" are an expression of internal conflicts or an effect of his political activities, the hunger occasioned by his poverty, or even opium. In some ways, however, this is precisely the point: with increasing emphasis, Gaskell represents John Barton's interior conflicts as originating in the external world. Most obviously captured in the Dives and Lazarus story, conflict—figured most consistently as a "dark gulf" that reflects some specific injustice—afflicts John Barton from his boyhood and as a consequence of his reading. In the climactic deathbed scene, he describes himself as being "tore in two" by his struggles to reconcile his sorrow for the suffering around him with the forgiveness the Bible recommends (p. 441). Thus his emotional conflict—the source of his will-

ingness to kill Harry Carson, which is in turn the source of his guilt—is not simply, or even primarily, psychological in a modern sense. Instead, Barton's interior "deep gulf" replicates the "deep gulf" that scars social relations, marked, as they are, both by economic inequalities and by the contradiction between the ethical rationality enunciated by the Bible and the economic rationality by which most men understand the acquisition of their daily bread.

I want to make four points about the (proto)psychological domain that begins to surface in *Mary Barton*. First, this domain is unmistakably social. What stands in the place of the modern psychological domain in this novel originates in, functions to protect, and is resolved by some image of social relations. Even though it intermittently resembles Freud's conceptualization of an autonomous psyche, in other words, Gaskell's depiction of interiority is at most a liminal arena, which partakes of inexpressible feelings *as they derive from and respond to* social relationships.

Second, what stands in the place of the psychological in *Mary Barton* is inflicted, *by and large*, on domesticity or its guardians (women) by events in the masculine worlds of work and politics. The turmoil that reduces Mary to convulsions and delirium, after all, originates in the economic and political disputes that set masters against workers, and its immediate cause is the piece of paper that has acquired its deadly meaning by lying around in a public street. Thus, paradoxically, what we now think of as the most personal, the most private, and, often, the most feminized domain—the psychological—appears in this early incarnation as the effect of the violation of domesticity by something else: the work, the politics, and the injustice that disfigure the masculine public sphere.[11] That the psychological is also inflicted on characters by books that are imaginatively engaging only complicates this picture of a feminized sphere that is violated by knowledge of an intolerable world of masculine complexity.

My third point about Gaskell's representation of a (proto)psychological domain follows from this last observation and also takes the form of a paradox. Although Gaskell figures domesticity as the heart of what she and her contemporaries were producing as a *social* domain, the social domain as such recedes from view as she explores that which political and social economy could not depict. As Gaskell begins to develop Mary's interior conflicts in relation to the murder of Harry Carson, not only do the detailed descriptions of working-class domesticity decrease in frequency, but Mary begins to resemble the middle-class heroines of novels like *Clarissa, Evelina,* or *Sense and Sensibility.* In the scenes set in Liverpool in particular, Gaskell emphasizes Mary's frailty, her delicacy, and her modesty. So marked are the indications of Mary's gentility that when the boatman takes her to his house for the night, Mary's virtue is instantly recognizable to her humble hosts—despite the fact that she has appeared in such a compromising situation. By the midpoint of the novel, in fact, Gaskell has all but discounted poverty as a source of meaningful distress, which is now figured as emotional pain. When Mary meets a starving child in the street in chapter 20, her first response is to discredit mere bodily woes: "Oh, lad, hunger is nothing," she murmurs, "—nothing!" (p. 284). In this novel, what takes the place of physical suffering is mental distress; and what takes the place of a concern to improve—or administer—the social domain are the two faces of what is primarily a social *emotion*: the sympathy or imaginative engagement that binds the reader to Mary; and the hysteria that curtails her speech.

Finally, as Gaskell adumbrates the dynamics of a domain that, even if not fully psychological in the modern sense, escapes the oversight of government administration, her writing also suggests that the emergence of this domain troubles the narrative conventions with which she gestures toward it. This suggestion appears in the four passages in *Mary Barton* in which the conventional barriers that separate author, narrator, and characters collapse.[12] In the most extended of these passages, which appears in chapter 18, the collapse occurs with the opening of a parenthetical digression.

> Already [Mrs. Wilson's] senses had been severely stunned by the full explanation of what was required of her,—of what she had to prove against her son, her Jem, her only child,—which Mary could not doubt the officious Mrs. Heming had given; and what if in dreams (that land into which no sympathy nor love can penetrate with another, either to share its bliss or its agony,—that land whose scenes are unspeakable terrors, are hidden mysteries, are priceless treasures to one alone,—that land where alone I may see, while yet I tarry here, the sweet looks of my dear child),—what if, in the horrors of her dreams, her brain should go still more astray, and she should waken crazy with her visions, and the terrible reality that begot them? (p. 259)

Such passages, which differ from the other narrative interpolations in *Mary Barton,* resemble the sympathetic identification that Gaskell advocates as an alternative to government interference in the social domain. So extreme is this identification, however, that Gaskell (or the narrator?) momentarily becomes a character in her novel. Instead of enforcing rules, as any form of administration must do, this identification undermines the conventions necessary to both the reader's trust in the novelist and the fictive nature of the novelistic world. These four passages suggest, then, that imaginative engagement may not be an adequate instrument for administering the social domain. Even more telling, they suggest that the emergent psychological domain both produces and requires new narrative conventions to represent its specific effects.

In this essay, I have argued that novelists' contributions to the debate about the condition of England tended to challenge the modes of representation that political and social economists deemed adequate to contemporary woes. Inevitably, this challenge recast the nature of the problem itself, for as writers like Disraeli and Gaskell abandoned abstractions for the kind of individualizing narratives that were conventional in the novel, they turned from quantifiable features of the urban landscape to the toll that dirt, disease, and debility extracted from the poor. Moreover, because social—and, more specifically, romantic—relationships had become the conventional site of readerly identification by the 1840s, novelists tended to embed stories of individual distress within narratives of affective, often erotic engagement. As a result, practitioners of this most feminized of discourses often linked their hopes for "improvement" not to specific government policies but to the utopian potential culturally ascribed to love.

Disraeli and Gaskell approached the condition-of-England question from very different perspectives, of course, and I do not want to overstate the similarities between *Coningsby* and *Mary Barton*. Disraeli's interest in political reform and his almost complete disregard (in this novel) for the details of impoverished life led to an emphasis very different from that of Elizabeth Gaskell, interested as she was in arousing sympathy for the suffering poor. Nevertheless, both writers suggested that no definition of the condition-of-England problem that omitted the roles played by such incalculable factors as erotic attraction and imaginative engagement could convey either the cost of England's overall prosperity or the resources available to offset it.

As novelists like Disraeli and Gaskell exposed the limitations of political- and social-economic contributions to the condition-of-England debate, they began to adumbrate a domain conceptually adjacent to the social, political, and economic domains that their contemporaries were trying to describe. While neither Disraeli's portrait of the homosociality of political intrigue nor Gaskell's characterization of hysteria ascribes full autonomy to the psychological domain, both novelists gesture toward a kind of experience in which conventional rules do not obtain. The specification of this domain—and the development of ways to represent and govern it—were to become definitive preoccupations of the modern novel. In the process of specifying this domain, of course, the modern novel has helped naturalize what we have come to think of as the psychological, just as it has helped sever this new domain from the social domain in relation to which it was initially conceptualized.

Eight

SPECULATION AND VIRTUE IN
OUR MUTUAL FRIEND

In 1819, David Ricardo formulated a rationality so specific to the economic domain that it seemed capable of severing the connection between poverty and the social body captured by the concept of pauperism. According to Ricardo, the economy is simply a distributional mechanism, governed by the laws of production, distribution, supply, and demand; it is oblivious to happiness, morality, and merit, and it acknowledges nature only in so far as it registers the variable fertility of land, not by accommodating biological facts about reproduction or hunger.[1]

Despite Ricardo's attempt to purge political economy of the moral considerations that the metaphor of a social body implied, throughout the next three decades contributors to the science of wealth continued to apply moral categories to economic transactions.[2] It was tempting to do so both because the connection between commerce and virtue, which had been forged with such difficulty in the eighteenth century,[3] had its own inertial power, and because the laws governing financial transactions tended to support the interpretation of bankruptcy as a punishment— or even a divine retribution—for unwise business practices. Before the passage of limited liability legislation in the 1850s, a shareholder in a bankrupted company stood to lose everything as punishment for his injudicious investment.

The persistence of a moralizing strain in discussions of things economic was also a function of the undeniable fact that unscrupulous individuals did take advantage of the opportunities offered by England's burgeoning economy. Even Ricardo's metaphor of a mechanism of production and distribution could not efface the critical role that investment—and risk—played in generating the wealth of the nation; where risk held out the possibility of wealth or destitution, the fantasies and fears that such possibilities aroused could not always be disciplined to the letter of the law. The 1840s constituted not only a decade of hunger for many but a period of unprecedented speculative opportunities for a few, especially in relation to the railways, whose completion helped catapult the English economy into general prosperity in the 1850s.

Beginning in the 1850s, the dramatic triumphs and the tragic collapse of investors both large and small provided irresistible material for novelists, and in the likes of Merdle (*Little Dorrit*) and Melmot (*The Way We Live Now*), the overreaching speculator became a figure for the moral pitfalls of the modern economy. Indeed, novelists like Dickens and Trollope were instrumental in defending the relevance of a moral vocabulary to transactions in the economic domain. To the former in particular, the ethically neutral language of classical political economy was no more appropriate to the shenanigans of unscrupulous investors than it was to the sufferings of the downtrodden factory hand.

In many ways, of course, novelists' efforts to defend a moral interpretation of business practices must be read as exactly that: a defense against the effort to enact juridical guarantees that finance capital would be free of inhibitions both moral and practical. This effort began to yield results in 1844, with the passage of the Registration Act, but its success was felt only in 1855, when the Limited Liability Act was passed. This act was reinforced by the Joint Stock Companies Act of 1856; then, in 1862, these acts were consolidated by the comprehensive Companies Act.[4] In part, the momentum behind this legislation reflects the achievement of a critical mass of support for Ricardo's position: according to this sentiment, the economy *is* a mechanism, which, if left alone, will produce and distribute the nation's wealth. Partly, the momentum behind the limited liability legislation suggests a growing conviction among England's legislators that, even if the economy was amoral, investors were moral agents, capable of self-regulation and judicious discrimination. Robert Lowe offered just this defense of limited liability in 1856, when he appealed to his colleagues in the House of Commons to "deal on the basis of confidence. Fraud and wickedness," he continued, "are not to be presumed in individuals."[5]

By the second half of the 1850s, then, the stage had been set for a contest over the relationship between economic transactions and a moralizing analytic carried over from evangelical theology. This essay focuses on the contribution that Dickens's *Our Mutual Friend* (1863–65) made to this contest. I will argue that Dickens's last completed novel took a paradoxical stance in relation to the constitution of modern British culture: on the one hand, the novel struggled against the modern disaggregation of domains by insisting that economic behavior *not* be freed from a moral analytic; on the other hand, *Our Mutual Friend* betrays the anxieties generated *by* this disaggregation. These anxieties, which focus on masculinity in particular, suggest the extent to which the modern form of culture that was being consolidated in the 1860s threatened to make both speculation *and* morality mere effects of representation. To forestall this triumph of modern representation, Dickens mobilized the assumption that his contemporaries had only begun to question: that the identity categories we call gender and race constituted natural bases for making moral discriminations about business and everything else.

In order to understand the semantic negotiations of *Our Mutual Friend*, it is necessary to survey the institutional and imaginative impact of limited liability and of speculation more generally. Limited liability was a legal provision that permitted corporations to be established where only partnerships and unincorporated companies had previously been allowed. This legislation enabled promoters to raise larger sums of capital for finance and investment than other kinds of business organizations, because limited liability decreased the fiscal responsibility of each investor. Because a limited corporation had its own legal personality, each shareholder was liable only for the capital he had invested in the business, not for all of his—and his family's—holdings "to the last shilling and acre," as the law of partnership had mandated. Limited companies therefore could not only engage more investors than a partnership generally could; they also drew investors from a much wider pool than the family network, which the partnership had often relied on to guarantee fiscal responsibility. The Joint Stock Companies Act and the more sweeping act of 1862 also helped facilitate company flotations by enabling as few as seven persons to incorporate a company merely by registering a memorandum of association; each shareholder, moreover, only had to subscribe to one share, with no minimum value and on which no money need have been paid.[6] As a consequence of this legislation, by 1862 England had the most permissive company law in the world. By the second half of the 1850s and early 1860s, England's joint-stock companies and corporations provided an extremely important source of monies for commercial expansion and capital improvements.

The speculative boom of which these company flotations were a part was fueled by a number of factors in addition to limited liability. Among these were the abandonment of trade restrictions between 1842 and 1860, improved and expanded transport systems both at home and abroad, the increase in "invisible exports" facilitated by Britain's transportation superiority, and the influx of gold from California and Australia in the 1850s.[7] As confidence grew and knowledge about the financial possibilities available in various parts of the world became more sophisticated, both individuals and banks aggressively sought investment opportunities that could return quick profits and high yields. In London, it even became common practice for some businessmen to borrow money for their regular transactions in order to be able to invest their own resources in potentially lucrative joint-stock companies or foreign loans. A general reluctance developed to keep even small amounts of capital idle. In the words of one modern economic historian, "everybody wanted [capital] to circulate and fructify the ground."[8]

Critical to the conditions that made such investment possible was the rapid expansion of banking and credit facilities.[9] Following the Joint Stock Bank Act (1844), the Bank Charter Act (1844), and the extension of limited liability to banks (1858), numerous joint-stock banks joined the central and still dominant Bank of England. Equally important was the establishment of a bill-broking business, much of which was consolidated in the London Discount Market, a series of houses and agents that allowed individuals and banks to raise capital quickly by discounting promissory notes at the cost of a proportionate service charge.[10] While this system of discounting bills was obviously essential to the liquidity and productivity of capital, it also contributed to the other side of the speculative boom—the increased opportunities for financial overextension and fraud. One factor that enhanced the likelihood of financial irresponsibility was that discount houses could rely on the Bank of England to back their loans. This guarantee encouraged discount houses to lend amounts far beyond the value of their own outstanding loans. The tendency of this unregulated system of discounting to generate a self-perpetuating cycle of borrowing and debt was further exacerbated in cases of overseas trade, for the sheer distances involved generated temporal gaps that could be turned to profit by wily investors. As early as 1847, the India trade was being described as a prototype of the abuses generated in colonial investment.

> The India trade has been one huge system of credit. If goods were bought in Manchester, by a house in London, they were paid for by bills at six months' date; and, as soon as shipped, an advance was obtained again by a bill at six months for a large part of the first cost, by the consignee, who,

again, in his turn, not infrequently drew upon the house in India, against the bills of lading when transmitted. The shipper and the consignee were thus both put in possession of funds, months before they actually paid for the goods; and, very commonly, these bills were renewed at maturity on pretence of affording time for the returns in a "long trade." Moreover, losses by such a trade, instead of leading to its contraction, led directly to its increase. The poorer men became, the greater need they had to purchase, in order to make up, by new advances, the capital they had lost on the past adventures. Purchases thus became, not a question of supply and demand, but the most important part of the finance operations of a firm labouring under difficulties.

But this is only one side of the picture. What took place in reference to the export of goods at home, was taking place in the purchase and shipment of produce abroad. Houses in India, who had credit to pass their bills, were purchasers of sugar, indigo, silk, or cotton,—not because the prices advised from London by the last overland mail promised a profit on the prices current in India, but because former drafts upon the London house would soon fall due, and must be provided for. What way so simple as to purchase a cargo of sugar, pay for it in bills upon the London house at ten months' date, transmit the shipping documents by the overland mail; and, in less than two months, the goods on the high seas, or perhaps not yet passed the mouth of the Hoogly, were pawned in Lombard Street,—putting the London house in funds *eight* months before the drafts against those goods fell due.[11]

During the 1850 and 1860s, the relationship between the discount market and the banking system grew increasingly complex and strained, and the reckless borrowing that followed from the Bank's guarantee culminated in a general financial crisis in 1857.[12] In 1858, in response to this crisis, the Bank withdrew its guarantee of support and imposed restrictions on the discount houses' ability to rediscount their bills with the Bank. The Bank's rule did not really check the instabilities of the bill-broking system, however, for simply the knowledge that the Bank was restricting its discounting services could generate a discount demand by scared investors that was all out of proportion to actual financial needs. This became clear in the spring of 1859, as fears that England would be drawn into the Franco-Austrian war led to a stock-market crisis that spread throughout the economy, largely because of the Bank's rule.[13]

In April 1860, the tension between the Bank and the discount houses reached new heights when the most important discount house, Overend, Gurney, & Co., tested the Bank's rule by withdrawing £1,650,000 from the Bank on the day before it had to issue dividends.

Despite this forcible attempt to make the Bank accept fiscal responsibility for the system of credit or for discriminating between bad bills and good, the Bank refused the role of moral guide and held fast to its noninterventionist position. As a result, the credit market remained extremely volatile, and the fate of finance capital became increasingly sensitive to the vagaries of investor confidence and the influence of external factors, such as the stability of the foreign governments to whom many companies made loans.[14]

At the same time that the Bank was refusing to regulate or underwrite the credit market, some discount houses were expanding into the much more dubious field of general finance. While many of the finance companies that sprang up in imitation of the International Finance Society, Ltd. (May 1863) were both honest and solvent, others were willing to invest in high-yield, questionable securities. Others were increasingly willing to extend credit to all kinds of projects without much preliminary investigation, to ignore the principle of lending "long" only when one borrowed "long," or even to accommodate bills that were either purely fraudulent or drawn against anticipated rather than secure resources.

Taken together, then, the same conditions that linked capital investment and speculation to potentially enormous profits also made fraudulent enterprises not only possible but virtually irresistible. The mania for profit—combined with legal provisions that encouraged (but did not oversee) company formations and credit facilities that generated finance capital vastly in excess of gold reserves or even good debts—produced a concentration of financial abuses, which, for sheer recklessness and audacity, surpassed even the credit frauds of the 1840s.[15] Although the most egregious deceits only became public after the crash of 1866, signs that the elaborate system of speculation was built on a precarious foundation began to appear in 1863 and 1864. By 1864 Bank rates had reached the unprecedented figure of 7 percent, and even though a market collapse was narrowly averted, numerous businesses failed.[16]

Between the winter of 1863 and November 1865, while Dickens was composing *Our Mutual Friend*, the vicissitudes of the English economy inspired numerous books, pamphlets, and articles in all kinds of periodicals and quarterlies. Among these were several long treatments of the speculation mania that appeared in Dickens's *All the Year Round* between March 1863 and August 1865—the three series by Malcolm Ronald Laing Meason on company flotations, the bill-broking system, and international speculation; and Charles Reade's *Hard Cash*.[17] Meason's works in particular deal with the moral ambiguities that were entwined with England's exhilarating new financial arrangements.

Meason's series on company flotations, for example, sees the narrator first solicited for a contribution to a nonexistent company by one "A. L.," and then, having learned from his mistakes, initiating his own speculative flotation.[18] From conjuring out of thin air a limited, joint-stock bank—the Bank of Patagonia—the narrator progresses to selling shares in his invention, then to circulating rumors about the bank's insolvency, then to overseeing—and selling the rights for litigating—its demise. At the end of the series, the narrator is content with the outcome of his "little speculation." "To get five thousand pounds for bringing a company into the world, and a year later netting a cool fifteen hundred for helping kill off the same concern, is what does not fall to the lot of every man," he coolly concludes.[19]

Meason's articles illustrate two aspects of the problematic inherent in the speculation mania. The first is the importance of international investments to the dynamic of speculation. While domestic investments continued to play an important role in the wealth of the nation and individuals, many company promoters tried to stress the superiority of overseas investments for those interested in high yields.[20] One form this argument took was developmental: England was adequate, the logic ran, for infant companies, because it provided a relatively protective environment where young companies could "cut their teeth," but as a company matured, it needed room to grow.[21] Another form the argument took stressed the difference, or lack thereof, between the English investor and the English working-class market. The English working classes, after all, were different enough from the English middle classes to want what the latter had, but not different enough to lack some of the services that yielded the greatest returns. Most obviously, the English working classes enjoyed the same banking facilities that all Englishmen used; in fact, favorable interest rates had been made available to the English working classes during the 1830s and 1840s in order to encourage saving and thrift.[22]

When company promoters celebrated overseas investment, they stressed two qualities of their enterprises, which positioned them in relation to the home market. On the one hand, they emphasized that the site of investment was sufficiently like the England with which investors were familiar to inspire confidence in the foreign country's political and economic stability.[23] On the other hand, they emphasized that the target country was sufficiently unlike England to want and need to emulate Britain's "success." At heart, these assumptions both projected and depended on an assumption about England's "natural" superiority. English investors, in other words, would most readily risk their money upon the assumptions that the peoples of their targeted markets both differed from and wanted to be like the "naturally" superior English man. The most salient mark of difference, in this regard, was nationality, and more specifically the "underdevelopment" that characterized colonial and other overseas countries. Hence, the current economic wisdom that a free market economy with high capital accumulation had to expand into foreign markets was built on assumptions about Englishmen at home as well as foreigners abroad.

The narrator of Meason's articles invokes these assumptions when he elaborates the fantasy that could be built on expectations about a foreign market. Here, the mirror that returns English investors' self-satisfied image is Patagonia—a real country, but sufficiently far away and unfamiliar to provide no obstacle to this nationalist and capitalist fantasy. To the narrator, in fact, the name of the country where he will locate his fictitious bank is more important than anything else, for his aim is to conjure visions of untapped natural resources *and* the assumption that this country will be both like and unlike England.[24] Such visionary possibilities are ultimately more important than any realistic description of the actual country. What Patagonia is like, in other words, is not as important as the fact that Patagonia wants to (and can) become (more) like England. Thus the narrator launches his lucrative enterprise with a blatantly fictitious prospectus.

> To draw out a prospectus for our bank, it was necessary both to study the commercial statistics of Patagonia, and to quote largely from papers and other documents relating to its produce and trade, or else to trust to chance, and write, as it were, a pleasantly coloured picture respecting our prospects of banking in that country. The former I was afraid would take up too much time, and therefore I chose the latter. . . . I commenced the document by stating that "This company has been formed for the purpose of extending the advantages of banking to the country of Patagonia, which was well known to be overwhelmingly rich in all kinds of natural produce." I then took a philanthropic view of the subject, and endeavoured to prove, that, in order to make men happy and prosperous, a banking establishment was of all things the most necessary in every country. After this I looked at the question from a missionary point of view, and showed that without banks there could be no Christian teaching. Lastly, I quoted extracts from letters—imaginary of course—written by Europeans resident in Patagonia, proving that with proper management a clear profit of not less than twenty per cent must be made out of any amount of capital employed in banking operations between London and that country. I then . . . ended by assuring the readers of the prospectus that we had promises of support from all the most influential native chiefs

in the land, and that, in a word, our success and triumph in the matter was certain.[25]

Obviously, Meason's fictitious prospectus capitalizes on the various rationales by which Englishmen had authorized their presence in less economically developed countries throughout the nineteenth century. In addition, it brings the earliest rationales for colonization—philanthropy and missionary conversion—into alignment with the latest, most explicitly economic rationale: in his description, banking—and, by extension, the flow of English currency—becomes the vehicle by which (English) profits confer happiness, prosperity, and Christianity upon the "natives," thereby simultaneously acknowledging their difference from Englishmen and beginning to close the enormous gulf between the two peoples.

The second point that Meason's articles make about such speculations is that they call upon and presumably appeal to a complex nexus of assumptions about familial relationships. If the projected bank is represented as bearing a benevolently paternal relation to this immature economy, then bringing the scheme to a profitable end deploys familial images of another kind: the imaginative work behind the bank is represented as the labor of begetting and then destroying a child. Calling his speculation a "child that we expected would have grown into so very large a man," the narrator repeatedly refers to the problem of "kill[ing], as it were, my own offspring."[26] Far from being a problem, however, killing the child has become another opportunity for the exercise of the founding father's ingenious wit. According to this metaphor, infanticide has been rendered painless—and, more to the point, lucrative—by the limited liability acts, which not only limited the investors' fiscal liability, but also absolved investors' families, as well as the corporation's (noninvesting) directors, from all fiscal responsibility. Because the new companies were internally free of the constraints of the investors' literal families, investors were free to alter—if not dispense with—the metaphorical familial bonds that the conditions as well as the language of the partnership involved.[27] Company founders could therefore dispense with ideas of parental responsibility and control, even though they retained a metaphorics of family to describe their actions.[28] Investors could figuratively beget, give birth to, and destroy companies without regret, as Meason's investors do here.

By the same token, of course, as the image of infanticide suggests, this situation was also hedged round with dangers. Freedom from parental responsibility and control for some meant the susceptibility of others to a situation without protection against loss or fraud, with no guarantee of loyalty, honesty, or even shared interest. More specifically, and more ominously, it meant an economic situation in which women were erased—not only literally, as dependents whose support rested on cautious investment, but also figuratively, as the mothers whose maternal instinct would compensate for and offset the sterner ambitions of the father. In fact, far from guaranteeing fiscal responsibility, as dependent women might have done, women under the new laws could facilitate fiscal irresponsibility, for husbands could use them to shelter monies otherwise at risk in corporate investments. In Meason's essay, significantly, there are no images of childbirth and thus no feminine influence to protect the infant company from the ruthless calculations of masculine self-interest. As men usurp the mother's place, the myth of bonded brothers, reproducing and supporting themselves for the sake of women, gives way to a more exhilarating and terrifying image of a world without women or a feminine function, where men not only bond together to beget little enterprises but also turn against each other to kill their offspring. This world without a feminine principle is the world made possible by the economic arrangements I have been discussing.

The issues of national (or "racial") otherness and gender anxiety that Meason discloses within the problematic of speculation also appear in *Our Mutual Friend*.[29] Dickens's explicit treatment of speculation seems to assuage some of the anxieties that Meason comically arouses, but the novel also draws out the connection, which Meason does not make, between the issues of racial difference raised by Patagonia, and the threat to men implicit in the image of infanticide. In order to tease out the strands of this connection, it is necessary to see how *Our Mutual Friend* works through the problematics of the speculation theme.

The fraud that accompanied the speculative boom of the late 1850s and early 1860s is explicitly addressed in *Our Mutual Friend* in Dickens's treatment of Alfred Lammle.[30] Lammle, who has generated the appearance of a substantial income and the reality of influential connections by speculating in shares, provokes the narrator's most vitriolic criticism of the groundlessness and power of speculative wealth. "As is well known to the wise in their generation," the narrator bemoans,

> traffic in Shares is the one thing to have to do with in this world. Have no antecedents, no established character, no cultivation, no ideas, no manners; have Shares. Have Shares enough to be on Boards of Direction in capital letters, oscillate on mysterious business between London and Paris, and be great. Where does he come from? Shares. Where is he going to? Shares. Has he any principles? Shares. What squeezes him into Parliament? Shares. Perhaps he never of himself achieved success in anything,

never originated anything, never produced anything? Sufficient answer to all; Shares. O mighty Shares! To set those blaring images so high, and to cause us smaller vermin, as under the influence of henbane or opium, to cry out, night and day, 'Relieve us of our money, scatter it for us, buy us and sell us, ruin us, only we beseech ye take rank among the powers of the earth, and fatten on us'![31]

The specific nature of the threat Dickens targets with this diatribe becomes clearer in another authorial aside concerning another stock exchange. While the Exchange referred to here is metaphorical, the stakes are even higher than in the literal Stock Exchange, because the commodity on offer consists not of shares or political power, but a child. This "orphan market" springs into being from the Boffins' desire to locate a child to replace John Harmon, who is missing and presumed dead.

> The instant it became known that anybody wanted the orphan, up started some affectionate relative of the orphan who put a price upon the orphan's head. The suddenness of an orphan's rise in the market was not to be paralleled by the maddest records of the Stock Exchange. He would be at five thousand per cent discount out at nurse making a mud pie at nine in the morning, and (being inquired for) would go up to five thousand percent premium before noon. The market was "rigged" in various artful ways. Counterfeit stock got into circulation. Parents boldly represented themselves as dead, and brought their orphans with them. . . . Likewise, fluctuations of a wild and South-Sea nature were occasioned, by orphan-holders keeping back, and then rushing into the market a dozen together. But, the uniform principle at the root of all these various operations was bargain and sale; and that principle could not be recognized by Mr and Mrs Milvey. (p. 244)

The target of Dickens's dark humor is obviously the infiltration of economic motives into the domestic sphere. In *Our Mutual Friend*, Dickens sets out to counteract the modern version of this tendency in the plot that inaugurates and vies to dominate the novel's action—the John Harmon deceit. This plot is specifically formulated as a speculation intended to convert Bella's lust for literal wealth into an appreciation of more emotionally substantive gratification, the "true golden gold" of domestic affection (p. 843). Thus the John Harmon plot works to rewrite "value," to exchange the false currency of literal money for the "true," metaphorical coin of love. As an "acquisition to the Boffins" (p. 361), Bella initially both wants money and stands for the commodification of human beings. At the beginning of his deceit, for example, Mr. Boffin tells Bella, "Value yourself. . . . These good looks of yours are worth money" (p. 526). Bella's moral education essentially takes the form of her learning to prefer honesty and affection to the rewards money can buy. As Bella learns this, the weight of the figuration associated with her shifts. Whereas Bella was previously converted into a figure of commodification, now money becomes the figure for value. In the process, Bella becomes a metaphorical rather than a literal commodity: "She's the true golden gold at heart," Boffin exclaims of the reformed Bella (p. 843).

Two critical moments in this process of conversion are the encounter between Lizzie and Bella in which Lizzie's statement that a woman does not seek to "gain" anything but belief through her love shames Bella into seeing her own aspirations as "mercenary" (p. 590), and the confrontation between Boffin and John Harmon, in which the Dustman's accusation that Harmon has turned Bella into a "speculation" makes her see her own selfishness (pp. 654–61). In the picnic in the counting house where Bella, her father, and John Harmon celebrate the triumph of love over riches, Rumpty Wilfer explicitly points out the apparent paradox involved in this rhetorical conversion: Bella, he says, "brings you a good fortune when she brings you the poverty she has accepted for your sake and the honest truth's" (p. 673). When Harmon, still disguised as Rokesmith, takes a job in the city, Dickens toasts another version of this conversion. Once more Bella is figured as a "commodity," but now the metaphorical status of the term is clear and powerful enough to displace the literal commodities in which the stock market trades: "He cared, beyond all expression, for his wife, as a most precious and sweet commodity, that was always looking up, and that never was worth less than all the gold in the world" (p. 750).

According to the logic of Dickens's plot, taking money literally, as a good and an end in itself, leads to the literal commodification of human beings. By contrast, recognizing the metaphorical nature of money facilitates exchanges that enhance domestic relations and bring out the humanity in people. Significantly, Dickens locates the action that effects this conversion in the domestic sphere, for there men are able to exercise precisely the kind of control that is not available in the unpredictable world of financial speculation. The John Harmon plot proves that in the domestic sphere, the return on a man's investment of intelligence and love satisfies all of his desires. Through his calculated deceit, Harmon turns Bella into the wife he wants, so that when he realizes her wishes at the end of the novel, he actually realizes his own.[32] In the long campaign of deceit that ultimately reforms Bella, John Harmon also transforms the iron yoke of his father's will into its opposite: far from limiting the son's opportunities to make decisions for himself, as it was intended to do, old Harmon's will becomes the occasion for the son to discover what he wants and calculate how to get it.

Converting the abstraction of commodification into a metaphorics of worth and the tyranny of a parent's will into permission to have what one wants takes place not only in the domestic sphere but, more specifically, on the cultural terrain of gender, for these transformations entail—and depend on—two assumptions about women. The first is that the "true" woman desires only what the man who (legally) represents her desires, that the law of coverture does not so much bind the wife's desires to those of the husband as recognize a community of interests that really does exist. The second assumption is that women can themselves stand in for the inhumane systems that control men. Literal women, in other words, can function like metaphors, which represent and displace something they are not. Thus, substituting a woman for stocks, as in John Harmon's depiction of his work, seems to allay the man's anxiety through literal displacement—because the domestic sphere apparently offers him an antidote to the demands and deceits of the marketplace. Actually, of course, this comfort depends on another kind of displacement—it depends on men effacing any desires that real women have that do not coincide with men's. Because of the two assumptions I have just described, this double displacement works—at least symbolically: because men assume that a good woman wants only to make a man happy and because women can stand in for other forces beyond men's control, the illusion can arise that what seems to be beyond man's control actually answers his deepest needs.

Through such logic, John Harmon's domestication of Bella can serve as a corrective substitution for the entire system of exploitation and fraud associated with speculation and debt. Yet in this novel, the domestic solution only works in what amounts to a narrative vacuum; by the end of *Our Mutual Friend,* the John Harmon story is almost completely cordoned off from the other plots, and the mutually gratifying partnership that Bella and John share cannot correct even the domestic imbalance that lies closest to Bella—the travesty of her parents' marriage—much less the economic system that has enabled the bill broker Fledgeby to profit while good men like Twemlow stay poor. If we turn for a moment to the subplot of *Our Mutual Friend* in which money and domestic virtue seem *least* entwined, we can begin to see why what happens in John Harmon's home cannot lay to rest all of the anxieties associated with speculation and deceit.

In *Our Mutual Friend,* the clearest example of domestic virtue free of mercenary interests is provided by Lizzie Hexam, the waterman's daughter. Lizzie's immunity to self-interest is figured both in her domestic loyalty and in her generosity. Her love for her father, Gaffer, has made her sacrifice her own education, and she has devoted her scant savings to her brother's training. Her virtuous passion for Eugene Wrayburn, moreover, is proof against short-sighted ambition, and Dickens presents it as so compelling that it eventually inspires emulative self-sacrifice, first in Bella, then in Eugene. At a deeper level, however, Lizzie's virtue can be seen to engender almost as many harmful effects as does the orphan market or the Lammles' plot to trade upon Georgiana Podsnap's loneliness. Not only is Lizzie implicitly responsible for the blame cast upon her father by Miss Abby Potterson; Lizzie also explicitly causes Eugene to feel like a criminal as he tracks Gaffer, to become a Peeping Tom as he spies on Lizzie, and to consort with Mr. Dolls as he seeks to discover where she is hiding. Unintentionally, of course, Lizzie is also the first cause of the assault upon Eugene and of the duplicitous conspiracy that results in the drownings of Bradley Headstone and Rogue Riderhood. In the scene of his agonized proposal, Bradley Headstone insists that Lizzie incarnates this dangerous doubleness: she can effect either evil or good because she has the power to precipitate in the desiring man either baseness or virtue. "You draw me to you," Headstone raves. . . .

> If I were shut up in a strong prison, you would draw me out. . . . If I were lying on a sick bed, you would draw me up—to stagger to your feet and fall there. . . . No man knows till the time comes, what depths are within him. . . . To me, you brought it; on me, you forced it; and the bottom of this raging sea . . . has been heaved up ever since. . . . I am under the influence of some tremendous attraction which I have resisted in vain, and which overmasters me. You could draw me to fire, you could draw me to water, you could draw me to the gallows, you could draw me to any death, you could draw me to any exposure and disgrace. . . . But if you would return a favourable answer to my offer of myself in marriage, you could draw me to any good—every good—with equal force. (pp. 454–55)

The power Headstone attributes to Lizzie assigns her the responsibility not only for gratifying his desire, but, more important, for domesticating his passion, for making him desire the right thing. Yet the doubleness he identifies in her ("you could draw me to the gallows . . . you could draw me to . . . good") renders this power dangerous to Headstone and all the other men who come under her influence. The precise nature of the danger Lizzie poses seems to reside in the fact that she is not only powerful but independent. Certainly, Dickens suggests that Lizzie's independence is dangerous when he repeatedly links it to sexual susceptibility, if not sexual agency. Not only does Lizzie betray a dangerously willful desire for Eugene (in explicit defiance of her brother's prohibition), but she also occupies both thematic and structural positions that imply a dangerous female autonomy: two of her occupations, that of seamstress and factory girl, epitomized female promiscuity for midcentury Victorians.[33] Her status as an unmarried lodger, first with Jenny Wren, then with Riah's friends, was also considered a state of "precocious independence" for a woman.[34] Her secret riverside meeting with Eugene, moreover, follows directly upon Bella's euphemistic announcement that she is pregnant, and thus acquires from the legitimate relationship the connotations of sexual activity to which the pregnancy explicitly alludes.[35]

The "precocious independence" associated with female sexuality reappears in Lizzie's economic agency. From the opening chapters of the novel, Lizzie has money—not much money, of course, but enough to underwrite her brother's education and his employment as a pupil teacher (pp. 115, 117). After her father's death, Lizzie becomes a seamstress who "keeps the stockroom of a seaman's outfitter" (p. 271); and after Wrayburn's and Headstone's unwanted advances drive her out of London, she becomes a factory girl in a paper mill. Even more ominously, Lizzie's agency is also figured in her physical strength. Lizzie literally saves Eugene not by her moral influence, but because the skills and strength she developed as a "female waterman" enable her to pull his broken body into the boat.

The combination of Lizzie's ambiguous "purity" with such stereotypically masculine traits as economic autonomy and muscular strength suggests that Lizzie's dangerous power may not so much originate in her independence from men as it expresses her assimilation to men. That is, despite the fact that Lizzie is said to have the ability to reform both Eugene and Bradley because she is different from them, she is actually, in some very basic ways, a better man than either of her suitors. Lizzie's "masculinity" is most obviously attributable to her class position: as a working-class woman, she lacks both the leisure and the resources to enhance her femininity. Yet Dickens specifically downplays Lizzie's class origins: she never speaks as a working-class woman; she (correctly) imagines that Eugene will see her as his equal; she never wants for resources or protectors; and at the end of the novel Twemlow decisively declares that she is a "lady" (p. 891). Moreover, the fact that her suitors' competition for *her* is transformed into an obsession with each *other* suggests that Lizzie's class position is, in some important senses, subordinate to her role in bringing these two men into a cross-class, homosocial relationship.[36]

Lizzie's ambiguous status—as a working-class "lady" and a "masculine" woman—begins to explain why the Harmon marriage can provide neither the moral center nor the organizing principle for *Our Mutual Friend,* as David Copperfield's marriage to Agnes was able to do in Dickens's earlier novel. The key to this insufficiency lies in the peculiar nature of Lizzie's ambiguity: she does not become a literal lady or a literal man but demonstrates instead that she can metaphorically cross class and gender barriers—that, in other words, class and gender identities are, in some sense at least, *only* metaphorical. Despite the fact, then, that Lizzie is Bella's opposite in being immune to the desire for money, she brings into the novel the same association between woman and representation that is thematically associated with Bella. In Lizzie, moreover, we see that the cultural association between woman and figuration posed threats as well as alleviating anxieties. In *Our Mutual Friend,* these threats acquire their peculiar urgency from the developments that distinguished the early 1860s.

In order to appreciate this urgency, we must place the developments of the 1850s and 1860s in the context of the historical relation between woman and figuration. As Catherine Gallagher has demonstrated, the figure of woman in the early eighteenth century was conceptually positioned in relation to the construction or redefinition of a number of critical concepts, including politics, virtue, the public, and fiction.[37] In a process I can only summarize here, woman and the feminine were conceptually linked to the anxieties generated by the new market economy and to the symbolic solutions formulated to resolve these anxieties. Thus, for example, femininity was associated with the fantasies and appetites unleashed in men by new commercial opportunities at the same time that social interactions with real women were expected to enhance the refined and polite behaviors that could theoretically control these excesses.

The financial revolution of the 1690s also generated a new model of politics as well as new anxieties about the nature of political discourse. This new politics was public in that it involved more people and was increasingly conducted in the newly expanded medium of the press. At the same time, however, the nature of this public political participation was shaped by the libel law, which virtually mandated anonymity, pseudonymity, and the use of allegorical or coded modes of description and analysis. The libel law, in other words, encouraged the use of fiction as a vehicle for political discourse. This use of fiction aroused the same kind of anxieties also generated by the newly expanded press, for both fiction and the press called attention to the possibility of creating a world of words that had no connection to the world outside language. As Gallagher explains, invoking the concept of "feminine" writing—and female practitioners of this writing like Mary Delarivier Manley—

constituted a basis for discriminating among kinds of writing and thus for alleviating anxiety about public writing per se. "Reputable" writing was considered legitimate, grounded, and constructive, while the "disreputable" writings of women like Manley were baseless scandals, which could discredit and even undermine the government.[38]

These anxieties about fiction and the press were exacerbated during this period by another set of worries, which also followed the financial revolution of the late seventeenth century. In making the English crown dependent on loans, this revolution bound the very formation of a national government to new forms of financial transaction, which in turn encouraged both speculative investment and new forms of paper property such as bills of exchange and stocks. Just as the combined effects of the libel law and the press threatened to convert politics into fiction, so these new forms of commerce threatened to turn property into sheer writing. Once more, the "feminine" genre of scandal—and scandalmongering women in particular—epitomized the danger inherent in this threat. Here is Gallagher: "The scandalmongering woman was . . . a creature displaying the dangers of the new marketplace in political literature with peculiar clarity. Her merchandise resembled an inflated paper currency, the crediting of which would lead to the discredit of those who held the public trust."[39]

By the early 1860s, the links welded in the eighteenth century between woman, fiction, politics, and new forms of commercial transaction like speculation had undergone significant alteration. In the first place, partly because of a general cultural shift after the French Revolution toward the moralism associated with the emergent bourgeoisie and partly because of the material role women played in helping men establish their credit-worthiness in the 1830s and 1840s,[40] "woman" increasingly came to be associated not with politics or with fiction as scandal but with morality and even "truth," both of which were held to be above or outside of politics. Coventry Patmore deified this cultural association in the mid-1850s in his celebration of the "angel in the house," but it is also important to recognize that Victorians believed this idealization to have a biological basis. The moralization of woman, in other words, was also a moralization of the female body—a displacement of the seventeenth-century obsession with female sexuality by an increasingly biologized focus on "maternal" instincts and the certainty of a woman's parental relation to her child. Here, for example, is J. W. Kaye, reviewing one of Caroline Norton's political pamphlets in 1855: "There is no confusion as regards the woman's knowledge of the true and false. Whether her offspring be legitimate or illegitimate, she knows it to be her own. But a man, in this the tenderest relation which humanity recognises, may be the prey of a miserable delusion all his life."[41] By the 1860s, then, woman was understood by middle-class Victorians literally to embody and thus metaphorically to guarantee truth and to stand as surety against both the economic vicissitudes of the market economy and the competitive drive of one man to deceive another even in the "tenderest" relation of all.

The second important change involved the relation between fiction and political discourse. On the one hand, the repeal of the libel law and various stamp acts had considerably loosened restrictions on public participation in politics, thus obviating the need for political discourse to disguise itself in fictions. On the other hand, of course, partly through the "feminizing" poetics of Romantic realists like Wordsworth, Scott, and Dickens, fiction had acquired a moral authority of its own, and authors could advance political positions through fictions, just as fictions were sometimes cited in Parliament to further political arguments. While the relationship between political discourse and fiction had not been severed, then, fiction, like woman, had undergone a process of moralization that helped cleanse it of connotations of excess and scandal.

Finally, the relationship between commerce and national stability had been radically transformed by the 1860s, partly through the financial vehicles I have already discussed. While diatribes against the national debt erupted periodically in the century after its institution, by the 1860s the English economy was ineluctably a system of credit and debt, and commercial transactions by individuals formed the backbone of the fiscal well-being of the now relatively bureaucratized and consolidated state. For my purposes, one of the most significant aspects of this transformation was the proliferation after 1757 of England's formal and informal colonies, which constituted sources of raw materials, markets for finished goods, and opportunities for investments of finance capital. An inevitable effect of England's growing dominance in a world market was a revaluation of the meaning of credit and debt. Whereas the Crown's status as debtor in the late seventeenth century had meant dependence on potentially seditious aristocrats at home, England's position as a creditor nation in a world economy in the 1860s meant that much of the debt was international and only enhanced England's independence as a nation and its domination in the world. Thus the "fiction" inherent in credit, paper money, and speculation did not automatically arouse the same kind of anxieties that it had in the early eighteenth century.

Given the revaluation of "woman" and "fiction," the naturalization of womanly virtue, and the removal of many of the threatening connotations previously associated with credit, why might Dickens reanimate the old anxieties once generated by the link between women and figuration? For this is exactly what Dickens's portrayal of Lizzie Hexam does: it ties what most Victorians thought to be the natural capacity of women to incarnate morality and value to a series of threats posed to the male characters. These threats, moreover, are specifically associated with the traditional connection between the fictional or metaphorical dimension of woman and the capacity of speculation to conjure something out of nothing. I want to suggest that this set of ominous meanings was available again in the early 1860s because of the historical conjunction between the economic factors I have already discussed and the emergence of the first specific challenge to the naturalization of female virtue. This challenge was articulated in the 1850s in a self-consciously politicized feminist movement, which was itself a response to the increasing number of women entering the workforce.[42] One of the first campaigns of this movement was to rectify the law that prohibited married women from being economic agents, capable of owning their own property or keeping the wages they earned. Even though the 1857 Married Women's Property bill did not become law, the controversy it aroused interjected the issues of women's rights, property, and work into parliamentary discussion, quarterly review articles, and popular novels as well.

Dickens's representation of Lizzie Hexam and Bella Wilfer must be read in the context of these developments. For the most part, Dickens's treatment of women is a conservative, even nostalgic, recuperation of the domesticated female in defiance of some contemporary feminists' claims that sexuality was not the determinate characteristic of women and therefore that woman's biology was not the natural ground of her character or of womanly truth. Like many of his conservative contemporaries, for example, Dickens consistently discredits Lizzie's waged work: either he idealizes and marginalizes this work, as in his depiction of her work in the paper mill,[43] or else he subordinates it to her domestic relationships, as he does with whatever labor generated the money that finances Charley's education. In keeping with this, Dickens represents Lizzie's education as a means of increasing her value as a wife or as the vehicle through which her suitors vie to establish their influence over her—not, as with Charley, as a means of making more money. Similarly, Dickens gives Lizzie's moral influence more narrative attention than any of her waged occupations, and he credits this—not her money—with making Charley aspire beyond a waterman's life. Finally, Lizzie's moral influence over Eugene is depicted as being more restorative than her brute strength (even though it wasn't working *before* she pulled him from the water), since, presumably, had Eugene not seen the error of his ways, he would have been morally better off dead than alive.

Despite these nostalgic recuperations, however, Dickens also (perhaps inadvertently) reveals the threat implicit in the challenge posed to the naturalization of womanly virtue by women working and demanding rights. That the form this threat takes reanimates the eighteenth-century link between woman and figuration poses a particular threat to Dickens's narrative project, for he finds himself trying to use a fiction about women to quiet old fears about the link between fiction and women. This threat is alluded to in Mortimer's defense of Lizzie Hexam. When, at the end of the novel, Mortimer is asked whether Lizzie has ever been "a female waterman," he answers firmly that she has not (p. 889). Mortimer's answer is correct in the strictest sense, since "waterman" was a term specifically applied to ferrymen and not to all-purpose boatmen like Gaffer, but while Mortimer's answer spares Lizzie the association with manual labor that his interlocutor is trying to insinuate, it misses the import of Lizzie's having assumed a metaphorical version of this role: Eugene is alive only because Lizzie *has* been a kind of "female waterman." Acknowledging the metaphorical nature of the term *waterman*, however, mobilizes the ominous nature of Lizzie's link to figuration. If Eugene's life depends on Lizzie's capacity to be like a man, yet his moral salvation depends on her being (like) a woman, then what is she by nature? Phrased differently, if Lizzie can be like a man when Eugene needs to be pulled from the water and like a woman when he is ready for a wife, then is it possible that her character is *not* an expression of some underlying female nature but merely the effect of a man's needs?

The implications of this question were far-reaching in the 1860s—and not just for the moralizing project of fiction. If the virtue men assigned to female nature proved to be only a figment of men's desire, then it might be possible that the sexed body did not guarantee moral difference. And if moral difference (or virtue) was not guaranteed by the female body, then it was possible that there was no basis for virtue at all—apart, that is, from men's desire that virtue exist. This structure of wishful projection is exactly the same principle that informs speculation and makes it so volatile and so threatening, for if nothing but (men's) desire underwrites value, then there will be nothing outside of (men's) desire to counteract the desirer's darker impulses. In *Our Mutual Friend*, Dickens explores the vertiginous possibilities this raises by creating, as Meason had also done, a brief fantasy of a world without women.

At the dark heart of this womanless world is the scene in which John Harmon, disguised as the sailor George Radfoot, is attacked just after his return to England. Everything about this episode signals ontological chaos. The assault itself is focused not just on Harmon, but on the other man who resembles him, and it quickly spreads to every man in the room. The attack is narrated as a distorted, almost hallucinatory memory, and its disclosure marks the moment of maximum narrative dislocation in the novel—the eight-page segment in which John Harmon wonders aloud whether to remain dead or to reclaim his life and name.[44] Here is part of Harmon's description: "I saw a figure like myself lying dressed in my clothes on a bed. What might have been, for anything I knew, a silence of days, weeks, months, years, was broken by a violent wrestling of men all over the room. The figure like myself was assailed, and my valise was in its hands. . . . I could not have said that my name was John Harmon. . . . I cannot possibly express it to myself without using the word I. But it was not I. There was no such thing as I, within my knowledge" (p. 426).

In one sense, as Rogue Riderhood explains it, the confusion of identity that Harmon experiences here is nothing unusual for a sailor. "There's fifty such [sailors] ten times as long as [Radfoot]," Riderhood laughs, "through entering in different names, re-shipping when the out'ard voyage is made, and what not" (p. 416). In another sense, it is only an extreme manifestation of the proclivity for disguise that men exhibit repeatedly in the novel, whether it be John Harmon miming secretary, Boffin playing miser, Bradley Headstone pretending to be Riderhood, or Twemlow counterfeiting Sophronia's father. The ontological instability these episodes figure is no laughing matter, however, as the assault and all its ramifications reveal. Such instability is both cause and effect of the violence that Harmon, Wrayburn, and Riderhood all suffer, because it is the characteristic feature of a world deprived of any reliable criterion of difference, without an external "other" to anchor appearances or adjudicate right and wrong. This instability follows from the same mental gesture by which Bella can be made to replace stocks. It follows, that is, from turning what had been the guarantor of difference into sheer metaphor, which reflects only male desire, not some nature beyond fantasy and language. As this scene and all the other masquerades in the novel suggest, the effect of this gesture is to locate difference inside of man, hence to imperil both the guarantee of virtue and the integrity of male identity itself.[45]

The threat posed to the natural guarantor of difference by the developments of the late 1850s momentarily exposed the possibility that difference resides not between men and women but within every individual man. Like, but also because of, its conjuncture with the passage of the limited liability laws, this exposure generated profoundly ambiguous effects. On the one hand, both limited liability and the obliteration of natural difference catapulted men into a giddy world beyond moral restraint, where nothing checked their ability to speculate and conceive (deceits, plots, disguises, money-making schemes). On the other hand, the two developments exposed each man to the rapacity of his brother's desire, mirror-image of his own, and in pitting one man against another for what they both desired, such developments created value out of nothing and violence from the general struggle for scarce resources. In *Our Mutual Friend*, the first of these two effects is figured in the general hysteria that characterizes the scene of John Harmon's assault and in the speculations that energize Alfred Lammle and Fascination Fledgeby. Even these explosions of energy have sinister effects, of course—effects that are elaborated in the scenes where sameness generates masquerade and finally a fight to the death. When one man can be "taken" for another, as Radfoot is taken for John Harmon, then a man can be taken down with another like himself, as Headstone takes Riderhood into their mutual, watery grave.

Even in *Our Mutual Friend*, Dickens's representation of the possibility that difference might not be natural and of the link between woman, figuration, and a world without grounded meanings is intermittent. In part, of course, this theme is intermittent because its challenge was so potentially ruinous to the social and psychological well-being of men like Charles Dickens. In part, however, the threat posed by the possibility that difference might not be anchored in sexual nature could be symbolically managed even as it was exposed, because another principle of differentiation had become available by the 1860s to compensate for—and complicate—the difference of sex. This difference was the difference of race, and its increasingly foundational status was shored up by both contemporary events and the institutionalization of anthropological discourses that represented the differences among peoples as immutable and decisive.[46] Dickens's textually marginal but ideologically central invocation of racial difference holds the key to his ability to recuperate the moralized image of woman.

Dickens invokes racial difference three times in *Our Mutual Friend*.[47] The first reference to a "coffee-coloured" man appears in Bella's fantasy about her own glamorous future. In one of the visions she conjures, Bella is married to "an Indian Prince, who was a Something-or-Other, who wore Cashmere shawls all over himself, and diamonds and emeralds blazing in his turban" (p. 374). The second black man is real but even more uncanny than Bella's fantasy. Struggling to be "exact" about his assault, John Harmon isolates one detail: "There was a black man

. . . wearing a linen jacket, like a steward, who put the smoking coffee on the table in a tray and never looked at me" (p. 425). The status of the third black man is even more indeterminate than the fantasy or the memory. This black man is supposedly a real king, but he exists only in a book "of African travel." When Mr. Wilfer alludes to this figure in describing his daughter's generosity to John Harmon, he obliterates whatever real king the traveler might have met by his demeaning cultural generalizations: black kings, Mr. Wilfer says, are "cheap" and "nasty"; they bear "whatever name the sailors might have happened to give [them]"; and they tend to wear only "one good article at a time" (p. 437). "The king is generally dressed in a London hat only, or a Manchester pair of braces, or one epaulet, or an uniform coat with his legs in the sleeves, or something of that kind" (p. 438).

Why do black men appear in these three passages—at the heart of Bella's materialistic fantasies, at the site of maximum stress on male identity, and in the comic figuration of Mr. Wilfer's sartorial embarrassment? The answer to this question is partially revealed by the content of the first reference. Bella's fantasy that she will marry an Indian prince is the last in a series of fantasies about her future in which she first imaginatively brings John Harmon back to life and marries him, and then "consign[s Harmon] to his grave again" and marries "a merchant of immense wealth" who gradually metamorphoses into the Indian prince. Bella's fantastic marital odyssey concludes with the comment that her "coffee-coloured" prince is "excessively devoted; though a little too jealous" (p. 374).

What this passage suggests is the power of language to conjure characters from sheer desire. Because of the coincidence between one of the figments of Bella's fantasy and Harmon, a character in this novel, this power refers to and comments upon Dickens's power to do the same thing, but it also links this power both to murder and to male jealousy. Bella's imaginative "murder" of Harmon repeats the "murder" with which the novel opens (the "murder" that frees Bella to dream and that Harmon tries to control with his deceit), and her reference to the prince's jealousy casts the shadow of male competition over the parade of husbands she entertains. Thus the coffee-colored prince is linked to figuration, desire, and the knot of deceptions and acts of homosocial violence that the assault on John Harmon most problematically describes. In this sense, the coffee-colored prince has something in common with women.

The second clue to the significance of the black men is provided by the relationship that the last two passages bear to each other; that is, the reference to black kings, which occurs in the chapter immediately following the narration of John Harmon's assault, is offered as an antidote to the black servant. Even if a black man dispensed the deranging drug, this placement suggests, such blacks are our puppets: we (white men) give them their names, their orders, and their desires. Just as Mr. Wilfer's story about Bella's generosity ostensibly offsets the heartlessness she has just displayed to John Harmon, then, and just as Mortimer Lightwood's assertion that Lizzie has never been a "female waterman" supposedly neutralizes the fact that she *has* been, the story of the black kings reveals that the black servant is really a projection of a white man's needs. In all three cases, however, the retraction does not actually cancel the initial assertion but merely completes a determinate contradiction central to *Our Mutual Friend* and to the structure of wishful projection that it addresses. This contradiction takes two forms: the fact that Bella and Lizzie are, in critical ways and at critical moments, *like* men is as important to the ideological work of *Our Mutual Friend* as is the fact that, for most of the novel, they are *not* like men; the fact that the deranging drug is passed to John Harmon by someone *like* him (a man "like a steward," who is dressed as a white man dresses) is as important as the fact that Harmon is drugged by someone *unlike* him (a black man).

This contradiction—the other is like me, the other is different—is essential to the economic and representational systems that *Our Mutual Friend* simultaneously participates in and resists. It is impossible to separate these two systems or to determine which had priority in the 1860s, for the social and economic developments of the mid-Victorian period brought the fantasies inherent in this system of representation home to Englishmen as never before, while the representational system of self and other gave a particular semantic cast to the activities in which the English were involved. The logic of this system is as follows. The power of English men (hence the "proof" of their "natural" superiority) rested upon their ability to make the world over in their own image. In the 1840s and early 1850s, this quest primarily took the form of religious conversion, as missionaries set about transforming "heathens" in India, South and Central America, and Africa into Christians with the carrot of philanthropy and the stick of brute force. Economic investment in these areas accelerated throughout this period, often, as Meason's depiction of his Bank of Patagonia suggests, by piggybacking on the missionary and philanthropic rhetorics that already defined relations with these countries.[48]

Events in the late 1850s and early 1860s, however, most notably the Indian Mutiny of 1857 and the Jamaica uprising of 1865, gave England's relationship to at least some of these countries a new cast. Reports in 1857 about the slaughter of women and children at the Well of Cawnpore stressed the inhumanity of the dark-skinned Indians and prompted Englishmen to speculate about the "savagery" of the "brutes." The fact that these reports did not mention British atrocities at Benares and Allahabad in June of 1857, for which Cawnpore might well have been a retaliation, suggests the extent to which the similarity between the English and the dark-skinned Indians was denied or repressed.[49] The "savagery" of dark-skinned peoples was proved once more—to some Englishmen at least—by the Jamaica uprising in early October 1865. This native rebellion and the brutal retaliation it occasioned from Governor Eyre caused the leading English men-of-letters to choose sides and publicly declare their positions on race.[50] To Dickens, who deplored what he saw as the inhumanity of "the black—or the Native or the Devil—afar off," this episode merely hardened the opinion he had expressed as early as 1853 in an essay satirically entitled "The Noble Savage": "cruel, false, thievish, murderous, addicted more or less to grease, entrails, and beastly customs, [the black man] is a wild animal with the questionable gift of boasting; a conceited, tiresome, bloodthirsty, monotonous humbug."[51]

By the early 1860s, then, even as the proliferating examples of speculative fraud and violent rhetorical and physical retaliations exposed rapacity in Englishmen, newly intensified meanings associated with the difference of race had become available to guarantee that the similarity between the "natives" and "us," which was so crucial to establishing English superiority, had its limit. Englishmen conquered the formal and informal colonies economically by creating in "natives" the desire to be like the English man; but they contained the threat implicit in that assertion of similarity by emphasizing the "natural" difference of race. The native in whose country English men invested was both like the investor (in his desires) and unlike him (in being "nasty" because black).

Here is where the neat parallelism between women and the racial other ends, for the fact that a woman—Bella Wilfer—symbolically drives home the difference between black men and white by giving her father what even a black king cannot have—a complete new suit of clothes—suggests that Dickens was not so much shoring up or even supplementing the difference of sex by invoking a parallel difference of race as he was establishing a relationship of mutual dependence between the two. That is, the same act with which Bella proves that her father is different from (read *better than*) a black king also proves her to be a good (read *virtuous*) woman. Bella's femininity, in other words, is momentarily stabilized as "other" to masculine self-interestedness through her relation to the black man, for femininity can now acquire its definition not only through acts of generosity to men but, more specifically, through charitable acts that also inscribe racial difference with moral meaning. The one troubling aspect of this symbolic solution, of course, remains Bella's fantasy of "killing" John Harmon and marrying the Indian prince. This trace of violence within the "woman" lingers as a reminder of the instability of the solution Dickens advances, for this fantasy, as the site of overdetermined meanings, concentrates the threats to difference posed by the artificiality upon which it is based. In one reading, this fantasy shows a woman wanting a man who is unlike John Harmon (in being black); in another, it shows a woman wanting (another) man who is like Harmon (in being jealous); in another, it shows the rapacity and violence within woman; in another, it shows that this violence is in everyone: the jealous black prince, the woman, and the man who imagines them both.

The twin fantasies that emerge in *Our Mutual Friend*—the fantasy of a world without women and the fantasy that feminine virtue is propped on a foundation of race—constituted a nightmare for Charles Dickens. This nightmare—which is one way of construing what we call modernity—entails both a picture of the world and a model of subjectivity. In the former, every thing and every distinction has been reduced to a mere effect of representation, which is, in turn, available on the open market, where every man is an instance of the same abstract entity. In the latter, *because* every man is an instance of the same kind of abstraction, identical desires rage endlessly for identical commodities; every man is an enemy to himself because he envies other men, and nothing determines value except the (aesthetic) will that some things be better than others.

   One man's nightmare may be another man's dream, of course, especially if that other "man" has been so gendered, classed, or racialized as to be excluded from the position whose privilege has long been masked by rhetorics of "representativeness" and "universality." While the 1860s did not realize this dream—for all women, for the men and women who constituted the "social body," or for the dark-skinned peoples whose labor helped underwrite British prosperity—this decade did witness the interrogation of some of the institutions and abstractions that had supported the traditional picture of Britain as a hierarchy of natural interests. As the power that had accrued to status was gradually usurped by the professionalization of various occupations, and as inherited distinctions were slowly challenged by modern categories that emphasized both individual responsibility and national identity, unforeseen sites of conflict emerged. The unexpected alliances that formed in relation to these conflicts undeniably gave some individuals and groups more access to what was fast becoming the currency of the realm: the images whose production and distribution increasingly determined how the British viewed themselves and were understood by the peoples they designated *other*.

NOTES

ONE

1. The notion that epistemology could be an analytic category (as opposed to a philosophical problem) has recently been questioned by Richard Rorty. Rorty's historicist account of the self-authorization of philosophy in the late eighteenth and early nineteenth centuries is, in many ways, compatible with my discussion of the disaggregation of domains. For Rorty, however, *epistemology* seems to be forever tainted by the nonempirical or *a priori* position that Kant assigned it late in the eighteenth century. Because the view of knowledge associated with epistemology—the view that knowledge is an "assemblage of representations"—is "optional" according to Rorty, then, again according to Rorty, "so is epistemology." By modifying *epistemology* with the adjective *historical,* I intend both to indicate that epistemology (even as Rorty understands it) has a history and that all modern institutions, concepts, and practices are formulated within a set of assumptions that pertain to epistemology as an analytic category—that is, a set of assumptions about the nature of knowledge and how one knows. See *Philosophy and the Mirror of Nature* (Princeton: Princeton University Press, 1979), especially pp. 132–38 and part 2. For the phrase *historical epistemology,* see Lorraine Daston, "Historical Epistemology," in *Questions of Evidence: Proof, Practice, and Persuasion Across the Disciplines,* ed. James Chandler, Arnold I. Davidson, and Harry Harootunian (Chicago: University of Chicago Press, 1994), pp. 282–89.

2. For a history of *culture,* see Raymond Williams, *Keywords: A Vocabulary of Culture and Society* (New York: Oxford University Press, 1976), pp. 76–82. The most recent analysis of culture during this period—and one of the most interesting—is Christopher Herbert's *Culture and Anomie: Ethnographic Imagination in the Nineteenth Century* (Chicago: University of Chicago Press, 1991), especially chapter 1. Whereas Herbert is interested in the emergence of

what we would call an anthropological view of culture, however, I am concerned with the uneven process by which the groundwork was laid for what looked like, and in some senses was, a single culture of consumption. This version of culture was a forerunner of the "mass culture" of the twentieth century. My analysis of this historical process has been informed by Daniel Denecke, "A Sort of Counterpoise: Social Economy in England: 1831–1863," unpublished paper (Johns Hopkins University, 1993).

3. See Gerald Newman, *The Rise of English Nationalism: A Cultural History, 1740–1830* (New York: St. Martin's Press, 1987), especially chapters 6–8.

4. For the history and persistence of national differences within Great Britain, see Hugh Kearney, *The British Isles: A History of Four Nations* (Cambridge: Cambridge University Press, 1989), especially chapters 7–9.

5. The notorious tables showing "Comparative Chances of Life in Different Classes of the Community" constitute part 4 of the *Sanitary Report*. [Edwin Chadwick], *Report on the Sanitary Condition of the Labouring Population of Great Britain*, ed. M. W. Flinn (1842; rpt., Edinburgh: Edinburgh University Press, 1965), pp. 219–54.

6. See Leonore Davidoff and Catherine Hall, *Family Fortunes: Men and Women of the English Middle Class, 1780–1850* (Chicago: University of Chicago Press, 1987), especially part 2; Barbara Taylor, *Eve and the New Jerusalem: Socialism and Feminism in the Nineteenth Century* (New York: Pantheon, 1983), especially chapter 4; Susan Staves, *Married Women's Separate Property in England, 1660–1833* (Cambridge, Mass.: Harvard University Press, 1990), especially chapters 6 and 7; and Mary Poovey, *Uneven Developments: The Ideological Work of Gender in Mid–Victorian England* (Chicago: University of Chicago Press, 1988), especially chapter 1.

7. See Sheila R. Herstein, *A Mid-Victorian Feminist, Barbara Leigh Smith Bodichon* (New Haven: Yale University Press, 1985), chapter 3; Lee Holcombe, *Wives and Property: Reform of the Married Women's Property Law in Nineteenth-Century England* (Toronto: University of Toronto Press, 1983), chapter 4; Mary Lyndon Shanley, *Feminism, Marriage, and the Law in Victorian England, 1850–1895* (Princeton: Princeton University Press, 1989), chapter 1; and Poovey, *Uneven Developments*, chapter 3.

8. For discussions of *race* in this period, see George W. Stocking, Jr., *Victorian Anthropology* (New York: Free Press, 1987), pp. 62–69 and passim; Douglas Lorimer, *Colour, Class, and the Victorians* (Leicester University Press, 1978); and Christine Bolt, *Victorian Attitudes Toward Race* (London and New York: Routledge & Kegan Paul, 1971).

9. A recent important contribution to the literature about a more-or-less homogeneous British culture is Linda Colley, *The Britons: Forging the Nation, 1707–1837* (New Haven: Yale University Press, 1992). Contributions to the idea that Britain was composed of several cultures often fall under the category of postcolonial studies. Relevant examples of this copious scholarship include Peter Freyer, *Staying Power: The History of Black People in Britain* (London: Pluto Press, 1987); Rozina Visram, *Ayahs, Lascars, and Princes: The Story of Indians in Britain, 1700–1947* (London: Pluto Press, 1986).

10. See Denecke, "Counterpoise," pp. 1–2.

11. See Daston, "Historical Epistemology," in Questions of Evidence, ed. Chandler, Arnold, and Harootunian, pp. 282–89. For examples of Daston's recent work, see "Baconian Facts, Academic Civility, and the Prehistory of Objectivity," Annals of Scholarship 8, nos. 3 and 4 (1991): 337–64; (with Peter Galison) "The Image of Objectivity," Representations 40 (Fall 1992): 81–128; and "Marvelous Facts and Miraculous Evidence in Early Modern Europe," Critical Inquiry 18 (1991): 93–124

12. The categories I am using harken back to the early Foucault. See especially Michel Foucault, "The Order of Discourse," in Untying the Text: A Post-Structuralist Reader, ed. Robert Young (Boston: Routledge & Kegan Paul, 1981), pp. 48–78; and Foucault, The Order of Things: An Archaeology of the Human Sciences, trans. anonymous (New York: Random House, 1970).

13. The classic discussion of the culture industry appears in Max Horkheimer and Theodor W. Adorno, Dialectic of Enlightenment, trans. John Cumming (New York: Seabury Press, 1972), pp. 120–67.

14. For relevant discussions of this aspect of modernity, see Fredric Jameson, "Postmodernism, or the Cultural Logic of Late Capitalism," New Left Review 146 (July–August): 59–92; Jürgen Habermas, The Philosophical Discourse of Modernity: Twelve Lectures, trans. Frederick G. Lawrence (Cambridge, Mass.: MIT Press, 1993), pp. 1–22; and Anthony J. Cascardi, The Subject of Modernity (Cambridge: Cambridge University Press, 1992), pp. 16–71.

It seems incumbent on me to clarify the sense in which I will be discussing representation in these essays, since I will be suggesting—although not properly arguing—that representation also has a history and therefore a modern form. In making this suggestion I am not claiming that some things lie outside of or existed before representation—or, more precisely, that some things can be known apart from representation. In alluding to a history of representation, I have stages like the following in mind: an early-modern stage, in which the belief that some kinds of knowing did not make a detour through figuration co-existed with the recognition that other kinds of knowing required this detour; another early-modern stage, in which it was generally believed that written (or even printed) images could stand in for and make (a kind of) sense of nonlinguistic things, but during which these images were not always or universally available (I have in mind here the example of maps, which were not available to every traveler for every part of the globe but which, when available, were generally considered aids to travel); a more properly modern stage, when mass production and mechanical printing made it possible for nearly everyone to know about nearly everything before actually encountering it; a postmodern stage, in which the infinitely replicable, often electronically transmitted image always precedes one's experience of the thing itself or even renders the thing redundant, because the image is both larger than life and amenable to commodification and consumption on a global scale. Obviously, these stages are not sequential in any simple sense and, just as obviously, each is uneven in development and application. While such a history of representation would clearly require far more than the suggestions I offer here, I want to indicate that when I write of a modern turn to representation, I have in mind a transition to the stage in which the image is mass-produced, (almost) universally available, and (almost always) encountered prior to the thing itself—yet not amenable (yet) to infinite seriality nor imagined to supersede the object for which it supposedly stands.

15. For discussions of the National Association for the Promotion of the Social Sciences, also known as the Social Science Association, or the SSA, see Philip Abrams, *The Origins of British Sociology: 1834–1914* (Chicago: University of Chicago Press, 1968), pp. 44–52; and Lawrence Goldman, "A Peculiarity of the English? The Social Science Association and the Absence of Sociology in Nineteenth-Century Britain," *Past and Present* 114 (1987): 133–71.

16. On the population as an aggregate, see Giovanna Procacci, "Social Economy and the Government of Poverty," in *The Foucault Effect: Essays in Governmentality,* ed. Graham Burchell, Colin Gordon, and Peter Miller (Chicago: University of Chicago Press, 1991), pp. 151–68. On the census and statistics as instruments of aggregation, see Michael J. Cullen, *The Statistical Movement in Early Victorian Britain: The Foundations of Empirical Social Research* (New York: Barnes and Noble, 1975), pp. 1–18.

17. Karl Marx and Frederick Engels, "Introduction to a Critique of Political Economy" in *The German Ideology,* ed. C. J. Arthur (New York: International Publishers, 1986), p. 144.

18. The most relevant discussion of the economic domain is Mitchell Dean, *The Constitution of Poverty: Toward a Genealogy of Liberal Governance* (London and New York: Routledge, 1991), especially "Introduction" and chapter 6. My argument differs from Dean's in some details and, primarily, in my insistence that examining the mode in which a conceptual entity like the economy is or was represented is crucial to understanding what could be said about it. For another relevant discussion, see Keith Tribe, *Land, Labour and Economic Discourse* (London: Routledge & Kegan Paul, 1978), especially chapter 6.

19. *Emergent, residual,* and *dominant* are terms taken from Raymond Williams. See *Marxism and Literature* (Oxford: Oxford University Press, 1977), pp. 121–27.

20. Another, less historically specific, account of the constitution of the social domain has been provided by Denise Riley, *"Am I That Name?" Feminism and the Category of "Women" in History* (Minneapolis: University of Minnesota Press, 1988), chapter 3. For an account that differs in emphasis from my own, see Dean, *Constitution,* pp. 217–19.

21. For a relevant use of the *body politic,* see Edward Forset, *A Comparative Discourse of the Bodies Natural and Politique* (London: Printed for John Bill, 1606). The classic discussion of the medieval, theological context in which this image was developed is Ernst H. Kantorowicz, *The King's Two Bodies: A Study in Medieval Political Theology* (Princeton: Princeton University Press, 1957).

22. See Cullen, *Statistical Movement,* p. 9.

23. See Cullen, *Statistical Movement,* part 2; T. S. Ashton, *Economic and Social Investigations in Manchester, 1833–1933: A Centenary History of the Manchester Statistical Society* (1933; rpt., Fairfield, Conn.: Augustus M. Kelley,

1977), chapter 2; David Elesh, "The Manchester Statistical Society: A Case Study of a Discontinuity of Empirical Social Research," *Journal of the History of the Behavioral Sciences* 8 (July–October 1972): 280–301, 407–17; Lawrence Goldman, "The Origins of British 'Social Science': Political Economy, Natural Science, and Statistics, 1830–1835," *The Historical Journal* 26 (September 1983): 587–616; and Mary Poovey, "'Figures of Arithmetic, Figures of Speech': The Discourse of Statistics in the 1830s," *Critical Inquiry* 19 (Winter 1993): 256–76. For the subdivisions instituted by the London Statistical Society, see *Journal of the Statistical Society of London* 1 (1833).

24. See Karl Marx on commodity fetishism in *Capital: A Critique of Political Economy*, vol. 1, trans. Ben Fowkes (Harmondsworth: Penguin Books, 1976), pp. 163–77; Georg Lukács on reification in "Reification and the Consciousness of the Proletariat," in *History and Class Consciousness: Studies in Marxist Dialectics*, trans. Rodney Livingstone (Cambridge, Mass.: MIT Press, 1971), especially pp. 83–109; and Sigmund Freud on the fetish in "Fetishism," in *The Standard Edition of the Complete Psychological Works of Sigmund Freud*, vol. 21, ed. James Strachey and Anna Freud (London: Hogarth Press and the Institute of Psychoanalysis, 1966–74), pp. 152–57.

25. See Michel Foucault, *Discipline and Punish: The Birth of the Prison*, trans. Alan Sheridan (New York: Vintage Books, 1979), pp. 182–84.

26. Dorothy Marshall, *The English Poor in the Eighteenth Century: A Study in Social and Administrative History* (London: George Routledge & Sons, 1926), p. 77.

27. On Bentham, see Charles F. Bahmueller, *The National Charity Company: Jeremy Bentham's Silent Revolution* (Berkeley and Los Angeles: University of California Press, 1981); on Malthus, see Dean, *Constitution*, chapters 4 and 5; on Chalmers, see Boyd Hilton, *The Age of Atonement: The Influence of Evangelicalism on Social and Economic Thought, 1795–1865* (Oxford: Clarendon Press, 1988), especially chapter 2.

28. The strongest case for the Benthamite nature of the New Poor Law is made by S. E. Finer, *The Life and Times of Sir Edwin Chadwick* (London: Methuen, 1952), book 2. See also Asa Briggs, *Age of Improvement* (New York: David McKay, 1959); and R. K. Webb, *Modern England* (Dodd, Mead, 1968), chapter 5. On the relationship between Tories and the New Poor Law, see Peter Mandler, "Tories and Paupers: Christian Political Economy and the Making of the New Poor Law," *The Historical Journal* 33, no. 1 (1990): 81–103.

29. On the history of Royal Commissions and their use of experts, see Hugh McDowall Clokie and J. William Robinson, *Royal Commissions of Inquiry: The Significance of Investigations in British Politics* (Stanford: Stanford University Press, 1937; rpt., New York: Octagon Books, 1969), pp. 54–148.

30. On the history of objectivity and facts in this period, see Daston and Galison, "The Image of Objectivity," pp. 81–128. On the reform of natural philosophy, which preceded its disaggregation from moral philosophy, see Julian Martin, *Frances Bacon, The State, and the Reform of Natural Philosophy* (Cambridge: Cambridge University Press, 1992), especially chapter 6.

31. On this distinction, see Gertrude Himmelfarb, *The Idea of Poverty: England in the Early Industrial Age* (New York: Vintage Books, 1985), chapter 6; and Dean, *Constitution,* pp. 156, 174–77.

32. Here is Chadwick on poverty: "Poverty . . . is the natural, the primitive, the general and the unchangeable state of man; . . . as labour is the source of wealth, so is poverty of labour. Banish poverty, you banish wealth." "The New Poor Law," *Edinburgh Review* 63 (1836), p. 501.

33. *First Annual Report of the Poor Law Commissioners* (London: W. Clowes and Sons, 1835), p. 6.

34. *First Annual Report,* p. 6

35. Riley offers a different interpretation of this point. See *"Am I That Name?,"* p. 49.

36. See Louis Althusser and Etienne Balibar, *Reading Capital,* trans. Ben Brewster (London: New Left Books, 1970), especially part 3; Pierre Bourdieu, "The Market as Symbolic Goods," *Poetics* 14 (1985): 13–44 and "The Field of Cultural Production, or the Economic World Reversed," trans. Richard Nice, *Poetics* 12 (1983): 261–56. See also John Guillory, *Cultural Capital: The Problem of Literary Canon Formation* (Chicago: University of Chicago Press, 1993), pp. 250, 304–5.

37. See Guillory, *Cultural Capital,* pp. 250, 304–5.

38. For discussions of these positions, see Cascardi, *Subject of Modernity,* especially chapter 1.

39. The New Historicist position has been developed most extensively in work on the Renaissance, but it is also present in many Victorian studies as well. For the prototype of this theoretical position, see Stephen Greenblatt, "Invisible Bullets: Renaissance Authority and Its Subversion, *Henry IV* and *Henry V,*" in *Political Shakespeare: New Essays in Cultural Materialism,* ed. Jonathan Dollimore and Alan Sinfield (Ithaca: Cornell University Press, 1985), pp. 18–47.

40. Ian Hunter, "Personality as a Vocation: The Political Rationality of the Humanities," *Economy and Society* 19, no. 4 (November 1990), pp. 424–27. See also *Culture and Government: The Emergence of Literary Education* (London: Macmillan, 1988); and Michel Foucault, "Governmentality," in *The Foucault Effect,* pp. 87–104.

41. Cascardi, *Subject of Modernity,* p. 3.

42. See Daston, "Marvelous Facts," pp. 93–124.

43. Dean, *Constitution,* pp. 216–17.

44. See Herstein, *A Mid-Victorian Feminist,* chapter 3; Holcombe, *Wives and Property,* chapter 4; Shanley, *Feminism,* chapter 1; and Poovey, *Uneven Developments,* chapter 3.

45. See Daniel Bivona, *"A Gladness of Abasement": Bureaucratic Discipline and European Subjects* (unpublished ms.), especially chapter 1.

46. E. P. Thompson, *The Making of the English Working Class* (New York: Alfred A. Knopf, 1966); Judith R. Walkowitz, *City of Dreadful Delight: Narratives of Sexual Danger in Late Victorian London* (Chicago: University of Chicago Press, 1992); Ellen Ross, *Love and Toil: Motherhood in Outcast London, 1870–1918* (New York: Oxford University Press, 1993).

47. Foucault's writings on power are numerous. See in particular the essays collected in *Power/Knowledge: Selected Interviews and Other Writings, 1972–1977*, trans. Colin Gordon (New York: Pantheon Books, 1980).

48. Some of the most exciting recent work on this period has focused on the factors that divided the interests of these white, propertied men in such as way as to render problematic the very concepts of class interests or ideology. These discussions are important contributions to the epistemological history I am describing here, even though their authors do not consistently place their studies in a larger theoretical context. See Catherine Hall, *White, Male, and Middle-Class: Explorations in Feminism and History* (Cambridge: Polity Press, 1992); Peter Mandler, *Aristocratic Government in the Age of Reform: Whigs and Liberals, 1830–1852* (Oxford: Clarendon Press, 1990); and Hilton, *Age of Atonement*.

49. For such a reading, see Catherine Gallagher, "The Bioeconomics of *Our Mutual Friend*," in *Subject to History: Ideology, Class, Gender*, ed. David Simpson (Ithaca: Cornell University Press, 1991), pp. 47–64.

50. Dean, *Constitution*, p. 218.

51. William Chambers, *Manuals for the Working Classes: [Robert] Chambers Social Science Tracts Embracing Subjects Connected with Social, Political, and Sanitary Economy*, vol. 2, *Political and Social Economy* (London: Chambers, 1861–62), p. 6.

52. Boyd Hilton, "Chalmers as Political Economist," in *The Practical and the Pious: Essays on Thomas Chalmers (1780–1847)*, ed. A. C. Cheyne (Edinburgh: Saint Andrew Press, 1985), pp. 141–56.

53. Hilton, "Chalmers," p. 151.

54. The phrase is that of R. H. Hutton, quoted in Hilton, "Chalmers," p. 153.

55. Quoted in Hilton, "Chalmers," p. 152.

56. John Hill Burton, *Political and Social Economy: Its Practical Application* (Edinburgh: W. and R. Chambers, 1849), p. 272.

57. Sir James Emerson Tennent, *Social Economy: An Address* (London: Emily Faithfull, 1860), p. 5.

Two

1. Henri Lefebvre, *The Production of Space*, trans. Donald Nicholson-Smith (Oxford: Basil Blackwell, 1991), p. 281.

2. The foundational texts are Frederick Engles, *The Condition of the Working Class in England* (1844–45; rpt., Oxford: Basil Blackwell, 1958); and Karl Marx, *Capital*, vol. 1 (1867; Harmondsworth: Penguin Books, 1976), chapters 10 and 15.

3. In particular, literary critics influenced by the middle phase of Foucault's work seem to believe that a totalized field of power dominates modern society. I have in mind Leonard Tennenhouse, *Power on Display: The Politics of Shakespeare's Genres* (New York: Methuen, 1986); and D. A. Miller, *The Novel and the Police* (Berkeley and Los Angeles: University of California Press, 1985).

4. I use the past tense in my discussion of abstraction, even though elements of this system are still obviously in place, in order to stress the historical dimension of its production.

5. Lefebvre, *Production*, p. 27.

6. Lefebvre, *Production*, p. 51.

7. See Richard Olson, *The Emergence of the Social Sciences, 1642–1792* (New York: Twayne Publishers, 1993), pp. 11, 24; and Steven Shapin and Simon Schaffer, *Leviathan and the Air-Pump: Hobbes, Boyle, and the Experimental Life* (Princeton: Princeton University Press, 1985), especially chapters 1 and 8.

8. See Steven Shapin, *A Social History of Truth: Civility and Science in Seventeenth-Century England* (Chicago: University of Chicago Press, 1994), especially chapters 1–3; and Lorraine Daston, "Baconian Facts, Academic Civility, and the Prehistory of Objectivity," *Annals of Scholarship* 8, nos. 3 and 4 (1991): 337–64.

9. The foundational texts for these three concepts are, for commodification, Marx, *Capital*, vol. I, chapter 1, part 4; for reification, Georg Lukács, "Reification and the Consciousness of the Proletariat," in *History and Class Consciousness: Studies in Marxist Dialectics*, trans. Rodney Livingstone (Cambridge. Mass.: MIT Press, 1971), pp. 83–222; and for the fetish, Sigmund Freud, "Fetishism," in *The Standard Edition of the Complete Psychological Works of Sigmund Freud*, vol. 21, ed. James Strachey and Anna Freud (London: Hogarth Press and the Institute of Psychoanalysis, 1966–74), pp. 152–57.

10. See Joan L. Richards, *Mathematical Visions: The Pursuit of Geometry in Victorian England* (San Diego: Academic Press, 1988), pp. 1–2.

11. Indeed, Augustine and other early medieval philosophers assumed that geometry simply *was* God's order. The theory of mimesis postdated such "conjunctive" thinking and laid the groundwork for the disjunction between material space and abstractions about that space. See Samuel Y. Edgerton, Jr., *The Heritage of Giotto's Geometry: Art and Science on the Eve of the Scientific Revolution* (Ithaca: Cornell University Press, 1991), p. 41.

12. See Edgerton, *Heritage*, p. 16.

13. My reading of Hobbes is indebted to Olson, *Emergence*, pp. 27–47.

14. See Joyce Oldham Appleby, *Economic Thought and Ideology in Seventeenth-Century England* (Princeton: Princeton University Press, 1978), especially chapter 7; Joseph A. Schumpeter, *History of Economic Analysis* (New York: Oxford University Press, 1954), pp. 121–22; and Michael Walzer, "On the Role of Symbolism in Political Thought," *Political Science Quarterly* 82 (1967): 191–204. See also Richard Olson, *Science Deified and Science Defied: The Historical Significance of Science in Western Culture*, vol. 2 (Berkeley and Los Angeles: University of California Press, 1990), p. 151.

15. Josiah Child, *Brief Observations Concerning Trade, and Interest of Money* (London: Elizabeth Calvert and Henry Mortlock, 1688).

16. William Letwin, *The Origins of Scientific Economics: English Economic Thought, 1660–1776* (New York: Methuen, 1963), pp. 221–28; and Olson, *Science*, pp. 149–51.

17. Thomas Hobbes, *Leviathan* (1651; rpt., Harmondsworth, England: Penguin Books, 1968), part 1, chap. 10, pp. 151–52.

18. Petty, *Verbum Sapienti* (1665) in *The Economic Writings of Sir William Petty*, ed. Charles Henry Hull (1899; rpt., Fairfield, N.J.: Augustus M. Kelley, 1986), pp. 99–120.

19. On these aspects of Petty's method, see Mary Poovey, "The Social Constitution of 'Class': Toward a History of Classificatory Thinking," in *Rethinking Class: Literary Studies and Social Formations*, ed. Wai Chee Dimock and Michael T. Gilmore (New York: Columbia University Press, 1994), pp. 15–56.

20. The camera obscura was an instrument that had been used for the scientific study of optics, popular entertainment, and artistic practice since at least the fifteenth century. It consists of an enclosure, one wall of which contains a small aperture that focuses light—and therefore projects an inverted image—onto an opposing wall. For a discussion of the history and phenomenology of this instrument, see Jonathan Crary, *Techniques of the Observer: On Vision and Modernity in the Nineteenth Century* (Cambridge, Mass.: MIT Press, 1990), chapter 2.

21. On the novelty of graphic plans in the Renaissance, see Edgerton, *Heritage*, chapter 5.

22. See Lefebvre, *Production*, p. 69.

23. "The rationality of space, according to this analysis, is not the outcome of a quality or property of human action in general, or human labour as such, of 'man,' or of social organization. On the contrary, it is itself the origin and source—not distantly but immediately, or rather inherently—of the rationality of activity" (Lefebvre, *Production*, pp. 71–72).

24. Lefebvre, *Production*, p. 85.

25. Lefebvre, *Production*, p. 95; Lukács, "Reification," p. 90.

26. Lefebvre writes that the history of abstract space "proceeds from nature to abstraction . . . towards the quantitative, towards homogeneity and towards the elimination of the body, which has had to seek refuge in art" (*Production*, pp. 110, 111).

27. Michel Foucault, *Discipline and Punish: The Birth of the Prison*, trans. Alan Sheridan (New York: Vintage Books, 1979), pp. 182–83.

28. Michel Foucault, "Governmentality," in *The Foucault Effect: Studies in Governmentality*, ed. Colin Gordon, Graham Burchell, and Peter Miller (Chicago: University of Chicago Press, 1991), pp. 87–104.

29. See David Hume, "Of the Rise and Progress of the Arts and Sciences," "Of Commerce," "Of Refinement in the Arts," and "Of the First Principles of Government" in *Essays Moral, Political, and Literary*, ed. Eugene F. Miller (Indianapolis: Liberty Classics, 1985), pp. 111–37, 253–67, 268–80, 32–42. See also Stefan Collini, Donald Winch, and John Burrow, *That Noble Science of Politics: A Study in Nineteenth-Century Intellectual History* (Cambridge: Cambridge University Press, 1983), p. 19; J. G. A. Pocock, "The Mobility of Property and the Rise of Eighteenth-Century Sociology," in *Virtue, Commerce, and History: Essays on Political Thought and History, Chiefly in the Eighteenth Century* (Cambridge: Cambridge University Press, 1985), pp. 103–124; and

Graham Burchell, "Peculiar Interests: Civil Society and Governing 'The System of Natural Liberty,'" in *The Foucault Effect,* ed. Gordon, Burchell, and Miller, pp. 128–29.

30. Adam Smith, *Theory of Moral Sentiments,* ed. D. D. Raphael and A. L. Macfie, vol. 3, i, 6 (1759; rpt., Indianapolis: Liberty Press, 1982), p. 113.

31. In his *Theory of Moral Sentiments,* Smith writes, "It is the impressions of our own senses only, not those of his, which our imaginations copy. By the imagination we place ourselves in his situation, we conceive ourselves enduring with all the same torments, we enter as it were into his body, and become in some measure the same person with him, and thence form some idea of his sensations, and even feel something which, though weaker in degree, is not altogether unlike them" (*TMS,* vol. 1, i, 1, p. 9). In *The Wealth of Nations,* Smith undeniably emphasizes the competition among individuals, but individuals compete because they are all instances of the same abstract entity—that is, they are characterized by the same "propensity to truck, barter, and exchange one thing for another" (*An Enquiry into the Nature and Causes of the Wealth of Nations* [1776; rpt., New York: Modern Library, 1937], p. 13). This is not to dismiss the famous "Adam Smith problem," but simply to suggest that there are continuities as well as differences between the two texts.

32. Smith, *Wealth,* p. 747.

33. Smith, *Wealth,* p. 734.

34. For an analysis of the role gender plays in Smith's argument, see Poovey, "The Social Constitution of 'Class,'" in *Rethinking Class,* ed. Dimock and Gilmore, pp. 46–47.

35. See Graham Burchell, "Peculiar Interests: Civil Society and Governing 'The System of Natural Liberty,'" in *The Foucault Effect,* ed. Gordon, Burchell, and Miller, pp. 137–39.

36. Jeremy Bentham's National Charity Company, which applied many of the strategies of his Panopticon to the management of the poor, was the most extreme version of the fusion of surveillance and administration. See Charles R. Bahmueller, *The National Charity Company: Jeremy Bentham's Silent Revolution* (Berkeley and Los Angeles: University of California Press, 1981), especially chapters 5–7.

37. Thomas Chalmers, *On the Christian and Economic Polity of a Nation,* vol. 14 of *The Works of Thomas Chalmers* (Glasgow: William Collins, 1845), p. 31.

38. [James Phillips Kay], "On the Establishment of County or District Schools, for the Training of the Pauper Children Maintained in Union Workhouses," *Journal of the Statistical Society of London* 1 (1838–39): 22. Future references will be cited in the text by page number.

39. [Kay], "Establishment," p. 22. This is the same principle of aggregation for the purpose of segregation that Chadwick wanted to implement in the New Poor Law.

40. On the logic of accounting, see Peter Miller, "Accounting and Objectivity: The Invention of Calculating Selves and Calculable Spaces," *Annals of Scholarship* 9, nos. 1 and 2 (1992): 61–86.

41. For his calculations of excrement, see [Edwin Chadwick], *Report on the Sanitary Condition of the Labouring Population of Great Britain* (1842; facsimile ed., Edinburgh: Edinburgh University Press, 1965), p. 123.

42. Thus, for example, Chadwick describes a servant woman whose appearance and temper "have been bourne down by the condition of the house" in which she lives (*Report*, p. 195).

43. Charles Babbage, *On the Economy of Machinery and Manufactures* (London: Charles Knight, 1832), p. vi. Future references will be cited in the text by page number. According to the preface Babbage added to the second edition, *Economy* sold 3,000 copies in two months, even though many booksellers "impeded its sale" (vi). Booksellers banded together against Babbage's book because in chapter 31 he used the example of booktraders to demonstrate how combinations of manufacturers could keep prices high by foreclosing competition. Such combinations, especially to fix the price of knowledge, widened the gap between the classes and thus exacerbated social unrest. Babbage printed the names of the men he claimed ran the booksellers' combination (p. 328) and went so far as to recommend a "counter-association of authors" (p. 331). It is noteworthy that he did not recommend unions for other aggrieved workers.

44. The history of the image of society as a machine extends at least into the seventeenth century, for René Descartes, Robert Boyle, and Thomas Hobbes all used mechanical imagery to describe social relations. During the eighteenth century, the image acquired new salience from both Scottish philosophers' elaborations of the "mechanisms" that made commercial society prosperous and William Paley's description of the universe as God's clockwork.

45. Men received 6 shillings per day for "tinning or whitening," whereas women, who required the same amount of time to make a pound of pins, received 3 shillings.

46. Recent studies of the nineteenth-century application of this image include Graeme Davison, "The City as a Natural System: Theories of Urban Society in Early Nineteenth-Century Britain," in *The Pursuit of Urban History*, ed. Derek Fraser and Anthony Sutcliffe (London: Edward Arnold, 1983), pp. 349–70; and Eileen Janes Yeo, *The Contest for Social Science in Britain in the Nineteenth and Twentieth Centuries: Relations and Representations of Gender and Class* (London: Virago, forthcoming), chapter 7. I am indebted to Yeo for allowing me to read this important manuscript prior to publication.

While Davison's essay is also an important study of the nineteenth century, ,he traces this image to Palcy's natural theology, which more consistently represents society as a machine. A longer view would identify William Petty's *Anatomy of Ireland* as one seventeenth-century revision of the medieval "body politick." Early in the eighteenth century, Daniel Defoe and Pierre Boiguilbert adapted Petty's idea that money and goods should be allowed to circulate as freely as blood as a defense of laissez-faire economic policy. At midcentury, this image was elaborated when François Quesnay and the other Physiocrats sought a way to explain the law-governed, natural domain that we call the economy.

47. Davison, "The City," p. 362.

48. See Thomas Southwood Smith, *A Treatise on Fever and Epidemics Con-*

*sidered With Relation to Their Common Nature and to Climate and Civiliza-
tion* (London: Longman, Rees, Orme, Brown, and Green, 1830); *The Philoso-
phy of Health* (1835; 11th ed. London: Longman, Green, Longman, Roberts &
Green, 1865); and "Use of the Dead to the Living," *The Westminster Review* 2
(July–October 1824): 59–97. On Smith, see C. L. Lewes, *Southwood Smith: A
Retrospect* (Edinburgh, 1889); and Davison, "The City," pp. 360–63.

49. Smith, "Lectures on Animal Economy at the London Institution,"
Monthly Repository 7 (1833), p. 51.

50. See Smith, *A Treatise on Fever and Epidemics*. See also Frank Mort, *Dangerous Sexualities: Medico-Moral Politics in England Since 1830* (London and
New York: Routledge & Kegan Paul, 1987), especially chapter 3.

51. In the introduction to the first edition of the *Philosophy of Health* (1835),
Smith states that "the bodily organization and the mental powers of the child
depend mainly on the management of the child" (p. xiii), and he admits that
mothers are entrusted with "the direction and control of the first impressions
that are made upon the human being" (p.xv). To Smith, however, this is scan-
dalous, because women have no training to be adequate managers: "What has
ever been done for you to enable you to understand the physical and mental
constitution of that human nature, the care of which is imposed on you?" Smith
scornfully demands of his female readers. "In what part of the course of your
education was instruction of this kind introduced? Over how large a portion of
your education did it extend? Who were your teachers? . . . " (This interrogation
continues for three pages: pp. xiii–xv.)

Smith erases the mother's body both in his description of the baby feeding,
where he reduces breast-feeding to the "function by which new matter is introduced into the system" (p. 21), and in his depiction of the infant's self-sufficiency, which implies that the newborn is isolated and simply awaits sensations
(p. 10). Smith's only reference to the mother in his description of infancy is a
passing reference to the child "leaving his maternal dwelling" (p. 10).

52. See Davison, "The City," p. 363; and Mary Poovey, "Anatomical Realism
and Social Analysis in Early Nineteenth-Century Manchester" in this volume.

53. Chalmers, *Christian and Economic Polity*, p. xiv. On antagonism to the
New Poor Law, see Nicholas C. Edsall, *The Anti-Poor Law Movement, 1834–
44* (Manchester: Manchester University Press, 1971); and John Knott, *Popular
Opposition to the 1834 Poor Law* (London: Croom Helm, 1986).

54. For a discussion of the tendency toward a mechanical mode of scientific
analysis, see Lorraine Daston and Peter Galison, "The Image of Objectivity,"
Representations 40 (1992), pp. 81–128.

55. See Ray Strachey, *The Cause* (1928; rpt., London: Virago, 1978), especially chapters 4 and 5; Jo Manton, *Mary Carpenter and the Children of the
Streets* (London: Heinemann, 1976); Lee Holcombe, *Wives and Property: Reform of the Married Women's Property Law in Nineteenth-Century England*
(Toronto: University of Toronto Press, 1983); Sheila R. Herstein, *A Mid-
Victorian Feminist: Barbara Leigh Smith Bodichon* (New Haven: Yale University Press, 1985); Jane Rendall, "'A Moral Engine'? Feminism, Liberalism, and
the *English Woman's Journal*," in *Equal or Different: Women's Politics, 1800–*

1914 (Oxford: Basil Blackwell, 1987), pp. 112–38; Jane Lewis, *Women and Social Action in Victorian and Edwardian England* (Aldershot: Edward Elgar, 1991), chapter 1; and Yeo, *The Contest for Social Science,* chapter 5.

56. The magazine sold for 3d. a month and was published between 1856 and 1864. That year, it was renamed the *Missing Link Magazine, or Bible Work at Home and Abroad,* under which title it was published until Ranyard's death in 1879. The collection, entitled *The Missing Link; or Bible-Women in the Homes,* was published in London by James Nisbet in 1859. All future references, which are to the second edition of this text (1861), will be cited by page number. Ranyard also trained nurses for the poor, beginning in 1868. For biographical information, see the *Dictionary of National Biography.* On Ranyard and the Female Bible Mission, see Leslie Howsam, *Cheap Bibles: Nineteenth-Century Publishing and the British and Foreign Bible Society* (Cambridge: Cambridge University Press, 1991), pp. 170–78; F. K. Prochaska, "Body and Soul: Bible Nurses and the Poor in Victorian London," *Historical Research* 60, no. 143 (October 1987): 336–48; and Françoise Ducrocq, "The London Biblewomen and Nurses Mission, 1857–1880: Class Relations/Women's Relations," in *Women and the Structure of Society: Selected Research from the Fifth Berkshire Conference on the History of Women,* ed. Barbara Harris and JoAnn McNamara (Durham: Duke University Press, 1984), pp. 98–107.

57. The Female Bible Mission was not the only woman's organization dedicated to Bible work, of course, nor was it the only society committed to collecting contributions from the poor. As early as 1809, for example, a Female Servants' Society was founded in Aberdeen "for promoting the diffusion of the Scriptures." This society, which charged its poor members a penny a week, followed the more customary practice of contributing to the British and Foreign Bible Society instead of benefiting from it. Thomas Chalmers was so impressed with the moral effects of this scheme that he instituted penny-a-week subscriptions in the Kilmany Bible Association. Rev. William Hanna, *Memoirs of the Life and Writings of Thomas Chalmers, D.D., LL. D.,* vol. 1 (New York: Harper and Brothers, 1851), pp. 271–72, and appendix K, p. 494.

58. John Matthias Weylland, *Round the Tower: The Story of the London City Mission* (London: S. W. Partridge, 1874), p. 291. All future references to this history of the LCM will be cited in the text by page number.

59. The British and Foreign Bible Society was founded in 1804 for the express purpose of distributing Bibles all over the world. See Howsam, *Cheap Bibles,* pp. 3–6.

60. This quotation is taken from p. 300 of the 1860 edition, published in New York. The first two sentences are not in the 1861 London edition, and in that edition the last sentence reads: "It is believed that there would be great evil in mixing the two departments of labor; and mistakes would be made in the accounts; while a particular benefit to be gained, by assembling the Women at a given hour at one place, would be lost likewise" (p. 278). The 1861 deletions obscure the Bible Society's role in maintaining the distinction in kinds of work. In 1859, the Bible Society had voted not to make additional outright grants to the Female Bible Mission but to donate Bibles to the mission instead. The pro-

ceeds of these sales were allowed to be taken as part payment of the expenses of the FBM (pp. 258–59; 1861 ed.). One wonders if the change in policy resulted not only from the depletion of the BFBS Jubilee fund (which had been used to pay the Bible women) but also from the society's recognition that the kind of records it required could not be supplied, because the separation of kinds of work could not be maintained. The alterations Ranyard made in the 1861 edition may express her desire to take some of the responsibility for attempting to enforce the distinction between mission and Bible work. In *The True Institution of Sisterhood; or, a Message and its Messengers* (1862), Ranyard reiterated her commitment to Bible selling as the "peculiar blessing" conferred by her organization (quoted in Howsam, *Cheap Bibles*, p. 175).

61. See Barry Supple, "Legislation and Virtue: An Essay on Working Class Self-Help and the State in the Early Nineteenth Century," in *Historical Perspectives: Studies in English Thought and Society,* ed. Neil McKendrick (London: Europa, 1974), pp. 211–54.

62. When Marian's visits were greeted with the complaint that she did not know how hard it was to live, she responded, "Oh yes I do. I am quite as poor as you are. I know it all; but get this book—it is the balm for all your sorrow—I bring it you, because I have found it so for myself" (p. 22).

63. "The 'woman' goes where the 'lady' might not enter, and performs offices which are most fittingly rendered by persons of the working class. The floor is scrubbed by a good 'woman' better than by a pious 'lady.' Yet the lady can find the scrubbing brush, and the soap, and materials for soup, and supplies of clothes, and the funds that are needful, and the sympathy and counsel which are indispensable, and be very blessed in her deed" (pp. 240–41).

64. Sarah Stickney Ellis, for example, referred to mothers as the "mainspring of the machinery by which social and domestic happiness is constantly supplied," yet her copious references to sympathy, influence, and maternal instinct suggest that she also considered social relations to be organic. See *The Mothers of England,* collected in *The Family Monitor and Domestic Guide* (New York: Henry G. Langley, 1844), p. 18.

65. In 1599, A. Hume employed this sense of *machine* in his *Hymnes*: "Be his wisdome . . . so wonderouslie of nocht, This machine round, this vniverse, this vther world he wrocht" (*OED*).

66. In expressing a commitment to limiting rather than extending the rationality associated with abstract space, the Female Bible Mission exemplifies a tendency that Leonore Davidoff has also identified in housework during this period. On the one hand, Davidoff argues, household guides instructed women about how "to make life more calculable, to balance expenditure with income in an effort to save." On the other hand, however, economic rationality always had limited success in households, partly because one of the goals of the household—"the maintenance of hierarchical boundaries and ego-servicing of superiors"—defies the logic of rational calculation. See "The Rationalization of Housework," in *Dependence and Exploitation in Work and Marriage,* ed. Diana Leonard Barker and Sheila Allen (London: Longman, 1976), pp. 131, 133.

67. See Joan W. Scott, "The Evidence of Experience," *Critical Inquiry* 17 (Summer 1991): 773–97.

68. The argument that patriarchy not only preceded but was taken up by and helped facilitate the new form of abstract rationality has been made by Rachel Harrison and Frank Mort, "Patriarchal Aspects of Nineteenth-Century State Formation: Property Relations, Marriage and Divorce, and Sexuality," in *Capitalism, State Formation and Marxist Theory: Historical Investigations,* ed. Philip Corrigan (London: Quartet Books, 1980), pp. 79–109; and Mitchell Dean, *The Constitution of Poverty: Towards a Genealogy of Liberal Governance* (London: Routledge, 1991), especially pp. 108–14, 216–17.

THREE

1. While it is not my purpose to analyze the nature of these historical conjunctures, in assuming the historicity of nationalism I am clearly taking a position within the debate about whether or not national (or even ethnic) identities always exist. For formulations of the historicist position, see Ernest Gellner, *Thought and Change* (London: Weidenfeld, 1964), and *Nations and Nationalism* (Oxford: Basil Blackwell, 1983); and John Breuilly, *Nationalism and the State* (Manchester: Manchester University Press, 1982). A recent proponent of the position that national identities are universal political forms is A. D. Smith, *The Ethnic Origins of Nations* (Oxford: Basil Blackwell, 1986). For a useful introduction to these debates, see John Foster, "Nationality, Social Change and Class: Transformations of National Identity in Scotland," in *The Making of Scotland: Nation, Culture and Social Change,* ed. David McCrone, Stephen Kendrick, and Pat Straw (Edinburgh: Edinburgh University Press, 1989), pp. 31–52.

2. Gerald Newman argues that the perception that there are aliens within characteristically targets those who govern. In the example I discuss, this is not the case. See Newman, *The Rise of English Nationalism: A Cultural History, 1740–1830* (New York: St. Martin's Press, 1987), pp. 163–64.

While England's imperial activities are clearly part of the articulation of "national values" during this period, constraints of space prevent me from discussing this here.

3. Catherine Hall also notes that nationalism is always crosscut and undercut by axes of gender, racial, and political identities. See "Missionary Stories: Gender and Ethnicity in England in the 1830s and 1840s," *White, Male and Middle Class: Explorations in Feminism and History* (Cambridge: Polity Press, 1992), pp. 205–54.

4. For biographical information on Kay, see Frank Smith, *The Life and Work of James Kay-Shuttleworth* (London: John Murray, 1923), chapter 1; and M. W. Flinn, "Introduction" to Edwin Chadwick, *Report on the Sanitary Condition of the Labouring Population of Great Britain* (1842; rpt., Edinburgh: Edinburgh University Press, 1965), pp. 32–34.

5. Quoted in Smith, *Life and Work,* pp. 13–14.

6. On the importance of the Manchester Statistical Society in providing a model for treating social problems, see Smith, *Life and Work*, pp. 25–26; T. S. Ashton, *Economic and Social Investigations in Manchester, 1833–1933: A Centenary History of the Manchester Statistical Society* (1933; rpt., Fairfield, Conn.: Augustus M. Kelley, 1977), chapters 1–2; David Elesh, "The Manchester Statistical Society: A Case Study in a Discontinuity in the History of Empirical Social Research," *Journal of the History of the Behavioral Sciences* 8, no. 3 (1972): 280–301 (part 1) and 8, no. 4 (1972): 407–17 (part 2); Victor L. Hilts, "*Aliis exterendum*, or, the Origins of the Statistical Society of London," *Isis* 69, no. 246 (1978): 21–43; Lawrence Goldman, "The Origins of British 'Social Science': Political Economy, Natural Science and Statistics, 1830–1835," *The Historical Journal* 26, no. 3 (1983): 587–616. For discussions of extra-parliamentary pressure groups, see Patricia M. Hollis, ed., *Pressure from Without in Early Victorian England* (London: Routledge & Kegan Paul, 1974); Biancamaria Fontana, *Rethinking the Politics of Commercial Society: The "Edinburgh Review," 1802–1832* (Cambridge: Cambridge University Press, 1985); and Peter Mandler, *Aristocratic Government in the Age of Reform: Whigs and Liberals, 1830–1852* (Oxford: Clarendon Press, 1990), especially chapter 4.

7. "Alfred" (Samuel H. G. Kydd) writes that Kay's tract was used, along with a pamphlet by W. R. Greg, to "accelerate [. . .] the growth of public opinion in favor of factory legislation." "It was the custom of Mr. Oastler and others to read extracts therefrom, corroborating the parliamentary evidence on the question, and either leaving out or replying to the educational and economical theories of the authors" (*The History of the Factory Movement* [1857; rpt., New York: Augustus M. Kelley, 1966], 1: 260; see also 1: 269).

8. Two editions of Kay's pamphlet were published in 1832. The first appeared before cholera struck Manchester; the second, Kay explains in his new dedication to the Rev. Thomas Chalmers, was delayed by cholera, "chiefly because new sources of information [were] opened" to him by his work with the newly established Manchester Board of Health (*The Moral and Physical Condition of the Working Classes Employed in the Cotton Manufacture in Manchester*, 2d ed., enlarged (London: James Ridgway, 1832), p. 3. All subsequent references are to this edition and will be cited in the text by page number. The first edition, which differs from this text primarily in lacking this long dedication, was also published by Ridgway in 1832. Because doctors understood neither the disease's nature nor its mode of transmission, because the disease struck suddenly and killed quickly, and because it was by origin foreign (Asiatic), cholera was easily assimilated to the plague, with all the connotations of judgment and apocalypse that this word would have carried for a Bible-reading population. For discussions of cholera, see R. A. Lewis, *Edwin Chadwick and the Public Health Movement, 1832–1854* (London: Longmans, Green, 1952), especially chapter 2; Anthony S. Wohl, *Endangered Lives: Public Health in Victorian Britain* (Cambridge, Mass.: Harvard University Press, 1983), chapter 5; and Margaret Pelling, *Cholera, Fever, and English Medicine, 1825–1865* (Oxford University Press, 1978).

9. The metaphor of the social body appears in a large number of texts in this

period, not all of which reach the same conclusions about "cure" that Kay does. Thomas Carlyle, for one, explicitly rejected the argument that repealing the Corn Laws would cure the "diseases of a world lying in wickedness." "Quite another alcahest is needed;—a long, painful course of medicine and regimen, surgery and physic," Carlyle asserted. Political reform was also useless, according to Carlyle; only moral reform was an effective "physic." See "Corn-Law Rhymes," *Edinburgh Review,* no. 110 (1832); rpt., *The Works of Thomas Carlyle,* vol. 28 (New York: Charles Scribner's Sons, 1904), pp. 150, 160; and "Signs of the Times," *Edinburgh Review,* no. 98 (1829); rpt., *Works,* vol. 27, p. 82.

10. The medical model Kay assumes is the same model set out by his friend and fellow doctor Thomas Southwood Smith in his enormously popular *Philosophy of Health* (1835; 11th ed., London: Longman, Green, Longman, Roberts & Green, 1865). According to this model, the human body is a system, itself composed of various vital systems, which constantly interacts with the environment. In its natural state, the body is healthy, and this health produces a "feeling of health" that is the source of human pleasure. Disease comes to the body from outside, carried by foul water, for example, or by atmospheric *miasmas,* which were thought to be the effluvia of decay or waste. For discussions of this model, see George Rosen, "Disease, Debility, and Death," in *The Victorian City: Images and Realities,* ed. H. J. Dyos and Michael Wolff, vol. 2 (London and Boston: Routledge & Kegan Paul, 1973), pp. 635–36; and Charles E. Rosenberg, "Florence Nightingale on Contagion: The Hospital as Moral Universe," in *Healing and History,* ed. Charles E. Rosenberg (New York: Dawson, 1979), pp. 116–36.

11. Robert Owen's writings began to be available as early as 1813. For a discussion of Owen and a bibliography of his work, see Barbara Taylor, *Eve and the New Jerusalem: Socialism and Feminism in the Nineteenth Century* (New York: Pantheon, 1983). John Francis Bray's *Labour Defended against the Claims of Capital* was published in 1825 and reprinted in extracts in the *Trades' Newspaper* in the second half of that year. Bray's *Labour's Wrongs and Labour's Remedy* began as a series of letters in the *Leeds Times* in 1835 and was published as a volume in 1839.

12. Quoted in J. C. D. Clark, *English Society, 1688–1832: Ideology, Social Structure, and Political Practices During the Ancien Regime* (Cambridge: Cambridge University Press, 1985), pp. 403–4.

13. Mandler notes that in the 1830s, demands for social and political reform often went hand-in-hand, especially for the Whigs. Even the Whigs, however, rarely endorsed the *principle* or *right* to vote. Instead, the Whig position was that the franchise should be extended only so as to reflect the influence that various groups already exercised in society. These groups were constituted by social criteria and by geography. See *Aristocratic Government,* pp. 2–6. Kay's position was more radical than that of most Whigs (although he also avoided any language of "rights"). Indeed, his involvement in political issues and "party conflict" eventually interfered in his medical practice and was one factor in his abandoning medicine for government service. See F. Smith, *Life and Work,* pp. 27–28.

14. For a discussion of the role assumptions about sexuality played in the early public health movement, see Frank Mort, *Dangerous Sexualities: Medico-Moral Politics in England Since 1830* (London and New York: Routledge & Kegan Paul, 1987), part 1. Catherine Gallagher discusses the impact of Malthus's representation of the sexualized working-class body in "The Body Versus the Social Body in the Works of Thomas Malthus and Henry Mayhew," *Representations* 14 (Spring 1986); reprinted in Catherine Gallagher and Thomas Laqueur, eds., *The Making of the Modern Body: Sexuality and Society in the Nineteenth Century* (Berkeley and Los Angeles: University of California Press, 1987), pp. 83–106.

15. For a discussion of Chadwick's assumptions about domesticity, see my essay, "Domesticity and Class Formation: Chadwick's 1842 *Sanitary Report*," in this volume. The relevant text by Hector Gavin is his *Sanitary Ramblings . . .* (1848; facsimile ed., London: Frank Cass, 1971). For typical speeches by Shaftesbury, see *Hansard's Parliamentary Debates*, 3d ser. vol. 73: March 15, 1844, c. 1073–1155; March 22, 1844, c. 1376–1387. It should be noted that Shaftesbury was a Tory, but found his own party "ten times more hostile to my views" than the Whigs (quoted in Mandler, *Aristocratic Government*, p. 82).

16. The transitional nature of the term *race* in the 1830s led writers such as Kay to conflate biological with cultural or ethnic characteristics. According to George W. Stocking, Jr., "Given the belief that the habitual behavior of human groups or different environments might become part of their hereditary physical makeup, cultural phenomenon were readily translatable into 'racial' tendencies" (*Victorian Anthropology* [New York: Free Press, 1987], p. 64). The "distinctly racial meaning," which *Anglo-Saxon* had taken on by the nineteenth century, emphasized the orderly, mature, disciplined, and devout nature of this group. By contrast, the Celts were held to be lawless, childlike, indolent, and superstitious. See Stocking, *Victorian Anthropology*, pp. 62–63; Richard Ned Lebow, *White Britain and Black Ireland: The Influence of Stereotypes on Colonial Policy* (Philadelphia: Institute for the Study of Human Issues, 1976), chapter 5; and Lynn Hollen Lees, *Exiles of Erin: Irish Migrants in Victorian London* (Ithaca: Cornell University Press, 1979), especially pp. 136–37. Lees argues that the widespread assumption that the Irish population increased more rapidly (and recklessly) than the English was inaccurate.

17. Some English writers did acknowledge the fact that different Irishmen and women had different religious faiths. Most often, predictably, these religious differences were mapped onto the "character" differences that corresponded to "race." Here, for example, is Nassau Senior, writing of the "two Irelands": "One is chiefly Protestant, the other is chiefly Roman Catholic. . . . The population of one is labourious but prodigal; no fatigue repels them—no amusement diverts them from the business of providing the means of subsistence and of enjoyment. . . . that of the other is indolent but parsimonious" (quoted in Richard Ned Lebow, "British Images of Poverty in Pre-Famine Ireland," in *Views of the Irish Peasantry, 1800–1916*, ed. Daniel J. Casey and Robert E. Rhodes [Hamden, Conn.: Archon Books, 1977], p. 73). Lebow discusses the various tensions and paradoxes of the English views of the Irish in this essay.

One of his conclusions is that "the real distinction in Ireland was not between Saxon and Celt or between Protestant and Catholic but between those Irishmen protected by custom and law and those exposed to the arbitrary power of the landlords" (p. 72).

18. In the late fifteenth century, for example, the definition of *English* was narrowed, partly by denigrating as different and inferior other "alien" peoples, among whom were the Irish. By the late eighteenth century, however, incorporating the Irish seemed more advantageous to "British" security than did excluding them.

Among the studies that discuss this process, I have found the following particularly helpful: Michael Hechter, *Internal Colonialism: The Celtic Fringe in British National Development, 1536–1966* (Berkeley and Los Angeles: University of California Press, 1975); Philip Corrigan and Derek Sayer, *The Great Arch: English State Formation as Cultural Revolution* (Oxford: Basil Blackwell, 1985), especially chapters 3, 5, and 6; Peter Stallybrass and Allon White, *The Politics and Poetics of Transgression* (Ithaca: Cornell University Press, 1986), chapters 1 and 3; Linda Colley, "Whose Nation? Class and National Consciousness in Britain, 1750–1830," *Past and Present* 113 (November 1986): 97–117; Keith Robbins, *Nineteenth-Century Britain: Integration and Diversity* (Oxford: Clarendon Press, 1988). On Ireland's place in this process, see Oliver MacDonagh, *States of Mind: A Study of Anglo-Irish Conflict 1780–1980* (London: George Allen and Unwin, 1983); David Cairns and Shaun Richards, *Writing Ireland: Colonialism, Nationalism and Culture* (Manchester: Manchester University Press, 1988), especially chapter 1; and Thomas E. Hachey and Lawrence J. McCaffrey, eds., *Perspectives on Irish Nationalism* (Lexington: University Press of Kentucky, 1989).

19. Mandler argues that one of the principle distinctions of the Whig party was that it was cosmopolitan, emphasizing national over local interests. See *Aristocratic Government*, p. 6.

20. By the 1840s, these two dangers came together in the Irish campaign to repeal the Act of Union. The connection between the agitation of Irish Catholics and more sweeping parliamentary reforms was identified by Isaac Butt in 1843. Butt, who later invented Home Rule, objected to repeal because of its democratic implications. "Repeal [is] revolution. . . . The proposition [is] not to return to any state of things which had previously existed in Ireland—not to adopt the constitution of any European state—but to enter on an untried and wild system of democracy" (quoted in MacDonagh, *States of Mind*, p. 57).

21. See McDonagh, *States of Mind*, pp. 105–7.

22. Here is Kay's suggestion in full: "We believe, however, that an impost on the rental of Ireland, might be applied with advantage in employing the redundant labour in great public works—such as draining bogs, making public roads, canals, harbours, &c., by which the entire available capital of the country would be increased, and the people would be trained in industrious habits, and more civilized manners. England would then cease to be, to the same extent as at present, the receptacle of the most demoralized and worthless hordes of the sister country" (p. 84). Notice that Kay devotes far more attention here to the im-

provements that could result from this tax revenue than to how it might be raised. Given the assumption held by many nineteenth-century English people that most of the Irish land was owned by absentee landlords, Kay probably intends for the tax to be imposed on this group. His solution, however, does not even address the land owned by resident landlords, nor does it take into consideration the fact that many landowners were also in debt—often to Catholics. Kay also leaves unspecified how this tax was to be collected or disbursed, and who is to oversee the public works projects—not to mention how the transition to this idealized state of public works is to be achieved, especially since Kay specifically argues against instituting an "unmodified" poor law in Ireland (p. 83).

The Irish "land question," which Kay sidesteps here, and which was to gain urgency during the course of the century, was partly at least a result of the relationship between England and Ireland. At the turn of the eighteenth century, the populations of the two countries held very different attitudes toward property. Whereas the three English "revolutions" had generated a model of property that depicted land as an individual possession that entailed absolute rights as well as responsibilities, the Irish experience had produced a competing image—of land as a communal trust whose ownership conferred obligations. The Act of Union subjected Ireland to the English assumption and policies, and the first decades of the century witnessed efforts by Irish landowners to extract rents from their tenants commensurate with these assumptions—despite, and often in bitter confrontation with, the claims of the latter.

For discussions of the Irish land question, see MacDonagh, *States of Mind,* pp. 34–41; Richard Ned Lebow, "Introduction" to *J. S. Mill and the Irish Land Question* (Philadelphia: Institute for the Study of Human Issues, 1979), pp. 3–12; Lebow, *White Britain,* chapter 4; and Michael J. Winstanley, *Ireland and the Land Question, 1800–1922* (London and New York: Methuen, 1984), pp. 1–27.

23. Among the most radical Whigs on this position was Poulett Thomson, for whom Kay campaigned in his successful run for Parliament in 1832.

24. Like many Liberal Tories, some moderate landed Whigs did think that repeal was inevitable, but they never saw it as a panacea. Whigs characteristically supported government noninterference in the economic sphere—laissez-rester—rather than the implicitly more dynamic, because permissive, laissez-faire. See Mandler, *Aristocratic Government,* p. 98.

25. Kay's position is closest to that of the Reverend Thomas Chalmers. Chalmers was the Professor of Moral Philosophy at St. Andrews and was called the "McCulloch of Malthusianism" and "greatest preacher of his age." Kay agreed with Chalmers's condemnation of Speenhamland, his support for abolishing the Corn Laws, and his advocacy of improved morality as the most effective cure for poverty; however, Kay did not oppose reform, as Chalmers did. On Chalmers, see Boyd Hilton, *The Age of Atonement: The Influence of Evangelicalism on Social and Economic Thought, 1785–1865* (Oxford: Clarendon Press, 1988), especially chapter 2.

26. See Boyd Hilton, *Corn, Cash, Commerce: The Economic Policies of the Tory Government, 1815–1830* (Oxford: Clarendon Press, 1977), chapter 1.

27. The inequality of these two parts of Great Britain was also clear in the

legislative reforms of the nineteenth century. The Reform Act of 1832, for example, did not reform Irish representation in Parliament or eliminate Ireland's rotten and pocket boroughs. State-aided elementary education was instituted in Ireland in 1831, with the explicit goal of combatting Irish "disorder." The police and new poor law seemed similar in the two countries, but "the Irish police constituted . . . a paramilitary force, while the Irish poor law could never attempt to deal with such questions as unemployment" (MacDonagh, *States of Mind*, p. 53). MacDonagh's summary comment is that "the same body controlled the legislative process for both, but in the case of Ireland its fundamental object was the maintenance of imperial control" (p. 54).

FOUR

1. Robert Vaughan, *The Age of Great Cities: or, Modern Society Viewed in its Relation to Intelligence, Morals, and Religion* (1843; rpt., New York: Garland Press, 1985), p. 1.

2. *Report from the Select Committee on the Health of Towns* (London: House of Commons, 1840). *Reprints of Economic Classics* (New York: Augustus M. Kelly, 1968), p. iii.

3. *Report*, p. xiv.

4. For contemporary reports of poverty, see the thirty-five volumes in the *Rise of Urban Britain* series, ed. Lynn and Andrew Lees (New York: Garland, 1985).

5. In this essay I do not address at length the party affiliations or disputes that characterized reformers. For my purposes, it is sufficient to note that the issue of government interference divided Whigs and high Tories who otherwise agreed that some reform—especially in the realm of trade—was crucial to social stability and prosperity. In general, the metaphor of the social body was used by Whigs and high Tories, who sought to establish that although what Adam Smith called "the great body of the People" resembled the economy in some ways, it was unlike the economy in requiring some kind of regulation. Most Whigs supported some form of poor relief, educational programs, and sanitary regulation; high Tories tended to endorse paternalism, if not these specific measures. One problem for the Whig program, as I discuss in this essay, was that the image of the social body did not provide any way to determine when and how interference should occur. Liberal Tories, by contrast, generally advocated laissez-faire in the social sphere as well as in trade; they tended to use the metaphor of the machine to describe society. For discussions of this important point, see Peter Mandler, "Tories and Paupers: Christian Political Economy and the Making of the New Poor Law," *The Historical Journal* 33, no. 1 (1990), pp. 81–103; and Boyd Hilton, *The Age of Atonement: The Influence of Evangelicalism on Social and Economic Thought* (Oxford: Clarendon Press, 1988), part 2, especially p. 220.

6. This was not the only image used to figure the city, of course. In addition to the metaphor of the machine, which I discuss in "The Production of Abstract Space" (in this volume), the early nineteenth-century city was represented as a "great wen," a vortex, and a forest. See William Cobbett, *Rural Rides* (1837;

rpt., London: Penguin Books, 1985), p. 321; James Grant, *The Great Metropolis*, vol. 1 (1837; rpt., New York: Garland Press, 1985), p. 17; and Vaughan, *Age of Great Cities*, p. 225.

7. For a general overview of this analogy, see Roy Porter, "Consumption: Disease of the Consumer Society?" in *Consumption and the World of Goods*, ed. John Brewer and Roy Porter (New York: Routledge, 1993), pp. 58–81.

8. Anatomical realism bears some obvious affinities with literary realism, although the latter postdated the former by a few years (cf. *Oliver Twist*). A particularly interesting point of similarity between the two versions of realism is the social analysts' use of scientific objectivity, the literary equivalent of which is narrative omniscience. For a discussion of this point, see Audrey Jaffe, *Vanishing Points: Dickens, Narrative, and the Subject of Omniscience* (Berkeley and Los Angeles: University of California Press, 1991). Other related discussions of realism include Lawrence Rothfield, *Vital Signs: Medical Realism in Nineteenth-Century Fiction* (Princeton: Princeton University Press, 1992), especially pp. 84–119; and Mark Seltzer, *Bodies and Machines* (New York: Routledge, 1992), especially pp. 43–44. Despite the provocative analogies these literary critics draw between various forms of scientific realism and literary realism, my contention is that each discourse conventionalized a variant of realism specific to it and not something abstractable as "realism" in general.

9. A symptomatic example of the mid-eighteenth-century use of abstractions is Henry Fielding's description of an imaginary "progress" through a poor neighborhood: "If we were to make a progress through the outskirts of this town, and look into the habitations of the poor, we should there behold such pictures of human misery as must move the compassion of every heart that deserves the name of human. What indeed, must be his compassion who could see whole families in want of every necessary of life, oppressed with hunger, cold, nakedness, and filth; and with diseases, the certain consequences of all these— what, I say, must be his composition who could look into such a scene as this, and be affected only in his nostrils?" (*A Proposal for Making an Effectual Provision for the Poor . . .* [1753]; reprinted in *The Complete Works of Henry Fielding*, vol. 13 [London: William Heinemann, 1903], p. 141). Typical of early nineteenth-century aristocratic guides to slumming is Pierce Egan, *Life in London* (1820; rpt., London: Methuen, 1904).

10. See Timothy Alborn, "Economic Man, Economic Machine: Images of Circulation in the Victorian Money Market," in *Natural Images of Economic Thought: "Markets Red in Tooth and Claw,"* ed. Philip Mirowski (Cambridge: Cambridge University Press, 1993), pp. 173–96.

11. See Rothfield, *Vital Signs*, pp. xii–xiv.

12. On the Manchester Statistical Society, see David Elesh, "The Manchester Statistical Society: A Case Study of a Discontinuity in the History of Empirical Social Research," *Journal of the History of the Behavioral Sciences* 8 (1972): 280–301, 407–17; and Thomas S. Ashton, *Economic and Social Investigations in Manchester, 1833–1933: A Centenary History of the Manchester Statistical Society* (1933; rpt., Fairfield, Conn.: Augustus M. Kelley, 1977), chapter 2. On the London Statistical Society, see Victor L. Hilts, "*Aliis exterendum,* or, The

Origins of the Statistical Society of London," *Isis* 69 (1978): 21–43. On the Statistical Section of the BAAS (British Association for the Advancement of Science), see Jack Morrell and Arnold Thackray, *Gentlemen of Science: Early Years of the British Association for the Advancement of Science* (Oxford: Oxford University Press, 1981), pp. 36–95. On the SSA, see Philip Abrams, *The Origins of British Sociology, 1834–1914* (Chicago: University of Chicago Press, 1968), pp. 1–52; and Lawrence Goldman, "The Origins of British 'Social Science': Political Economy, Natural Science, and Statistics, 1830–1835," *The Historical Journal* 26 (1983): 587–616.

13. Christopher Lawrence, "The Nervous System and Society in the Scottish Enlightenment," in *Natural Order: Historical Studies of Scientific Culture,* ed. Barry Barnes and Steven Shapin (London: Sage, 1979), pp. 19–40.

14. See Frank Smith, *The Life and Work of Sir James Kay-Shuttleworth* (London: Murray, 1923), chapters 1 and 2; and Ian Inkster, "Marginal Men: Aspects of the Social Role of the Medical Community in Sheffield, 1790–1850," in *Health Care and Popular Medicine,* ed. John Woodward and David Richards (New York: Holmes and Meier, 1979), pp. 128–63.

15. Maxine Berg, *The Machinery Question and the Making of Political Economy, 1815–1848* (Cambridge: Cambridge University Press, 1980), pp. 9–42.

16. Berg, *Machinery,* p. 23.

17. On this aspect of Kay's work, see Frank Mort, *Dangerous Sexualities: Medico-Moral Politics in England Since 1830* (London: Routledge & Kegan Paul, 1987), pp. 18–25; Mary Poovey, "Curing the Social Body in 1832," in this volume; and Anita Levy, *Other Women: The Writing of Class, Race, and Gender, 1832–1898* (Princeton: Princeton University Press, 1991), pp. 20–47.

18. James Phillips Kay, *The Moral and Physical Condition of the Working Classes Employed in the Cotton Manufacture in Manchester,* 2d ed. (London: James Ridgway, 1832), p. 18. All future references will be to this edition and will be cited in the text by page number.

19. Lawrence, "Nervous System and Society," pp. 19–40.

20. Lawrence, "Nervous System and Society," pp. 23–28.

21. The most famous literary use of this term appears in Laurence Sterne's *Tristram Shandy.*

22. On the nature of scientific truth in the nineteenth century, see Lorraine Daston and Peter Galison, "The Image of Objectivity," *Representations* 40 (1992): 81–128.

23. Quoted in Ludmilla Jordanova, "Gender, Generation, and Science: William Hunter's *Obstetrical Atlas,*" in *William Hunter and the Eighteenth-Century Medical World,* ed. W. F. Bynum and Roy Porter (Cambridge: Cambridge University Press, 1985), p. 394.

24. See Jordanova, "Gender, Generation, and Science," p. 394; and Londa Schiebinger, *The Mind Has No Sex? Women in the Origins of Modern Science* (Cambridge, Mass.: Harvard University Press, 1989), p. 201.

25. Quoted in Jordanova, "Gender, Generation, and Science," p. 394.

26. Daston and Galison, "Image," pp. 84–85.

27. See Barbara Maria Stafford, *Body Criticism: Imaging the Unseen in Enlightenment Art and Medicine* (Cambridge, Mass.: MIT Press, 1991), p. 28.

28. Schiebinger, *Mind Has No Sex?*, pp. 201–6.

29. Daston and Galison, "Image," pp. 87–98.

30. Ruth Richardson, *Death, Dissection, and the Destitute* (London: Routledge & Kegan Paul, 1987), pp. 30–51.

31. See Karl Figlio, "Theories of Perception and the Physiology of Mind in the Late Eighteenth Century," *History of Science* 12 (1975), p. 177.

32. Steven Shapin and Simon Schaffer, *Leviathan and the Air-Pump: Hobbes, Boyle, and the Experimental Life* (Princeton: Princeton University Press, 1985), pp. 3–21.

33. The holistic nature of Scottish knowledge as late as the 1830s is clear in this statement by John Barclay, who was a disciple of the philosopher Dugald Stewart and a prominent anatomist: "On the least reflection, it is obvious that man is not only a physical but a moral being; that his physical and moral nature are conjoined, but not confounded" (quoted in Karl Figlio, "The Metaphor of Organization: An Historiographical Perspective on the Bio-Medical Sciences of the Early Nineteenth Century," *History of Science* 14 [1976], p. 41).

34. Lawrence, "Nervous System and Society," pp. 33–34; Steven Shapin, "Property, Patronage, and the Politics of Science: The Founding of the Royal Society of Edinburgh," *British Journal for the History of Science* 7 (1974), pp. 3–40; and Steven Shapin, "The Audience for Science in Eighteenth-Century Edinburgh," *History of Science* 12 (1974), pp. 102–4.

35. L. S. Jacyna, "Images of John Hunter in the Nineteenth Century," *History of Science* 21 (1983), pp. 97–99.

36. See the frontispiece to George Godwin, *London Shadows: A Glance at the "Homes" of the Thousands* (1854; rpt., New York: Garland Press, 1985).

37. On the miasmatic theory of disease, see Charles E. Rosenberg, "Florence Nightingale on Contagion: The Hospital as Moral Universe," in *Healing and History*, ed. Charles E. Rosenberg (New York: Dawson, 1979), pp. 121–23.

38. See Thomas Southwood Smith, *The Philosophy of Health, or, an Exposition of the Physiological and Sanitary Conditions Conducive to Human Longevity and Happiness*, 11th ed. (London: Longman, Green, Longman, Roberts & Green, 1865), pp. 193, 386.

39. See Roger Cooter, "The Power of the Body: The Early Nineteenth Century," in *Natural Order: Historical Studies of Scientific Culture* ed. Barry Barnes and Steven Shapin (London: Sage, 1979), p. 75; Rosenberg, "Florence Nightingale," pp. 117–19.

40. A. J. Youngson, *The Scientific Revolution in Victorian Medicine* (New York: Holmes and Meier, 1979), pp. 12–19.

41. See Poovey, "Curing," in this volume.

42. See Mary Poovey, "Speaking of the Body: Mid-Victorian Constructions of Female Desire," in *Body/Politics: Women and the Discourses of Science*, ed. Mary Jacobus, Evelyn Fox Keller, and Sally Shuttleworth (New York: Routledge, 1990), pp. 30–38.

43. Amanda Anderson, *Tainted Souls and Painted Faces: The Rhetoric of*

Fallenness in Victorian Culture (Ithaca: Cornell University Press, 1993), pp. 22–65,

44. "Moral and Physical Evils of Great Towns," *Foreign Quarterly Review* 38 (1837), p. 182. All future references to this article, the author of which the *Wellesley Index to Victorian Periodicals* does not identify, will be cited in the text by page number.

45. Mary Poovey, "'Figures of Arithmetic, Figures of Speech': The Discourse of Statistics in the 1830s," *Critical Inquiry* 19 (1993), pp. 272–76.

46. See Sally Shuttleworth, "Female Circulation: Medical Discourse and Popular Advertising in the Mid-Victorian Era," in *Body/Politics*, ed. Jacobus, Keller, and Shuttleworth, pp. 48–52, 57–58.

47. From *Prostitution Considered in its Moral, Social, and Sanitary Aspects*. Excerpt in *The Sexuality Debates*, ed. Sheila Jeffreys (New York: Routledge & Kegan Paul, 1987), pp. 53–54.

48. Ludmilla Jordanova, *Sexual Visions: Images of Gender in Science and Medicine between the Eighteenth and Twentieth Centuries* (Madison: University of Wisconsin Press, 1989), pp. 45, 55, 93–98.

49. Jordanova, "Gender, Generation, and Science," pp. 395, 401.

50. W. R. Greg, "Prostitution," *Westminister Review* 53, no. 105 (1850), p. 238.

51. Jordanova, "Gender, Generation, and Science," p. 388.

52. See William A. Cohen, "Manual Conduct in *Great Expectations*," *English Literary History* 60, no. 1 (1993), 221; and D. A. Miller, "Anal *Rope*," *Representations* 32 (1990), p. 118.

53. The SSA was composed of five sections (which suggest just how unlike the modern divisions of the social sciences the subdivisions of this discipline still were in 1857): jurisprudence and amendment of the law; education; punishment and reformation; public health; and social economy. Prostitution was assigned to the social economy section. See *Transactions of the National Association for the Promotion of the Social Sciences* 1 (1858): 605–8.

54. Daston and Galison, "Image," pp. 98–117.

55. Herbert Spencer, "The Social Organism," in *Essays: Scientific, Political, and Speculative* (New York: Appleton, 1891), pp. 265–307.

FIVE

1. See S. E. Finer, "The Transmission of Benthamite Ideas," in *Studies in the Growth of Nineteenth-Century Government*, ed. Gillian Sutherland (Totowa, N.J.: Rowman and Littlefield, 1972), pp. 11–32.

2. See Oliver MacDonagh, "The Nineteenth-Century Revolution in Government," *The Historical Journal* 1 (1958): 52–67. A useful summary of this debate is provided in S. T. Stokes, "Bureaucracy and Ideology: Britain and India in the Nineteenth Century," *Transactions of the Royal Historical Society*, series 5, 80 (1980): 131–36. The relevant documents have been collected in Peter Stansky, ed., *The Victorian Revolution: Government and Society in Victoria's Britain* (New York: New Viewpoints, 1973).

3. Max Weber, "Bureaucracy," and "The Nature of Charismatic Authority," in *Max Weber on Charisma and Institution Building,* ed. S. N. Eisenstadt (Chicago: University of Chicago Press, 1968), pp. 70, and 51–52.

4. On Chalmers's popularity, see Boyd Hilton, *The Age of Atonement: The Influence of Evangelicalism on Social and Economic Thought, 1785–1865* (Oxford: Clarendon Press, 1988), pp. 36–70; and Hugh Watt, *Thomas Chalmers and the Disruption, Incorporating the Chalmers Lectures for 1940–44* (Edinburgh and London: Thomas Nelson and Sons, 1943), pp. 103–7.

5. See Mary T. Furgol, "Chalmers and Poor Relief: An Incidental Sideline?" in *The Practical and the Pious: Essays on Thomas Chalmers (1780–1847),* ed. A. C. Cheyne (Edinburgh: Saint Andrew Press, 1988), pp. 115–29.

6. See Stewart T. Brown, *Thomas Chalmers and the Godly Commonwealth in Scotland* (Oxford: Oxford University Press, 1982), pp. 143–47.

7. Brown, *Thomas Chalmers,* pp. 249–50.

8. On the Disruption, see Watt, *Thomas Chalmers and the Disruption;* and Brown, *Thomas Chalmers,* chapter 6.

9. Quoted in Brown, *Thomas Chalmers,* p. 11.

10. Henry Cockburn, *Memorials of his Time* (Edinburgh and London: T. N. Foulis, 1910), pp. 391, 392.

11. Quoted in Rev. William Hanna, *Memoirs of the Life and Writings of Thomas Chalmers, D.D., LL.D.,* vol. 2 (New York: Harper and Brothers, 1851), pp. 15, 16.

Chalmers's contemporaries and historians alike have repeated this young student's struggle. The efforts to account for the effect of Chalmers's preaching range from phrenological explanations (see Hanna, *Memoirs,* 2:15) to the somewhat more pedestrian suggestion that Chalmers simply told his audiences what they wanted to hear (Owen Chadwick, "Chalmers and the State," in *The Practical and the Pious,* ed. Cheyne, p. 69). Chalmers's eloquence was often compared to both music and theatrical performances (Hanna, *Memoirs,* 3:231; 2:157–58)—comparisons that were made manifest in 1824, when the organizers of an appearance in Manchester advertised that Chalmers would preach with "an orchestra of at least 100 people, three rows of female singers . . . [and] a number of amateurs." Complaining that this arrangement made his sermon "a theatrical performance," Chalmers insisted on retiring from the stage while the orchestra played to the audience of approximately 3,500 people (Hanna, *Memoirs,* 3:64).

12. Quoted in Hanna, *Memoirs,* 2:158.

13. Hanna, *Memoirs,* 2:157.

14. Quoted in A. C. Cheyne, "Introduction," in *The Practical and the Pious,* ed. Cheyne, p. 14.

15. Brown, *Thomas Chalmers,* p. 151; Michel Foucault, *Discipline and Punish: The Birth of the Prison,* trans. Alan Sheridan (New York: Random House, 1979), p. 189.

16. Robert Castel associates this kind of individualism with what he calls "contractual society." "This notion of a 'contractual society,'" is central to

Castel's work on psychiatry, Peter Miller explains in his review of *L'Ordre Psychiatrique;* it "derives from what he terms the 'juridico-administrative fiction' of the contract regulating the circulation and exchange of goods, wealth and social subjects. The citizen in a liberal society is both subject and sovereign and need never encounter the repressive form of State power unless he voluntarily transgresses those laws through which his liberty is defined" ("The Territory of the Psychiatrist," *Ideology and Consciousness* 7 [1980], p. 69).

17. See Joseph A. Schumpeter, *History of Economic Analysis* (New York: Oxford University Press, 1954), pp. 121–22; Michael Walzer, "On the Role of Symbolism in Political Thought," *Political Science Quarterly* 82 (1967): 191–204; and Joyce Oldham Appleby, *Economic Thought and Ideology in Seventeenth-Century England* (Princeton: Princeton University Press, 1978), especially pp. 190–91.

18. The best concise discussion of Chalmers's political economy is Boyd Hilton, "Thomas Chalmers as Political Economist," in *The Practical and the Pious,* ed. Cheyne, pp. 141–56.

19. Thomas Chalmers, "Political Economy of the Bible," *North British Review* 2 (1845): 40.

20. See Hilton, "Thomas Chalmers," pp. 145–51.

21. Thomas Chalmers, *Works of Thomas Chalmers* (Glasgow: William Collins, 1836–42), 14:31.

22. Chalmers, *Works,* 6:266.

23. Brown, *Thomas Chalmers,* p. 238.

24. Brown, *Thomas Chalmers,* pp. 275–78.

25. See Brown, *Thomas Chalmers,* pp. 275–78.

26. E. T. Stokes, "Bureaucracy and Ideology," pp. 143–44.

27. The "imperialism" with which I associate the "coercion" of charisma was absolutely clear in the British and Foreign Bible Society, from which Chalmers derived the organizational details of his cherished "principle of locality." This society was founded in 1804 for the purpose of providing cheap Bibles to readers who could not otherwise own them. Chalmers was particularly impressed by the activities of the Aberdeen Female Servants' Society (founded 1809), for their local branch of the Bible Society attracted members from every class by the simple expedient of requiring a penny-a-week subscription. So taken was Chalmers with the self-improvement that such regular contributions exacted from the female servants that he adopted the principle of a penny-a-week in the Kilmany Bible Association, which he supported throughout his service there. See Hanna, *Memoirs* 1:271 and appendix K, p. 494; Brown, *Thomas Chalmers,* p. 237; and Iain F. Maciver, "Chalmers as 'Manager' of the Church, 1831–1840," in *The Practical and the Pious,* ed. Cheyne, p. 89. On the missionary spirit shared by Chalmers and the Bible Society, see John Roxborough, "Chalmers' Theology of Mission," and Harry R. Sefton, "Chalmers and the Church: Theology and Mission," in *The Practical and the Pious,* ed. Cheyne, pp. 181 and 168, respectively.

28. The phrase "A Despot and a Bureaucrat," which comes from *The Econo-*

mist, is quoted by Anthony Brundage, *England's "Prussian Minister": Edwin Chadwick and the Politics of Government Growth, 1832–1854* (University Park, Pa.: Pennsylvania State University Press, 1988), p. 156.

29. Sidney and Beatrice Webb, *English Poor Law Policy* (London and New York: Longmans, Green, 1910), p. 2.

30. Sidney and Beatrice Webb, *English Local Government from the Revolution to the Municipal Corporations Act: The Manor and the Borough,* vol. 2 (London: Longmans, Green, 1908), p. 76. See also *First Annual Report of the Poor Law Commissioners for England and Wales* (London: W. Clowes and Sons, 1835), p. 97.

31. S. and B. Webb, *Local Government,* pp. 81–82; S. E. Finer, *The Life and Times of Sir Edwin Chadwick* (London: Methuen, 1953), p. 67.

32. This point was not lost on Chadwick's most important modern biographer, S. E. Finer. Chadwick's program, Finer points out, constituted "a ruthless and bureaucratic attempt to keep the ring clear for individual initiative wherever customs or vested interests stood in its way. It meant not merely the removal of obstructive and obsolete laws such as the law of settlement, but a new framework of laws devised to break the connexions between the individual and any institution which prevented him from standing on his own feet" (*Life and Times,* p. 26).

33. Peter Mandler, "The Making of the New Poor Law *Redivivus,*" *Past and Present* 117 (1987), p. 156.

34. *First Annual Report,* p. 62.

35. "The New Poor Law," *Edinburgh Review* 63 (1836), pp. 495, 532.

36. "The New Poor Law," p. 490.

37. "The New Poor Law," p. 504.

38. "The New Poor Law," p. 512.

39. "The New Poor Law," pp. 506, 507, 508.

40. "The New Poor Law," pp. 514, 516.

41. "The New Poor Law," p. 530.

42. "The New Poor Law," p. 524.

43. G. Kitson Clark, "'Statesmen in Disguise': Reflexions on the History of the Neutrality of the Civil Service," *The Historical Journal* 2, no. 1 (1959): 32, 29.

44. Brundage, *England's "Prussian Minister,"* p. 172.

45. Brundage, *England's "Prussian Minister,"* p. 172.

46. Clark, "'Statesmen in Disguise,'" p. 38.

47. *Fourth Annual Report of the Poor Law Commissioners for England and Wales* (London: W. Clowes and Sons, 1838), p. 94.

48. *Fourth Annual Report,* p. 100.

49. *Fourth Annual Report,* p. 100.

50. Finer, *Life and Times,* pp. 24–25.

51. Mandler, "The Making of the New Poor Law," p. 156.

52. Mandler, "The Making of the New Poor Law," p. 157.

53. Jennifer Hart, "Nineteenth-Century Social Reform: A Tory Interpretation of History," *Past and Present* 31 (1965): 59–61.

54. MacDonagh, "The Nineteenth-Century Revolution," p. 54.

55. David Roberts, *Victorian Origins of the British Welfare State* (New Haven: Yale University Press, 1960), p. 103; Hart, "Nineteenth-Century Social Reform," p. 39.

Six

1. Philip Corrigan and Derek Sayer, *The Great Arch: English State Formation as Cultural Revolution* (Oxford: Basil Blackwell, 1985), p. 129.

2. In addition to Corrigan and Sayer's *The Great Arch*, readers interested in the relationship between the public health movement and the consolidation of English government should consult the following: S. E. Finer, *The Life and Times of Sir Edwin Chadwick* (London: Methuen, 1953); R. A. Lewis, *Edwin Chadwick and the Public Health Movement* (London: Longmans, Green, 1952); M. W. Flinn, "Introduction" to [Edwin Chadwick], *Report on the Sanitary Condition of the Labouring Population of Great Britain* (1842; rpt., Edinburgh: Edinburgh University Press, 1965); William C. Lubenow, *The Politics of Government Growth: Early Victorian Attitudes Toward State Intervention, 1833–1848* (Newton Abbot: David & Charles, Archon Books, 1971), chapter 3; John M. Eyler, *Victorian Social Medicine: The Ideas and Methods of William Farr* (Baltimore and London: The Johns Hopkins University Press, 1979); F. B. Smith, *The People's Health, 1830–1910* (New York: Holmes and Meier, 1979); Anthony S. Wohl, *Endangered Lives: Public Health in Victorian Britain* (Cambridge, Mass.: Harvard University Press, 1983); and Frank Mort, *Dangerous Sexualities: Medico-Moral Politics in England Since 1830* (London and New York: Routledge & Kegan Paul, 1987).

3. In this essay, I will use the word *class* in the modern sense, which is loosely derived from Marx's discussion about the determining role played by one's relationship to the mode of production. Elsewhere I have argued that the concept of class has its own history and that the modern usage was being stabilized in the 1830s and 1840s ("The Social Constitution of 'Class': Towards a History of Classificatory Thinking," in *Rethinking Class: Literary Studies and Social Formations,* ed. Wai Chee Dimock and Michael T. Gilmore [New York: Columbia University Press, 1994], pp. 15–16). Here, I want simply to note that the *Sanitary Report* was one of the texts that rendered class status a matter of *calculable* features like longevity. Chadwick's own use of *class* is not consistently modern, however, and sometimes he uses *status* where we would use *class*. For related discussions of the history of *class*, see the essays in Penelope J. Corfield, ed., *Language, History and Class* (Oxford: Basil Blackwell, 1991).

4. Accounts of Chadwick's role in these enterprises can be found in Flinn's "Introduction" to [Chadwick], *Report on the Sanitary Condition*; and Finer, *The Life and Times.*

5. Finer, *The Life and Times,* p. 222. Michael Cullen argues that between 1839 and 1841 Chadwick was converted to the belief that the solution to the

sanitary problem lay in external drainage and sanitation rather than in the improvement of the actual houses themselves, and that this accounts for Chadwick's antipathy toward Robert A. Slaney, who advocated a general building act rather than Chadwick's "arterial system" (*The Statistical Movement in Early Victorian Britain: The Foundations of Empirical Social Research* [New York: Barnes and Noble, 1975], pp. 55–56). As I will argue, however, the fact that Chadwick emphasizes the links between houses and sewers or water supplies places all of these in one system, an urban or social body analogous to the individual body. In none of his projects does Chadwick fully turn away from his focus on the home. He never, for example, takes full account of the time individuals spent away from the home, especially in the streets, the workplace, and so on.

6. [Edwin Chadwick], *Report on the Sanitary Condition of the Labouring Population of Great Britain* (1842; rpt., Edinburgh: Edinburgh University Press, 1965), p. 219. All future references will be cited in the text by page number.

7. See Flinn, "Introduction," in [Chadwick], *Report on the Sanitary Condition*, p. 48.

8. Alexander Welch points out that the term *overcrowding* was new in the nineteenth century and that its use conveyed both a norm and the violation of that norm. See *The City of Dickens* (Oxford: Clarendon Press, 1971), p. 17.

9. Quoted in Cullen, *The Statistical Movement*, p. 72.

10. Hector Gavin, *Sanitary Ramblings, Being Sketches and Illustrations of Bethnal Green. A Type of the Condition of the Metropolis and Other Large Towns* (1848; facsimile ed. London: Frank Cass, 1971); and Henry Mayhew, *The Unknown Mayhew: Selections from the "Morning Chronicle," 1849–50*, ed. Eileen Yeo and E. P. Thompson (Harmondsworth: Penguin, 1973).

11. The New Poor Law encouraged migrant labor because it put an end to the assumption that one's parish would automatically provide relief. After 1834, manufacturers in northern industrial towns encouraged the poor-law commissioners to help transfer redundant agricultural laborers to Lancastershire and Yorkshire. About 4,000 laborers and their families were sent north under this scheme between 1835 and 1837. When industrial depression hit in 1837, however, many of the migrants found themselves out of work. See Michael Rose, ed., *The English Poor Law, 1780–1930* (Newton Abbot: David & Charles, 1971), pp. 102, 107–9.

One could also argue that the number of itinerant workers was swelled by the unpopularity of the New Poor Law. Many people would do anything—including tramp—rather than go to a workhouse. See Gavin, *Sanitary Ramblings*, p. 42. On the so-called wandering tribes, see Raphael Samuel, "Comers and Goers," in *The Victorian City: Images and Realities*, ed. H. J. Dyos and Michael Woolf, vol. 1 (London and Boston: Routledge & Kegan Paul, 1973), pp. 123–60. Samuel points out that "the distinction between the nomadic life and the settled one was by no means hard and fast. Tramping was not the prerogative of the social outcast . . . ; it was a normal phase in the life of entirely respectable classes of working men; it was a frequent resort of the out-of-works; and it was a very principle of existence for those who followed the itinerant callings and trades. Within the wandering tribes themselves the nomadic phase and the settled were often intertwined, with men and women exchanging a fixed occupation for a roving one whenever conditions were favourable" (pp. 152–53).

12. See Brian Harrison, "Pubs," in *The Victorian City*, ed. Dyos and Woolf (London and Boston: Routledge & Kegan Paul, 1973), 1: 175–81.

13. Mayhew's description of the pantomime displays many of these anxieties. See Henry Mayhew, *London Labour and the London Poor*, vol. 1 (New York: Dover, 1969), pp. 40–42.

14. See Mary Poovey, *Uneven Developments: The Ideological Work of Gender in Mid-Victorian England* (Chicago: University of Chicago Press, 1988), chapter 1.

15. See Leonore Davidoff and Catherine Hall, *Family Fortunes: Men and Women of the English Middle Class, 1780–1850* (Chicago: University of Chicago Press, 1987), p. 199.

16. See Peter Stallybrass and Allon White, *The Politics and Poetics of Transgression* (Ithaca: Cornell University Press, 1986), pp. 89–90.

17. See Davidoff and Hall, *Family Fortunes*, part 2.

18. Stallybrass and White, *Politics and Poetics*, pp. 82–84, 94–100. See also Harold Perkin, *The Origins of Modern English Society, 1780–1880* (London: Routledge & Kegan Paul, 1969), chapters 7 and 8.

19. The literature on Chartism is vast. Works I found particularly useful include the following: R. G. Gammage, *The History of the Chartist Movement* (1854; facsimile ed. 1976); M. Hovell, *The Chartist Movement* (Manchester, 1918); Iorwerth Prothero, "Chartism in London," *Past and Present* 44 (1969): 76–105; W. H. Maehl, "Chartist Disturbances in Northeastern England, 1839," *International Review of Social History* 8 (1963): 389–414; J. Epstein and Dorothy Thompson, *The Chartist Experience: Studies in Working Class Radicalism and Culture, 1830–1860* (London: Macmillan, 1982); and Gareth Stedman Jones, "Rethinking Chartism," in G. S. Jones, *Languages of Class: Studies in English Working-Class History, 1832–1982* (Cambridge: Cambridge University Press, 1983), pp. 90–178.

20. For a discussion of nationalism as ideology, see Hugh Kearney, *The British Isles: A History of Four Nations* (Cambridge: Cambridge University Press, 1989), especially chapters 7 and 8.

SEVEN

1. The "romance" of everyday life and the phrase "feelings and passions" are Elizabeth Gaskell's own descriptions of what she wanted to dramatize in *Mary Barton*. See *Mary Barton: A Tale of Manchester Life* (1848; rpt., London: Penguin, 1985), pp. 37, 457. All future references will be to this edition and cited in the text by page number.

Although I have presented the discourse of political economy as "effacing" and "obscuring" an interior world of feelings, I do not want to foreclose the possibility that, far from hiding something that was always present, the discourse of political economy—by hastening the consolidation of the mode of aesthetic-cum-psychological representation I discuss here—actually *created*(the effect of) that which it could not specify. In formulating this dynamic as one of effacement, I am following the conceptualization offered by Gaskell and her contemporaries of the relationship between political-economic discourse and feelings. As I discuss below, however, this conceptualization itself can be seen as a stage in the gradual consolidation of an autonomous psychological domain.

2. On the gendering of modes of knowing in this period, see John Barrell, "The Public Prospect and the Private View: The Politics of Taste in Eighteenth-Century Britain," "The Dangerous Goddess: Masculinity, Prestige, and the Aesthetic in Early Eighteenth-Century Britain," and "Visualising the Division of Labour: William Pyne's *Microcosm*," in *The Birth of Pandora and the Division of Knowledge* (Philadelphia: University of Pennsylvania Press, 1992), pp. 41–62, 63–88, 89–118; David Simpson, *Romanticism, Nationalism, and the Revolt Against Theory* (Chicago: University of Chicago Press, 1993), pp. 104–125; and Mary Poovey, "Aesthetics and Political Economy in the Eighteenth Century: The Place of Gender in the Social Constitution of Knowledge," in *Aesthetics and Ideology,* ed. George Levine (New Brunswick: Rutgers University Press, 1994), pp. 79–105.

3. Quoted in Thom Braun, "Introduction" to *Coningsby, or the New Generation* (1845; rpt. London: Penguin, 1983), p. 15.

4. This depiction of modern subjectivity—which is an effect of the conjuncture of a model of personal maturation figured as growth, the specification of a character's choice of love object as the signifier of that growth, and the refinement of novelistic conventions capable of conveying both interior complexity and change—is best exemplified by Jane Austen's novels. For an argument about the historical specificity of this ensemble, see Clifford Sisken, *The Historicity of Romantic Discourse* (Oxford: Oxford University Press, 1988), chapter 6.

5. Benjamin Disraeli, *Coningsby, or the New Generation* (1845; rpt., London: Penguin Books, 1983), p. 94. All future references will be cited in the text by page number.

6. My suggestion that the aesthetic domain, and the novel in particular, constitutes a totalizing vision of society available nowhere else in modern culture is indebted to Georg Lukács, *The Theory of the Novel,* trans. Anna Bostock (Cambridge, Mass.: MIT Press, 1977).

7. In this discussion of homoeroticism, I am indebted to Eve Kosofsky Sedgwick, *Between Men: English Literature and Male Homosocial Desire* (New York: Columbia University Press, 1985).

8. In *Sybil,* Disraeli does give a female character more prominence, but even there the title character primarily serves as a source of inspiration for the man who reunites the classes in the style of Young England. When she is called on to act, Sybil becomes confused and lost; she fails to reach her father in time, and then she falls senseless in a faint.

9. For discussions of the treatment of domesticity in works by Kay and Chadwick, see my essays "Curing the Social Body in 1832" and "Domesticity and Class Formation: Chadwick's 1842 *Sanitary Report*," in this volume.

10. For discussions of the range of plots in *Mary Barton,* see Catherine Gal-

lagher, *The Industrial Reformation of English Fiction: Social Discourse and Narrative Form, 1832–1867* (Chicago: University of Chicago Press, 1985), pp. 62–87.

11. This point is underscored by Gaskell's characterizations of politics and work. In her accounts, both carry overtones of the gothic horrors with which she also associates psychological turmoil. Here is Gaskell's description of the Chartists' visitations to the Barton home: "Strange faces of pale men, with dark glaring eyes, peered into the inner darkness, and seemed desirous to ascertain if her father were at home. Or a hand and arm (the body hidden) was put within the door, and beckoned him away" (p. 162). Here is Gaskell's depiction of the conditions in which Jem works: "A deep and lurid red glared over all. . . . The men, like demons, in their fire-and-soot colouring, stood swart around. . . . The heat was intense, and the red glare grew every instant more fierce" (p. 214).

12. In addition to the parenthetical digression I discuss, these passages are the last paragraph on p. 301; the last nine lines of the first, incomplete paragraph on p. 303; and the phrase "I am one" on p. 313.

EIGHT

1. David Ricardo, *On the Principles of Political Economy* [1819], vol. 4 of *The Works and Correspondence of David Ricardo*, ed. Piero Sraffa (Cambridge: Cambridge University Press, 1962). For a discussion of the relationship between Ricardo's theories about wealth and contemporary discussions of poverty, see Mitchell Dean, *The Constitution of Poverty: Toward a Genealogy of Liberal Governance* (New York: Routledge, 1991), pp. 148–55.

2. The so-called Christian economists constituted the most prominent example of this tendency. See Boyd Hilton, *The Age of Atonement: The Influence of Evangelicalism on Social and Economic Thought, 1785–1865* (Oxford: Clarendon Press, 1988), especially parts 1 and 2.

3. J. G. A. Pocock, "The Mobility of Property and the Rise of Eighteenth-Century Sociology," in *Virtue, Commerce, and History: Essays on Political Thought and History, Chiefly in the Eighteenth Century* (Cambridge: Cambridge University Press, 1985), pp. 103–124.

4. Helpful discussions of limited liability include H. A. Shannon, "The Coming of General Limited Liability," in *Economic History,* ed. J. M. Keynes and D. H. MacGregor, vol. 2 (London: Macmillan and Co., 1933), pp. 267–91; J. B. Jeffreys, "The Denomination and Character of Shares, 1855–1885," in *Essays in Economic History,* ed. E. M. Carus-Wilson, vol. 1 (London: Edward Arnold, 1954), pp. 344–57; S. G. Checkland, *The Rise of Industrial Society in England, 1815–1885* (London: Longmans, Green, 1964), pp. 39, 43, 104–7, 129–30; and W. T. C. King, *History of the London Discount Market* (London: George Routledge & Sons, 1936), pp. 238–45. One nineteenth-century view of limited liability is provided by David Morier Evans, *Speculative Notes and Notes on Speculation, Ideal and Real* (London: Groombridge and Sons, 1864), pp. 228–36.

A helpful discussion of the differences among partnerships, unincorporated companies, and corporations is provided by P. L. Cottrell. "The key legal difference was that a corporation had its own legal personality, which was independent of that of its shareholders. In the case of a partnership, its rights and liabilities were simply the sum of those who constituted it. The unincorporated company was in a 'grey' area of the law, a consequence of being in some ways the product of opportunism—attempts to establish as close an approximation to a corporation or rather some of the attributes of a corporation without being subject to the scrutiny of the state" (*Industrial Finance, 1830–1914: The Finance and Organization of English Manufacturing Industry* [London and New York: Methuen, 1980], p. 39). See also Leland Hamilton Jenks, *The Migration of British Capital to 1875* (New York & London: Alfred A. Knopf, 1927), pp. 233–62.

5. Quoted in Boyd Hilton, "Chalmers as Political Economist," in *The Practical and the Pious: Essays on Thomas Chalmers (1780–1847)*, ed. A. C. Cheyne (Edinburgh: Saint Andrew Press, 1985), p. 152. Hilton's article is an extremely important interpretation of the limited liability legislation.

6. See Cottrell, *Industrial Finance*, p. 52. Unlike England, other countries, including France, Germany, Belgium, and Italy, imposed safeguards on company formations. These included a minimum of paid-up capital, the registration of the company's prospectus, and the oversight of a registrar.

7. For a discussion of these factors, see Checkland, *Rise of Industrial Society,* pp. 22–26. "Invisible exports" in the 1850s and early 1860s largely consisted of services that produced income for English companies and investors. The largest source of service income was shipping, but monies were also generated by foreign trade, overseas banking, administrative service, and pensions charged to colonial governments (see Peter Mathias, *The First Industrial Nation: An Economic History of Britain, 1700–1914* [New York: Charles Scribner's Sons, 1969], pp. 303–20). In 1864, David Morier Evans estimated that the gold from California and Australia was contributing £21,000,000 per year to the precious-metal reserves of England (Evans, *Speculative Notes*, p. 46).

8. Sir John H. Clapham, *An Economic History of Modern Britain: Free Trade and Steel, 1850–1886* (Cambridge: Cambridge University Press, 1932), p. 371.

9. Here is Checkland on the effect of new forms of mobilizing capital: "The rise of banks and finance companies meant that the centripetal forces were much strengthened—bringing into the money market all kinds of savings scattered about the country and concentrating them for investment. But the newly created centrifugal forces generated by the new institutions were even stronger—seeking means of placing capital with increasing skill. The net effect was a closer mobilization of capital for the more hectic exploitation of a boom, both at home and abroad" (*Rise of Industrial Society,* pp. 50–51).

10. D. Morier Evans noted in 1864 that the banking system was in "a transition stage," and he speculated that the private system would soon be replaced by a joint-stock system (*Speculative Notes,* p. 29). For a history of the bill-discounting system, see King, *London Discount Market.*

11. Quoted in King, *London Discount Market,* pp. 135–36.

12. In 1858, Sheffield Neave testified before the Select Committee on the

Bank Act that the system of "money at call" was responsible for the stress placed on the system, not to mention the creation of dubious paper. "I wished to state that the system of money at call necessarily compels the broker, as well as the banker who takes it, to make immediate use of it, because he could not afford to allow interest if it was not employed at the same instant at a better rate of interest, for the sake of his profit; it therefore occasions the party who takes the money at call to look out for securities wherever he can find them; and not to be very chary in the selection of them, when there is no difficulty in getting them. It leads therefore to the encouragement of an inferior class of bills, and is in some degree instrumental in giving currency to bills that probably ought not to be discounted" (quoted in King, *London Discount Market*, p. 188).

13. See King, *London Discount Market*, pp. 206–7.

14. See King, *London Discount Market*, pp. 207–16.

15. King, *London Discount Market*, p. 238.

16. Here is Evans's densely metaphorical depiction of the spirit of the times: "Gaunt panic, with uncertain gait and distorted visage, stalks hurriedly through the land. Like the leper of old, downcast in mien and paralyzed in limb, his presence is the signal for immediate apprehension, lest his contagious touch should strike with disease sound constitutions, and bleach white the bones of living men. The slightest blast from his lividly scorching breath remorselessly crumples up credit, and destroys, as by the fell wand of the necromancer, the good fame and fortune acquired by long years of toil and steady accumulation" (*Speculative Notes*, p. 36).

17. Meason's articles include one on speculation and joint-stock banks: "Promoters of Companies" (*AYR* 11 [March 12, 1864]: 110–15); "How We 'Floated' the Bank" (*AYR* 12 [December 31, 1864]: 493–97); "'The Bank of Patagonia' (Limited)" (*AYR* 13 [June 17, 1865]: 485–90); "How the Bank Was Wound Up" (*AYR* 13 [April 15, 1865]: 276–82); one on bill broking and accommodation: "Wanted to Borrow, One Hundred Pounds" (*AYR* 13 [March 11, 1865]: 164–68); "Accommodation" (*AYR* 13 [April 8, 1865]: 260–64); "How I Discounted My Bill" (*AYR* 13 [July 8, 1865]: 557–61); one entitled "Going into Business": "Part the First" (*AYR* 13 [May 13, 1865]: 378–82), "Part the Second" (*AYR* 13 [May 20, 1865]: 404–8), "Part the Third" (*AYR* 13 [May 27, 1865]: 428–32); and one entitled "Amateur Finance": "Part 1" (*AYR* 14 [August 12, 1865]: 57–60), "Part 2" (*AYR* 14 [August 19, 1865]: 87–91), "Part 3" (*AYR* 14 [August 26, 1865]: 110–15). Meason also contributed an article entitled "Insurance and Assurance" to *AYR* 13 (June 3, 1865): 437–40. Some of these articles were collected and published as *The Bubble of Finance: Joint-Stock Companies, Promoting Companies, Modern Commerce, Money Lending, and Life Insurance* (London: Sampson Low, Son, and Marston, 1865).

The first number of Charles Reade's *Hard Cash* (serialized as *Very Hard Cash*) appeared in *AYR* 9 (March 28, 1863). The last number appeared in *AYR* 10 (December 26, 1863).

18. This is the series on speculation and joint-stock banks, cited above.

19. Meason, "'The Bank of Patagonia' (Limited)," p. 490.

20. Shannon, who analyzed the limited companies registered in London, es-

timates that 15.15% of all registered companies and 17.18% of all companies formed between 1856 and 1862 were overseas companies. See H. A. Shannon, "The First Five Thousand Limited Companies and Their Duration," in *Economic History,* ed. J. M. Keynes and D. H. MacGregor, vol. 2 (London: Macmillan, 1933), pp. 396–24. See also P. L. Cottrell, *British Overseas Investment in the Nineteenth Century* (London: Macmillan, 1975), p. 29; and Jenks, *Migration of British Capital,* p. 239.

The question of the relative importance of home and overseas markets has been extensively discussed in the literature. Neil McKendrick in particular stresses the importance of home demand, but his focus is primarily the early part of the Industrial Revolution. See "Home Demand and Economic Growth: A New View of the Role of Women and Children in the Industrial Revolution," in *Historical Perspectives: Studies in English Thought and Society,* ed. Neil McKendrick (London: Europa Press, 1974), pp. 152–210. Recent treatments of this subject include P. J. Cain, *Economic Foundations of British Overseas Expansion, 1815–1914* (Basingstoke: Macmillan Education, 1980); Cottrell, *British Overseas Investment;* and Michael Edelstein, *Overseas Investment in the Age of High Imperialism, The United Kingdom, 1850–1914* (New York: Columbia University Press, 1982). Edelstein emphasizes England's superiority in relation to other European nations in its rate of net foreign loans, especially in the 1860s and 1870s (p. 3).

21. McKendrick, "Home Demand," p. 181.

22. See Barry Supple, "Legislation and Virtue: An Essay on Working-Class Self-Help and the State in the Early Nineteenth Century," in *Historical Perspectives,* ed. McKendrick, pp. 211–54.

Some proponents of the limited liability acts argued specifically that the new laws would overcome what differences remained between owners and employees. The new corporations, they argued, by promoting investments by workers in the concerns in which they worked, "would prevent the recurrence of those differences which ending in strikes are a disgrace to our age and to our laws" (quoted in Cottrell, *British Overseas Investment,* p. 48).

23. Jenks points out that promoters of overseas companies organized their firms in forms that would be attractive to British investors partly because they could not be sure that indigenous investors could support them. Thus securities had to be in pounds sterling, and headquarters had to be in Britain (*Migration of British Capital,* p. 239). Edelstein stresses the importance of British perceptions of law, order, and commercial regularity in the countries in which new firms were proposed (*Overseas Investment,* p. 39).

24. The critical point at which Argentina became sufficiently like England to inspire investor confidence was passed after the dictator Juan Manuel de Rosas was driven into exile in 1852 and the country was unified under an American-style constitution in 1862. During the remainder of the 1860s, the Indians in Argentina were suppressed. See Charles A. Jones, "Great Capitalists and the Direction of British Overseas Investment in the Late Nineteenth Century: The Case of Argentina," *Business History* 22 (1980): 153, 157.

25. Meason, "'The Bank of Patagonia' (Limited)," p. 488.

26. Meason, "'The Bank of Patagonia' (Limited)," pp. 485, 488. See also "How the Bank Was Wound Up," p. 277.

27. For a discussion of the relationship between limited liability and the family, see Leonore Davidoff and Catherine Hall, *Family Fortunes: Men and Women of the English Middle Class, 1780–1850* (Chicago: University of Chicago Press, 1987), pp. 200–5.

28. The persistence of familial metaphors, especially those involving growth, also distinguishes modern discussions of company formation. Shannon, for example, writes of "abortive companies" ("The First Five Thousand," p. 401); Jenks describes the creation of a finance company from the "parent" International Land Company as a "birth," and the joining of the two as "incestuous nuptials" (*Migration of British Capital*, p. 250). Jenks also describes company formation as "company obstetrics" (p. 251).

29. The word *race* was used in various ways in mid-Victorian England. Ethnologists in the Prichardian school of thought used the word to refer to differences that could arise from educational, religious, or climatic factors. As early as 1850, the word was also used to designate physical traits that were hereditary. Dickens's and Meason's works embody this imprecision, for they show national differences bleeding into what we would now call racial differences. For Dickens, however, skin color receives more attention than it does in Meason's articles. See George W. Stocking, Jr., *Victorian Anthropology* (New York: Free Press, 1987), especially pp. 64–65.

30. Other treatments of speculation in Victorian novels include N. N. Feltes, "Community and the Limits of Liability in Two Mid-Victorian Novels," *Victorian Studies* 17 (June 1974): 362–67; and Michael Cotsell, "The Book of Insolvent Facts: Financial Speculation in *Our Mutual Friend*," *Dickens Studies Annual* 13 (1985): 125–43.

Characters specifically associated with various kinds of metaphorical and literal speculation include Silas Wegg; that "happy pair of swindlers," the Lammles; Mr. Veneering, who invests £5,000 in the initials "M. P."; and Fascination Fledgeby and his parents.

31. Charles Dickens, *Our Mutual Friend*, ed. Stephen Gill (1864–65; rpt., Harmondsworth: Penguin Books, 1971), p. 160. All future references are to this edition and will be cited in the text.

32. Laurie Langbauer gives this principle more ahistorical significance than I do, but her description of its dynamics is shrewd. She argues that "our forms of representation attempt to order our existence in a way that will establish for the male subject a comfortable relation to what controls him." Langbauer's thesis is that a woman is typically assigned the role of representing—so as to displace— whatever controls the male subject. "Although he cannot ignore or escape it, the system offers him this consolation: it directly reflects his desires . . . and is always there to minister to his needs" ("Woman in White, Men in Feminism," *Yale Journal of Criticism* 2 [April 1989]: 230–31).

33. See Elizabeth K. Helsinger, Robin Lauterbach Sheets, and William Veeder, eds., *The Woman Question: Social Issues, 1837–83* (New York: Garland, 1983), pp. 114–33; and Mary Poovey, "Speaking of the Body: Mid-Victorian

Constructions of Female Desire," in *Body/Politics: Women and the Discourses of Science,* ed. Mary Jacobus, Evelyn Fox Keller, and Sally Shuttleworth (New York and London: Routledge, 1990), pp. 29–46.

34. See Leonore Davidoff, "The Separation of Home and Work? Landladies and Lodgers in Nineteenth and Twentieth-Century England," in *Fit Work for Women,* ed. Sandra Burman (London: Croom Helm, 1979), pp. 74.

35. Lizzie shares the name of another fictional good girl, who does become pregnant out of wedlock: the title character of Elizabeth Gaskell's "Lizzie Leigh," which was published in Dickens's *Household Words* in 1850.

36. For a discussion of this dimension of *Our Mutual Friend,* see Eve Kosofsky Sedgwick, *Between Men: English Literature and Male Homosocial Desire* (New York: Columbia University Press, 1985), pp. 161–79.

37. See Catherine Gallagher, *British Women Writers and the Literary Marketplace* (Berkeley and Los Angeles: University of California Press, forthcoming).

38. According to Gallagher, "as the press became an increasingly important political forum, the correspondence between the words that poured out of it and their putative referents became a topic of concern. Had politics become 'mere' words? . . . Was political discourse 'fictional'? One strategy for answering these questions and containing their attendant anxiety was to divide political writings into the reputable and the disreputable. Foremost in the latter category were the excessively 'feminine' writings of Delarivier Manley, for these were worse than mere fictions with no relation to reality; they were scandals, *discreditings,* that bore a potentially negative relationship to the polity" (*British Women Writers,* p. 176).

39. Gallagher, *British Women Writers,* p. 193.

40. See Davidoff and Hall, *Family Fortunes,* chapter 6.

41. J. W. Kaye, "The 'Non-Existence' of Women," *North British Review* 23 (August 1855): 295.

42. Useful recent works on the Victorian feminist movement include Lee Holcombe, *Wives and Property: Reform of the Married Women's Property Law in Nineteenth-Century England* (Toronto: University of Toronto Press, 1983); Sheila R. Herstein, *A Mid-Victorian Feminist: Barbara Leigh Smith Bodichon* (New Haven: Yale University Press, 1985); Philippa Levine, *Victorian Feminism, 1850–1900* (Tallahassee: Florida State University Press, 1987); and Mary Lyndon Shanley, *Feminism, Marriage, and the Law in Victorian England, 1850–1895* (Princeton: Princeton University Press, 1989).

43. Dickens even has Lizzie say that this work has "softened" her hands (pp. 590–91). This is a particularly ostentatious dismissal of women's work, because women's labor in paper mills was actually one of the hardest and most poorly paid of women's occupations. See Wanda Neff, *Victorian Working Women: An Historical and Literary Study of Women in British Industries and Professions, 1831–1850* (1929; New York: Humanities Press, 1966), p. 100.

44. In his introduction to the Penguin edition of *Our Mutual Friend,* Stephen

Gill calls the Harmon plot "the albatross about Dickens's neck" and book 2, chapter 13—the scene of Harmon's deliberation—"a confession of [narrative] breakdown" (p. 22).

45. In addition to the psychological instability figured in John Harmon's assault, obliterating difference also both creates and destroys any basis for value. This is clear in the inherent structure of speculation. Speculation works as a form of investment because every investor imagines all desire to be the same (other men will want what I want); this similarity of desire, and not intrinsic worth, therefore confers value upon the desired object at the same time that it sets up a competitive relationship among men. Just as value rises out of the sameness of desire, however, so, too, does worthlessness. As every speculator knew, one rumor of insolvency could trigger a panic capable of breaking a bank; one lapse of faith could plummet the price of shares. The structure of speculation is mirrored in the relationship between men and women once difference has been erased. As projections of male desire, women are like stocks. Their "value" is sheerly the effect of male desire, and the more men's desires mirror each other, the greater the value of the woman who is desired. As with stocks again, the rise in a woman's value primarily intensifies the competitive relationships among men. As *Our Mutual Friend* suggests, such competition—whether for money or love—soon turns to violence and a fight to the death.

46. The Anthropological Society of London was established by James Hunt in 1863. Hunt's extreme racist views informed the society and were articulated in papers such as "On the Negro's Place in Nature" (*Memoirs Read Before the Anthropological Society of London* 1 [1863]). The membership of the society had expanded to 500 by 1865. See Ronald Rainger, "Race, Politics, and Society: The Anthropological Society of London in the 1860s," *Victorian Studies* 22 (1978): 51–70. On race and Victorian anthropology, see George W. Stocking, Jr., *Victorian Anthropology* (New York: Free Press, 1987), especially chapters 2, 3, 6, and 7.

47. Angus Wilson makes the following comment on Dickens's attitude toward race: "Gradually, and markedly after the Indian Mutiny in 1857, [Dickens] . . . had come to believe that the white man must dominate and order the world of the blacks and the browns" ("Introduction" to Charles Dickens, *The Mystery of Edwin Drood* [1870]; rpt., Harmondsworth, England: Penguin Books, 1987], p. 25).

48. Useful works on Victorian imperialism include Lance E. Davi and Robert A. Huttenback, *Mammon and the Pursuit of Empire: The Economics of British Imperialism* (Cambridge: Cambridge University Press, 1988), abridged ed.; and Patrick Brantlinger, *Rule of Darkness: British Literature and Imperialism, 1830–1914* (Ithaca: Cornell University Press, 1988).

49. See Brantlinger, *Rule of Darkness*, p. 201 and chapter 7 in general. There is a vast literature on the Indian Mutiny. Some helpful analyses include Sashi Bhussan Chaudhuri, *Theories of the Indian Mutiny (1857–1959)* (Calcutta: World Press, 1968); Pratul Chandra Gupta, *Nana Sahib and the Rising at Cawnpore* (Oxford: Clarendon Press, 1963); Christopher Hibbert, *The Great Mu-*

tiny: India in 1857 (New York: Viking, 1978); Ramesh Chandra Majumdar, *The Sepoy Mutiny and the Revolt of 1857* (Calcutta: Firma K. L. Mukhopadhyay, 1963); Karl Marx and Frederick Engels, *The First Indian War of Independence, 1857–1859* (Moscow: Progress Publishers, 1959); Eric Stokes, *The Peasant Armed: The Indian Revolt of 1857* (Oxford: Clarendon Press, 1986); and Evelyn E. P. Tisdall, *Mrs. Duberly's Campaigns: An English-woman's Experiences in the Crimean War and Indian Mutiny* (London: Jar-rod's, 1963).

Charles Dickens's opinion about the Indian Mutiny was unequivocal. In 1857, he wrote to Angela Burdett-Coutts that "I wish I were Commander in Chief in India. The first thing I would do to strike that Oriental race with amazement (not in the least regarding them as if they lived in the Strand, London, or at Camden Town) should be to proclaim to them in their language that I considered my holding that appointment by leave of God, to mean that I should do my utmost to exterminate the Race upon whom the stain of the late cruelties rested; and that I was there for that purpose and no other, and was now proceeding, with all convenient dispatch and merciful swiftness of execution, to blot it out of mankind and rase it off the face of the Earth" (*Letters*, ed. Walter Dexter [Bloomsbury: Nonesuch Press, 1937–38], 2:889; see also 2:894). See also William Oddie, "Dickens and the Indian Mutiny," *Dickensian* 68 (1972): 3–15.

50. John Stuart Mill, Thomas Carlyle, and Charles Dickens were among those who engaged actively in the Governor Eyre controversy. For accounts of this incident and the controversy it provoked, see Gillian Workman, "Thomas Carlyle and the Governor Eyre Controversy," *Victorian Studies* 18 (1974): 77–102; Don Robotham, *"The Notorious Riot": The Socio-economic and Political Bases of Paul Bogle's Revolt* (Kingston: Institute of Social and Economic Research), Working Paper #28; Bernard Semmel, *The Governor Eyre Controversy* (London: MacGibbon and Kee, 1962); Lorna Simmonds, "Civil Disturbances in Western Jamaica 1838–1865," *Jamaica Historical Review* 14 (1984): 1–17; and Catherine Hall, "Competing Masculinities: Thomas Carlyle, John Stuart Mill and the Case of Governor Eyre," *White, Male and Middle Class: Explorations in Feminism and History* (Cambridge: Polity Press, 1992), pp. 255–95.

51. "The Noble Savage," *Household Words* 168 (June 11, 1853), p. 337. Essays about Dickens and race include Arthur A. Adrian, "Dickens on American Slavery: A Carlylean Slant," *PMLA* 67 (1952): 315–29; Charles Barker, "Muscular Christianity, Race, and *Edwin Drood*," unpublished manuscript (Johns Hopkins University, 1991); William Oddie, *Dickens and Carlyle* (London: Centenary Press, 1972), especially pp. 92–93, 135–42; Donald H. Simpson, "Charles Dickens and Empire," *Library Notes of the Royal Commonwealth Society*, n.s. 162 (June–July 1970): 1–28; and John O. Waller, "Dickens and the American Civil War," *Studies in Philology* 57 (1960): 535–48.

BIBLIOGRAPHY

Abrams, Philip. *The Origins of British Sociology: 1834–1914.* Chicago: University of Chicago Press, 1968.

Acton, William. *Prostitution Considered in Its Moral, Social, and Sanitary Aspects.* Excerpted in *The Sexuality Debates,* edited by Sheila Jeffreys. New York: Routledge, 1987.

Adrian, Arthur A. "Dickens on American Slavery: A Carlylean Slant." *PMLA* 67 (1952): 315–29.

Alborn, Timothy. "Economic Man, Economic Machine: Images of Circulation in the Victorian Money Market." In *Natural Images of Economic Thought: "Markets Red in Tooth and Claw,"* edited by Philip Mirowski, pp. 173–96. Cambridge: Cambridge University Press, 1993.

All the Year Round. Vols. 11–14 (1864–65).

Althusser, Louis, and Etienne Balibar. *Reading Capital.* Translated by Ben Brewster. London: New Left Books, 1970.

Anderson, Amanda. *Tainted Souls and Painted Faces: The Rhetoric of Fallenness in Victorian Culture.* Ithaca: Cornell University Press, 1993.

Appleby, Joyce Oldham. *Economic Thought and Ideology in Seventeenth-Century England.* Princeton: Princeton University Press, 1978.

Ashton, T. S. *Economic and Social Investigation in Manchester, 1833–1933; a Centenary History of the Manchester Statistical Society.* 1933. Reprint. Fairfield, CT: Augustus M. Kelley, 1977.

Babbage, Charles. *On the Economy of Machinery and Manufactures.* London: Charles Knight, 1832.

Bahmueller, Charles F. *The National Charity Company: Jeremy Bentham's Silent Revolution.* Berkeley: University of California Press, 1981.

Barker, Charles. "Muscular Christianity, Race, and *Edwin Drood*." Unpublished ms., Johns Hopkins University.

Barrell, John. "The Dangerous Goddess: Masculinity, Prestige and the Aesthetic in Early Eighteenth-Century Britain." In *The Birth of Pandora and the Division of Knowledge,* pp. 63–88. Philadelphia: University of Pennsylvania Press, 1992.

———. "The Public Prospect and the Private View: The Politics of Taste in Eighteenth-Century Britain." In *The Birth of Pandora and the Division of Knowledge,* pp. 41–62. Philadelphia: University of Pennsylvania Press, 1992.

———. "Visualising the Division of Labour: William Pyne's *Microcosm*." In *The Birth of Pandora and the Division of Knowledge,* pp. 89–118. Philadelphia: University of Pennsylvania Press, 1992.

Berg, Maxine. *The Machinery Question and the Making of Political Economy, 1815–1848.* Cambridge: Cambridge University Press, 1980.

Bivona, Daniel. "'A Gladness of Abasement': Bureaucratic Discipline and European Subjects." Unpublished ms., n.d.

Bolt, Christine. *Victorian Attitudes Toward Race.* London and New York: Routledge & Kegan Paul, 1971.

Bordieu, Pierre. "The Field of Cultural Production, or the Economic World Reversed." Translated by Richard Nice. *Poetics* 12 (1983): 261–56.

———. "The Market as Symbolic Goods." *Poetics* 14 (1985): 13–44.

Brantlinger, Patrick. *Rule of Darkness: British Literature and Imperialism, 1830–1914.* Ithaca: Cornell University Press, 1988.

Breuilly, John. *Nationalism and the State.* Manchester: Manchester University Press, 1982.

Briggs, Asa. *The Age of Improvement.* New York: David McKay, 1959.

Brown, Stewart T. *Thomas Chalmers and the Godly Commonwealth in Scotland.* Oxford: Oxford University Press, 1982.

Brown, Thom. Introduction to *Coningsby, or The New Generation,* by Benjamin Disraeli. 1845. Reprint. London: Penguin, 1983.

Brundage, Anthony. *England's "Prussian Minister": Edwin Chadwick and the Politics of Government Growth, 1832–1854.* University Park, PA: Penn State University Press, 1988.

Burchell, Graham. "Peculiar Interests: Civil Society and Governing 'The System of Natural Liberty.'" In *The Foucault Effect: Studies in Governmentality,* edited by Graham Burchell, Colin Gordon, and Peter Miller, pp. 119–50. Chicago: University of Chicago Press, 1991.

Burton, John Hill. *Political and Social Economy: Its Practical Application.* Edinburgh: W. and R. Chambers, 1849.

Cain, P. J. *Economic Foundations of British Overseas Expansion 1815–1914*. Basingstoke: Macmillan Education, 1980.

Cairns, David, and Shaun Richards. *Writing Ireland: Colonialism, Nationalism, and Culture*. Manchester: Manchester University Press, 1988.

Carlyle, Thomas. "Corn-Law Rhymes." *Edinburgh Review* 110 (1832). Reprint. *The Works of Thomas Carlyle*. Vol. 28. New York: Charles Scribner's Sons, 1904.

———. "Signs of the Times." *Edinburgh Review* 98 (1829). Reprint. *The Works of Thomas Carlyle*. Vol. 27. New York: Charles Scribner's Sons, 1904.

Cascardi, Anthony J. *The Subject of Modernity*. Cambridge: Cambridge University Press, 1992.

Chadhuri, Sashi Bhussan. *Theories of the Indian Mutiny (1857–1959)*. Calcutta: World Press, 1968.

Chadwick, Edwin. "The New Poor Law." *Edinburgh Review* 63 (1836): 487–573.

———. *Report on the Sanitary Condition of the Labouring Population of Great Britain*. 1842. Reprint. Edinburgh: Edinburgh University Press, 1965.

Chadwick, Owen. "Chalmers and the State." In *The Practical and the Pious: Essays on Thomas Chalmers (1780–1847)*, edited by A. C. Cheyne, pp. 65–83. Edinburgh: Saint Andrew Press, 1988.

Chalmers, Thomas. *On the Christian and Economic Polity of a Nation*. Vol. 14 of *The Works of Thomas Chalmers*. Glasgow: William Collins, 1836–42, 1845.

———. "Political Economy of the Bible." *North British Review* 2 (1845): 1–52.

Chambers, William. *Manuals for the Working Classes: [Robert] Chambers Social Science Tracts. Embracing Subjects Connected with Social, Political, and Sanitary Economy*. Vol. 2 of *Political and Social Economy*. London: Chambers, 1861–62.

Checkland, S. G. *The Rise of Industrial Society in England, 1818–1885*. London: Longmans, Green, 1964.

Cheyne, A. C. Introduction to *The Practical and the Pious: Essays on Thomas Chalmers (1780–1847)*, pp. 9–30. Edinburgh: Saint Andrew Press, 1988.

Child, Josiah. *Brief Observations Concerning Trade, and Interest of Money*. London: Elizabeth Calvert and Henry Mortlock, 1688.

Clapham, Sir John H. *An Economic History of Modern Britain: Free Trade and Steel, 1850–1886*. Cambridge: Cambridge University Press, 1932.

Clark, J. C. D. *English Society 1688–1832: Ideology, Social Structure, and Political Practices During the Ancien Régime*. Cambridge: Cambridge University Press, 1985.

Clokie, Hugh McDowall, and J. William Robinson. *Royal Commissions of In-*

quiry: The Significance of Investigations in British Politics. Stanford: Stanford University Press, 1937. Reprint. New York: Octagon Books, 1969.

Cobbett, William. *Rural Rides.* 1830. Reprint. London: Penguin Books, 1985.

Cockburn, Henry. *Memorials of His Time.* Edinburgh and London: T. N. Foulis, 1910.

Cohen, William A. "Manual Conduct in *Great Expectations.*" *English Literary History* 60 (1993): 217–59.

Colley, Linda. *Britons: Forging the Nation, 1707–1837.* New Haven: Yale University Press, 1992.

———. "Whose Nation? Class and National Consciousness in Britain, 1750–1830." *Past and Present* 113 (1986): 97–117.

Collini, Stefan, Donald Winch, and John Burrow. *That Noble Science of Politics: A Study in Nineteenth-Century Intellectual History.* Cambridge: Cambridge University Press, 1983.

Cooter, Roger. "The Power of the Body: The Early Nineteenth Century." In *Natural Order: Historical Studies of Scientific Culture,* edited by Barry Barnes and Steven Shapin, pp. 73–90. London: Sage, 1979.

Corfield, Penelope J., ed. *Language, History and Class.* Oxford: Basil Blackwell, 1991.

Corrigan, Philip, and Derek Sayer. *The Great Arch: English State Formation as Cultural Revolution.* Oxford: Basil Blackwell, 1985.

Costell, Michael. "The Book of Insolvent Facts: Financial Speculation in *Our Mutual Friend.*" *Dickens Studies Annual* 13 (1985): 125–43.

Cottrell, P. L. *British Overseas Investment in the Nineteenth Century.* London: Macmillan Press, 1975.

———. *Industrial Finance, 1830–1914: The Finance and Organization of English Manufacturing Industry.* London and New York: Methuen, 1980.

Crary, Jonathan. *Techniques of the Observer: On Vision and Modernity in the Nineteenth Century.* Cambridge, MA: MIT Press, 1990.

Cullen, Michael J. *The Statistical Movement in Early Victorian Britain: The Foundations of Empirical Social Research.* New York: Barnes and Noble, 1975.

Daston, Lorraine. "Baconian Facts, Academic Civility, and the Prehistory of Objectivity." *Annals of Scholarship* 8 (1991): 337–64.

———. "Historical Epistemology." In *Questions of Evidence: Proof, Practice, and Persuasion Across the Disciplines,* edited by James Chandler, Arnold I. Davidson, and Harry Harootunian, pp. 282–89. Chicago: University of Chicago Press, 1994.

———. "Marvelous Facts and Miraculous Evidence in Early Modern Europe." *Critical Inquiry* 18 (1991): 93–124.

————, and Peter Galison. "The Image of Objectivity." *Representations* 40 (1992): 81–128.

Davi, Lance E., and Robert A. Huttenback. *Mammon and the Pursuit of Empire: The Economics of British Imperialism.* Abridged ed. Cambridge: Cambridge University Press, 1988.

Davidoff, Leonore. "The Rationalization of Housework." In *Dependence and Exploitation in Work and Marriage,* edited by Diana Leonard Barker and Sheila Allen, pp. 121–51. London: Longmans, 1976.

————. "The Separation of Home and Work? Landladies and Lodgers in Nineteenth and Twentieth-Century England." In *Fit Work for Women,* edited by Sandra Burman, pp. 64–97. London: Croom Helm, 1979.

————, and Catherine Hall. *Family Fortunes: Men and Women of the English Middle Class, 1780–1850.* Chicago: University of Chicago Press, 1987.

Davison, Graeme. "The City as Natural System: Theories of Urban Society in Early Nineteenth-Century Britain." In *The Pursuit of Urban History,* edited by Derek Fraser and Anthony Sutcliffe, pp. 349–70. London: Edward Arnold, 1983.

Dean, Mitchell. *The Constitution of Poverty: Toward a Genealogy of Liberal Governance.* London and New York: Routledge, 1991.

Denecke, Daniel. "A Sort of Counterpoise: Social Economy in England: 1831–1863." Unpublished paper, Johns Hopkins University, 1993.

Dickens, Charles. *Letters.* Edited by Walter Dexter. Vol. 2. Bloomsbury: Nonesuch Press, 1937–38.

————. "The Noble Savage." *Household Words* 168 (1853): 337.

————. *Our Mutual Friend.* 1864–65. Reprint. Harmondsworth: Penguin Books, 1971.

Disraeli, Benjamin. *Coningsby, or the New Generation.* 1845. Reprint. London: Penguin Books, 1983.

Ducrocq, Françoise. "The London Biblewomen and Nurses Mission, 1857–1880: Class Relations/Women's Relations." In *Women and the Structure of Society: Selected Research from the Fifth Berkshire Conference on the History of Women,* edited by Barbara Harris and JoAnn McNamara, pp. 98–107. Durham, NC: Duke University Press, 1984.

Edelstein, Michael. *Overseas Investment in the Age of High Imperialism: The United Kingdom, 1850–1914.* New York: Columbia University Press, 1982.

Edgerton, Samuel Y., Jr. *The Heritage of Giotto's Geometry: Art and Science on the Eve of the Scientific Revolution.* Ithaca: Cornell University Press, 1991.

Edsall, Nicholas C. *The Anti-Poor Law Movement, 1834–44.* Manchester: University of Manchester Press, 1971.

Egan, Pierce. *Life in London.* 1820. London: Methuen, 1904.

Elesh, David. "The Manchester Statistical Society: A Case Study of a Discontinuity in the History of Empirical Social Research." *Journal of the History of the Behavioral Sciences* 8 (1972): 280–301 and 407–17.

Ellis, Sarah Stickney. *The Mothers of England*. In *The Family Monitor and Domestic Guide*. New York: Henry G. Langley, 1844.

Engels, Frederick. *The Condition of the Working Class in England*. 1844–45. Reprint. Oxford: Basil Blackwell, 1958.

Epstein, James, and Dorothy Thompson. *The Chartist Experience: Studies in Working-Class Radicalism and Culture, 1830–1860*. London: Macmillan, 1982.

Evans, David Morier. *Speculative Notes and Notes on Speculation, Ideal and Real*. London: Groombridge and Sons, 1864.

Eyler, John M. *Victorian Social Medicine: The Ideas and Methods of William Farr*. Baltimore, MD: Johns Hopkins University Press, 1979.

Feltes, N. N. "Community and the Limits of Liability in Two Mid-Victorian Novels." *Victorian Studies* 17 (1974): 362–67.

Fielding, Henry. *A Proposal for Making an Effectual Provision for the Poor . . . 1753. The Complete Works of Henry Fielding*. Vol. 13. London: William Heinemann, 1903.

Figlio, Karl. "The Metaphor of Organization: An Historical Perspective on the Bio-Medical Sciences of the Early Nineteenth Century." *History of Science* 14 (1976): 17–53.

———. "Theories of Perception and the Physiology of the Mind in the Late Eighteenth Century." *History of Science* 12 (1975): 177–212.

Finer, S. E. *The Life and Times of Sir Edwin Chadwick*. London: Methuen, 1952–53.

———. "The Transmission of Benthamite Ideas." In *Studies in the Growth of Nineteenth-Century Government*, edited by Gillian Sutherland, pp. 11–32. Totowa, NJ: Rowman and Littlefield, 1972.

First Annual Report of the Poor Law Commissioners for England and Wales. London: W. Clowes and Sons, 1835–36.

Flinn, M. W. Introduction to *Report on the Sanitary Condition of the Labouring Population of Great Britain*, by Edwin Chadwick. 1842. Reprint. Edinburgh: Edinburgh University Press, 1965.

Fontana, Biancamaria. *Rethinking the Politics of Commercial Society: The "Edinburgh Review" 1802–1832*. Cambridge: Cambridge University Press, 1985.

Forset, Edward. *A Comparative Discourse of the Bodies Natural and Politique*. London: Printed for John Bill, 1606.

Foster, John. "Nationality, Social Change, and Class: Transformations of National Identity in Scotland." In *The Making of Scotland: Nation, Culture, and Social Change*, edited by David McCrone, Stephen Kendrick, and Pat Straw, pp. 31–52. Edinburgh: Edinburgh University Press, 1989.

Foucault, Michel. *Discipline and Punish: The Birth of the Prison.* Translated by Alan Sheridan. New York: Vintage Books, 1979.

———. "Governmentality." In *The Foucault Effect: Essays in Governmentality,* edited by Graham Burchell, Colin Gordon, and Peter Miller, pp. 87–104. Chicago: University of Chicago Press, 1991.

———. "The Order of Discourse." In *Untying the Text: A Post-Structuralist Reader,* edited by Robert Young, pp. 48–78. Boston: Routledge & Kegan Paul, 1981.

———. *The Order of Things: An Archaeology of the Human Sciences.* Anonymous translator. New York: Random House, 1970.

———. *Power/Knowledge: Selected Interviews and Other Writings, 1972–1977.* Translated by Colin Gordon. New York: Pantheon Books, 1980.

Fourth Annual Report of the Poor Law Commissioners for England and Wales. London: W. Clowes and Sons, 1838.

Freud, Sigmund. "Fetishism." In *The Standard Edition of the Complete Psychological Works of Sigmund Freud,* vol. 21, pp. 152–57. Edited by James Strachey and Anna Freud. London: Hogarth Press and the Institute of Psychoanalysis, 1966–74.

Freyer, Peter. *Staying Power: The History of Black People in Britain.* London: Pluto Press, 1987.

Furgol, Mary T. "Chalmers and Poor Relief: An Incidental Sideline?" In *The Practical and the Pious: Essays on Thomas Chalmers (1780–1847),* edited by A. C. Cheyne, pp. 115–29. Edinburgh: Saint Andrew Press, 1988.

Gallagher, Catherine. "The Bioeconomics of *Our Mutual Friend.*" In *Subject to History: Ideology, Class, Gender,* edited by David Simpson, pp. 47–64. Ithaca: Cornell University Press, 1991.

———. "The Body Versus the Social Body in the Works of Thomas Malthus and Henry Mayhew." *Representations* 14. Reprinted in *The Making of the Modern Body: Sexuality and Society in the Nineteenth Century,* edited by Gallagher and Thomas Laqueur, pp. 83–106. Berkeley: University of California Press, 1987.

———. *British Women Writers and the Literary Marketplace.* Berkeley: University of California Press, forthcoming.

———. *The Industrial Reformation of English Fiction: Social Discourse and Narrative Form, 1832–1867.* Chicago: University of Chicago Press, 1985.

Gammage, R. G. *The History of the Chartist Movement.* 1854. Reprint. New York: A. M. Kelley, 1976.

Gaskell, Elizabeth. *Mary Barton: A Tale of Manchester Life.* 1848. Reprint. London: Penguin, 1985.

Gavin, Hector. *Sanitary Ramblings, Being Sketches and Illustrations of Bethnal Green. A Type of the Condition of the Metropolis and Other Large Towns.* 1848. Reprint. London: Frank Cass, 1971.

Gellner, Ernest. *Nations and Nationalism.* Oxford: Basil Blackwell, 1983.

———. *Thought and Change.* London: Weidenfeld, 1964.

Godwin, George. *London Shadows: A Glance at the "Homes" of the Thousands.* 1854. Reprint. New York: Garland Press, 1985.

Goldman, Lawrence. "The Origins of British 'Social Science': Political Economy, Natural Science, and Statistics, 1830–1835." *The Historical Journal* 26 (1983): 587–616.

———. "A Peculiarity of the English? The Social Science Association and the Absence of Sociology in Nineteenth-Century Britain." *Past and Present* 114 (1987): 133–71.

Grant, James. *The Great Metropolis.* Vol. 1. 1830. Reprint. New York: Garland Press, 1985.

Greenblatt, Stephen. "Invisible Bullets: Renaissance Authority and Its Subversion, *Henry IV* and *Henry V.*" In *Political Shakespeare: New Essays in Cultural Materialism,* edited by Jonathan Dollimore and Alan Sinfield, pp. 18–47. Ithaca: Cornell University Press, 1985.

Greg, W. R. "Prostitution." *Westminster Review* 53 (1850): 238–68.

Guillory, John. *Cultural Capital: The Problem of Literary Canon Formation.* Chicago: University of Chicago Press, 1993.

Gupta, Pratul Chandra. *Nana Sahib and the Rising at Cawnpore.* Oxford: Clarendon Press, 1963.

Habermas, Jürgen. *The Philosophical Discourse of Modernity: Twelve Lectures.* Translated by Frederick G. Lawrence. Cambridge, MA: MIT Press, 1993.

Hall, Catherine. "Competing Masculinities: Thomas Carlyle, John Stuart Mill, and the Case of Governor Eyre." In *White, Male, and Middle Class: Explorations in Feminism and History,* pp. 255–95. Cambridge: Polity Press, 1992.

———. "Missionary Stories: Gender and Ethnicity in England in the 1830s and 1840s." In *White, Male, and Middle Class: Explorations in Feminism and History,* pp. 205–54. Cambridge: Polity Press, 1992.

———. *White, Male, and Middle Class: Explorations in Feminism and History.* Cambridge: Polity Press, 1992.

Hanna, Rev. William. *Memoirs of the Life and Writings of Thomas Chalmers, D.D., LL.D.* 3 vols. New York: Harper and Brothers, 1851.

Hansard's Parliamentary Debates, 3d series, vol. 73 (1844).

Harrison, Brian. "Pubs." In *The Victorian City: Images and Realities,* vol. 1, edited by H. J. Dyos and Michael Woolf, pp. 175–81. London and Boston: Routledge & Kegan Paul, 1973.

Harrison, Rachel, and Frank Mort. "Patriarchal Aspects of Nineteenth-Century State Formation: Property Relations, Marriage and Divorce, and Sexuality." In *Capitalism, State Formation, and Marxist Theory: Historical Investigations,* edited by Philip Corrigan, pp. 79–109. London: Quartet Books, 1980.

Hart, Jennifer. "Nineteenth-Century Social Reform: A Tory Interpretation of History." *Past and Present* 31 (1965): 39–61.

Hatchey, Thomas E., and Lawrence J. McCaffrey, eds. *Perspectives on Irish Nationalism.* Lexington: University Press of Kentucky, 1989.

Hechter, Michael. *Internal Colonialism: The Celtic Fringe in British National Development, 1536–1966.* Berkeley: University of California Press, 1975.

Helsinger, Elizabeth K., Robin Lauterbach Sheets, and William Veeder, eds. *The Woman Question: Social Issues, 1837–83.* 3 vols. New York: Garland, 1983.

Herbert, Christopher. *Culture and Anomie: Ethnographic Imagination in the Nineteenth Century.* Chicago: University of Chicago Press, 1991.

Herstein, Sheila R. *A Mid-Victorian Feminist, Barbara Leigh Smith Bodichon.* New Haven: Yale University Press, 1985.

Hibbert, Christopher. *The Great Mutiny: India in 1857.* New York: Viking, 1978.

Hilton, Boyd. *The Age of Atonement: The Influence of Evangelicalism on Social and Economic Thought, 1795–1865.* Oxford: Clarendon Press, 1988.

———. *Corn, Cash, Commerce: The Economic Policies of the Tory Government, 1815–1830.* Oxford: Clarendon Press, 1977.

———. "Thomas Chalmers as Political Economist." In *The Practical and the Pious: Essays on Thomas Chalmers (1780–1847),* edited by A. C. Cheyne, pp. 141–56. Edinburgh: Saint Andrew Press, 1988.

Hilts, Victor L. "*Aliis exterendum,* or, the Origins of the Statistical Society of London." *Isis* 69 (1978): 21–43.

Himmelfarb, Gertrude. *The Idea of Poverty: England in the Early Industrial Age.* New York: Vintage Books, 1985.

Hobbes, Thomas. *Leviathan.* 1651. Harmondsworth: Penguin Books, 1968.

Holcombe, Lee. *Wives and Property: Reform of the Married Women's Property Law in Nineteenth-Century England.* Toronto: University of Toronto Press, 1983.

Hollis, Patricia, ed. *Pressure from Without in Early Victorian England.* London: Routledge & Kegan Paul, 1974.

Horkheimer, Max, and Theodor Adorno. *Dialectic of Enlightenment.* Translated by John Cumming. New York: Seabury Press, 1972.

Hovell, M. *The Chartist Movement.* Manchester: Manchester University Press, 1918.

Howsam, Leslie. *Cheap Bibles: Nineteenth-Century Publishing and the British and Foreign Bible Society.* Cambridge: Cambridge University Press, 1991.

Hume, David. "Of Commerce." In *Essays Moral, Political, and Literary,* edited by Eugene F. Miller, pp. 253–67. Indianapolis: Liberty Classics, 1985.

————. "Of Refinement in the Arts." In *Essays Moral, Political, and Literary*, edited by Eugene F. Miller, pp. 268–80. Indianapolis: Liberty Classics, 1985.

————. "Of the First Principles of Government." In *Essays Moral, Political, and Literary*, edited by Eugene F. Miller, pp. 32–42. Indianapolis: Liberty Classics, 1985.

————. "Of the Rise and Progress of the Arts and Sciences." In *Essays Moral, Political, and Literary*, edited by Eugene F. Miller, pp. 111–37. Indianapolis: Liberty Classics, 1985.

Hunt, James. "On the Negro's Place in Nature." *Memoirs Read Before the Anthropological Society of London* 1 (1863).

Hunter, Ian. *Culture and Government: The Emergence of Literary Education*. London: Macmillan, 1988.

————. "Personality as a Vocation: The Political Rationality of the Humanities." *Economy and Society* 19 (1990): 391–430.

Inkster, Ian. "Marginal Men: Aspects of the Social Role of the Medical Community in Sheffield, 1790–1850." In *Health Care and Popular Medicine*, edited by John Woodward and David Richards, pp. 128–63. New York: Holmes and Meier, 1979.

Jacyna, L. S. "Images of John Hunter in the Nineteenth Century." *History of Science* 21 (1983): 85–108.

Jaffe, Audrey. *Vanishing Points: Dickens, Narrative, and the Subject of Omniscience*. Berkeley: University of California Press, 1991.

Jameson, Fredric. "Postmodernism, or the Cultural Logic of Late Capitalism." *New Left Review* 146: 59–92.

Jeffreys, J. B. "The Denomination and Character of Shares, 1855–1885." In *Economic History*, vol. 1, edited by E. M. Carus-Wilson, pp. 344–57. London: Edward Arnold, 1954.

Jenks, Leland Hamilton. *The Migration of British Capital to 1875*. New York and London: Alfred P. Knopf, 1927.

Jones, Charles A. "Great Capitalists and the Direction of British Overseas Investment in the Late Nineteenth Century: The Case of Argentina." *Business History* 22 (1980): 152–69.

Jordanova, Ludmilla. "Gender, Generation, and Science: William Hunter's Obstetrical Atlas." In *William Hunter and the Eighteenth-Century Medical World*, edited by W. F. Bynum and Roy Porter, pp. 385–412. Cambridge: Cambridge University Press, 1985.

————. *Sexual Visions: Images of Gender in Science and Medicine between the Eighteenth and Twentieth Centuries*. Madison: University of Wisconsin Press, 1989.

Journal of the Statistical Society of London 1 (1833).

Kantorowicz, Ernst H. *The King's Two Bodies: A Study in Medieval Political Theology*. Princeton: Princeton University Press, 1957.

Kay, James Phillips. *The Moral and Physical Condition of the Working Classes Employed in the Cotton Manufacture in Manchester*. 2d ed. enlarged. London: James Ridgway, 1832.

[Kay, James Phillips]. "On the Establishment of County or District Schools, for the Training of the Pauper Children Maintained in Union Workhouses." *Journal of the Statistical Society of London* 1 (1833): 14–27.

Kaye, J. W. "The 'Non-Existence' of Women." *North British Review* 23 (1855): 288–302.

Kearney, Hugh. *The British Isles: A History of Four Nations*. Cambridge: Cambridge University Press, 1989.

King, W. T. C. *History of the London Discount Market*. London: George Routledge & Sons, 1936.

Kitson Clark, G. "'Statesmen in Disguise': Reflexions on the History of the Neutrality of the Civil Service." *The Historical Journal* 2 (1959): 19–39.

Knott, John. *Popular Opposition to the 1834 Poor Law*. London: Croom Helm, 1986.

Kydd, Samuel H. G. [Alfred, pseud.]. *The History of the Factory Movement*. 1857. Reprint. New York: Augustus M. Kelley, 1966.

Langbauer, Laurie. "Woman in White, Men in Feminism." *Yale Journal of Criticism* 2 (1989): 219–43.

Lawrence, Christopher. "The Nervous System and Society in the Scottish Enlightenment." In *Natural Order: Historical Studies of Scientific Culture*, edited by Barry Barnes and Steven Shapin, pp. 19–40. London: Sage, 1979.

Lebow, Richard Ned. "British Images of Poverty in Pre-Famine Ireland." In *Views of the Irish Peasantry, 1800–1916*, edited by Daniel J. Casey and Robert E. Rhodes, pp. 57–85. Hamden, CT: Archon Books, 1977.

———. Introduction to *J. S. Mill and the Irish Land Question*, pp. 3–12. Philadelphia: Institute for the Study of Human Issues, 1979.

———. *White Britain and Black Ireland: The Influence of Stereotypes on Colonial Policy*. Philadelphia: Institute for the Study of Human Issues, 1976.

Lees, Lynn Hollen. *Exiles of Erin: Irish Migrants in Victorian London*. Ithaca: Cornell University Press, 1979.

———, and Andrew Lees, eds. *Rise of Urban Britain*. 35 vols. New York: Garland, 1985.

Lefebvre, Henri. *The Production of Space*. Translated by Donald Nicholson-Smith. Oxford: Basil Blackwell, 1991.

Letwin, William. *The Origins of Scientific Economics: English Economic Thought, 1660–1776*. New York: Methuen, 1963.

Levine. Philippa. *Victorian Feminism, 1850–1900.* Tallahassee: Florida State University Press, 1987.

Levy, Anita. *Other Women: The Writing of Class, Race, and Gender, 1832–1898.* Princeton: Princeton University Press, 1991.

Lewes, C. L. *Southwood Smith: A Retrospect.* Edinburgh: Edinburgh University Press, 1889.

Lewis, Jane. *Women and Social Action in Victorian and Edwardian England.* Aldershot: Edward Elgar, 1991.

Lewis, R. A. *Edwin Chadwick and the Public Health Movement, 1832–1854.* London: Longmans, Green, 1952.

Lorimer, Douglas. *Colour, Class, and the Victorians.* Leicester: Leicester University Press, 1978.

Lubenow, William C. *The Politics of Government Growth: Early Victorian Attitudes Toward State Intervention, 1833–1848.* Newton Abbot: David & Charles, Archon Books, 1971.

Lukács, Georg. "Reification and the Consciousness of the Proletariat." In *History and Class Consciousness: Studies in Marxist Dialectics,* translated by Rodney Livingstone, pp. 83–222. Cambridge, MA: MIT Press, 1971.

———. *The Theory of the Novel.* Translated by Anna Bostock. Cambridge, MA: MIT Press, 1977.

MacDonagh, Oliver. "The Nineteenth-Century Revolution in Government." *The Historical Journal* 1 (1958): 52–67.

———. *States of Mind: A Study of Anglo-Irish Conflict 1780–1980.* London: George Allen and Unwin, 1983.

Maciver, Iain F. "Chalmers as 'Manager' of the Church, 1831–40." In *The Practical and the Pious: Essays on Thomas Chalmers (1780–1847),* edited by A. C. Cheyne, pp. 84–97. Edinburgh: Saint Andrew Press, 1988.

Maehl, W. H. "Chartist Disturbances in Northeastern England, 1839." *International Review of Social History* 8 (1963): 389–414.

Majumdar, Ramesh Chandra. *The Sepoy Mutiny and the Revolt of 1857.* Calcutta: Firma K. L. Mukhopadhyay, 1963.

Mandler, Peter. *Aristocratic Government in the Age of Reform: Whigs and Liberals, 1830–1852.* Oxford: Clarendon Press, 1990.

———. "The Making of the New Poor Law *Redivivus.*" *Past and Present* 117 (1987): 131–57.

———. "Tories and Paupers: Christian Political Economy and the Making of the New Poor Law." *The Historical Journal* 33 (1990): 81–103.

Manton, Jo. *Mary Carpenter and the Children of the Streets.* London: Heinemann, 1976.

Marshall, Dorothy. *The English Poor in the Eighteenth Century: A Study in Social and Administrative History*. London: George Routledge & Sons, 1926.

Martin, Julian. *Francis Bacon, The State, and the Reform of Natural Philosophy*. Cambridge: Cambridge University Press, 1992.

Marx, Karl. *Capital: A Critique of Political Economy*. 1867. Translated by Ben Fowkes. Harmondsworth: Penguin Books, 1976.

————, and Frederick Engels. *The First Indian War of Independence 1857–1859*. Moscow: Progress Publishers, 1959.

————, and Frederick Engels. "Introduction to a Critique of Political Economy." In *The German Ideology*, edited by C. J. Arthur. New York: International Publishers, 1986.

Mathias, Peter. *The First Industrial Nation: An Economic History of Britain, 1700–1914*. New York: Charles Scribner's Sons, 1969.

Mayhew, Henry. *London Labour and the London Poor*. 4 volumes. New York: Dover, 1969.

————. *The Unknown Mayhew: Selections from the "Morning Chronicle" 1849–50*. Edited by Eileen Yeo and E. P. Thompson. Harmondsworth: Penguin, 1973.

McKendrick, Neil. "Home Demand and Economic Growth: A New View of the Role of Women and Children in the Industrial Revolution." In *Historical Perspectives: Studies in English Thought and Society*, edited by Neil McKendrick, pp. 152–210. London: Europa Press, 1974.

Meason, Malcolm Ronald Laing. *The Bubble of Finance: Joint-Stock Companies, Promoting Companies, Modern Commerce, Money Lending, and Life Insurance*. London: Sampson Low, Son, and Marston, 1865.

Miller, D. A. "Anal *Rope*." *Representations* 32 (1990): 114–33.

————. *The Novel and the Police*. Berkeley: University of California Press, 1985.

Miller, Peter. "Accounting and Objectivity: The Invention of Calculating Selves and Calculable Spaces." *Annals of Scholarship* 9 (1992): 61–86.

————. "The Territory of the Psychiatrist." *Ideology and Consciousness* 7 (1980): 63–105.

"Moral and Physical Evils of Great Towns." *Foreign Quarterly Review* 38 (1837): 181–91.

Morrell, Jack, and Arnold Thackray. *Gentlemen of Science: Early Years of the British Association for the Advancement of Science*. Oxford: Oxford University Press, 1981.

Mort, Frank. *Dangerous Sexualities: Medico-Moral Politics in England Since 1830*. London and New York: Routledge & Kegan Paul, 1987.

Neff, Wanda. *Victorian Working Women: An Historical and Literary Study of*

Women in British Industries and Professions, 1831–1850. 1929. New York: Humanities Press, 1966.

Newman, Gerald. *The Rise of English Nationalism: A Cultural History, 1740–1830*. New York: St. Martin's Press, 1987.

Oddie, William. *Dickens and Carlyle*. London: Centenary Press, 1972.

———. "Dickens and the Indian Mutiny." *Dickensian* 18 (1972): 3–15.

Olson, Richard. *The Emergence of the Social Sciences, 1642–1792*. New York: Twayne Publishers, 1993.

———. *Science Deified and Science Defied: The Historical Significance of Science in Western Culture*. 2 volumes. Berkeley: University of California Press, 1990.

Pelling, Margaret. *Cholera, Fever, and English Medicine, 1825–1865*. Oxford: Oxford University Press, 1978.

Perkin, Harold. *The Origins of Modern English Society, 1780–1880*. London: Routledge & Kegan Paul, 1969.

Petty, Sir William. *Verbum Sapienti* (1665). In *The Economic Writings of Sir William Petty*, edited by Charles Henry Hull, pp. 99–120. 1899. Reprint. Fairfield, NJ: Augustus M. Kelley, 1986.

Pocock, J. G. A. "The Mobility of Property and the Rise of Eighteenth-Century Sociology." In *Virtue, Commerce, and History: Essays on Political Thought and History, Chiefly in the Eighteenth Century*, pp. 103–24. Cambridge: Cambridge University Press, 1985.

Poovey, Mary. "Aesthetics and Political Economy in the Eighteenth Century: The Place of Gender in the Social Constitution of Knowledge." In *Aesthetics and Ideology*, edited by George Levine, pp. 79–105. New Brunswick: Rutgers University Press, 1994.

———. "'Figures of Arithmetic, Figures of Speech': The Discourse of Statistics in the 1830s." *Critical Inquiry* 19 (1993): 256–76.

———. "The Social Constitution of 'Class': Toward a History of Classificatory Thinking." In *Rethinking Class: Literary Studies and Social Formations*, edited by Wai Chee Dimock and Michael T. Gilmore, pp. 15–56. New York: Columbia University Press, 1994.

———. "Speaking of the Body: Mid-Victorian Constructions of Female Desire." In *Body/Politics: Women and the Discourses of Science*, edited by Mary Jacobus, Evelyn Fox Keller, and Sally Shuttleworth, pp. 29–46. New York: Routledge, 1990.

———. *Uneven Developments: The Ideological Work of Gender in Mid-Victorian England*. Chicago: University of Chicago Press, 1988.

Porter, Roy. "Consumption: Disease of the Consumer Society?" In *Consumption and the World of Goods*, edited by John Brewer and Roy Porter, pp. 58–81. New York: Routledge, 1993.

Procacci, Giovanna. "Social Economy and the Government of Poverty." In *The Foucault Effect: Essays in Governmentality,* edited by Graham Burchell, Colin Gordon, and Peter Miller, pp. 151–68. Chicago: University of Chicago Press, 1991.

Prochaska, F. K. "Body and Soul: Bible Nurses and the Poor in Victorian London." *Historical Research* 60 (1987): 336–48.

Prothero, Iorwerth. "Chartism in London." *Past and Present* 44 (1969): 76–105.

Rainger, Ronald. "Race, Politics, and Society: The Anthropological Society of London in the 1860s." *Victorian Studies* 22 (1978): 51–70.

Ranyard, Ellen. *The Missing Link; or Bible-Women in the Home.* London: James Nisbet, 1859. 2d ed. 1861.

Rendall, Jane. "'A Moral Engine'? Feminism, Liberalism, and the *English Woman's Journal.*" In *Equal or Different: Women's Politics, 1800–1914,* edited by Jane Rendall, pp. 112–38. Oxford: Basil Blackwell, 1987.

Report from the Select Committee on the Health of Towns. London: House of Commons, 1840. Reprint. *Reprints of Economic Classics.* New York: Augustus M. Kelly, 1968.

Ricardo, David. *On the Principles of Political Economy.* 1819. Vol. 4 of *The Works and Correspondence of David Ricardo.* Edited by Piero Straffa. Cambridge: Cambridge University Press, 1962.

Richards, Joan. *Mathematical Visions: The Pursuit of Geometry in Victorian England.* San Diego: Academic Press, 1988.

Richardson, Ruth. *Death, Dissection, and the Destitute.* London: Routledge & Kegan Paul, 1987.

Riley, Denise. *"Am I That Name?" Feminism and the Category of "Women" in History.* Minneapolis: University of Minnesota Press, 1988.

Robbins, Keith. *Nineteenth-Century Britain: Integration and Diversity.* Oxford: Clarendon Press, 1988.

Roberts, David. *Victorian Origins of the British Welfare State.* New Haven: Yale University Press, 1960.

Robotham, Don. *"The Notorious Riot": The Socio-economic and Political Bases of Paul Bogle's Revolt.* Kingston: Institute of Social and Economic Research, Working Paper 28.

Rorty, Richard. *Philosophy and the Mirror of Nature.* Princeton: Princeton University Press, 1979.

Rose, Michael, ed. *The English Poor Law, 1780–1930.* Newton Abbot: David & Charles, 1971.

Rosen, George. "Disease, Debility, and Death." In *The Victorian City: Images and Realities,* vol. 2, edited by H. J. Dyos and Michael Wolff, pp. 624–68. London and Boston: Routledge & Kegan Paul, 1973.

Rosenberg, Charles. "Florence Nightingale on Contagion: The Hospital as Moral Universe." In *Healing and History*, edited by Rosenberg, pp. 116–36. New York: Dawson, 1979.

Ross, Ellen. *Love & Toil: Motherhood in Outcast London, 1870–1918*. New York: Oxford University Press, 1993.

Rothfield, Lawrence. *Vital Signs: Medical Realism in Nineteenth-Century Fiction*. Princeton: Princeton University Press, 1992.

Roxborough, John. "Chalmers' Theology of Mission." In *The Practical and the Pious: Essays on Thomas Chalmers (1780–1847)*, edited by A. C. Cheyne, pp. 174–85. Edinburgh: Saint Andrew Press, 1988.

Samuel, Raphael. "Comers and Goers." In *The Victorian City: Images and Realities*, vol. 1, edited by H. J. Dyos and Michael Woolf, pp. 123–60. London and Boston: Routledge & Kegan Paul, 1973.

Schiebinger, Londa. *The Mind Has No Sex? Women in the Origins of Modern Science*. Cambridge, MA: Harvard University Press, 1989.

Schumpeter, Joseph A. *History of Economic Analysis*. New York: Oxford University Press, 1954.

Scott, Joan W. "The Evidence of Experience." *Critical Inquiry* 17 (1991): 773–97.

Sedgwick, Eve Kosofsky. *Between Men: English Literature and Male Homosocial Desire*. New York: Columbia University Press, 1985.

Sefton, Harry R. "Chalmers and the Church: Theology and Mission." In *The Practical and the Pious: Essays on Thomas Chalmers (1780–1847)*, edited by A. C. Cheyne, pp. 166–73. Edinburgh: Saint Andrew Press, 1988.

Seltzer, Mark. *Bodies and Machines*. New York: Routledge, 1992.

Semmel, Bernard. *The Governor Eyre Controversy*. London: MacGibbon and Kee, 1962.

Shanley, Mary Lyndon. *Feminism, Marriage, and the Law in Victorian England, 1850–1895*. Princeton: Princeton University Press, 1989.

Shannon, H. A. "The Coming of General Limited Liability." In *Economic History*, vol. 2, edited by J. M. Keynes and D. H. MacGregor, pp. 267–91. London: Macmillan, 1933.

———. "The First Five Thousand Limited Companies and their Duration." In *Economic History*, vol. 2, edited by J. M. Keynes and D. H. MacGregor, pp. 396–424. London: Macmillan, 1933.

Shapin, Steven. "The Audience for Science in Eighteenth-Century Edinburgh." *History of Science* 12 (1974): 95–121.

———. "Property, Patronage, and the Politics of Science: The Founding of the Royal Society of Edinburgh." *British Journal for the History of Science* 7 (1974): 3–40.

———. *A Social History of Truth: Civility and Science in Seventeenth-Century England*. Chicago: University of Chicago Press, 1994.

————, and Simon Schaffer. *Leviathan and the Air-Pump: Hobbes, Boyle, and the Experimental Life.* Princeton: Princeton University Press, 1985.

Shuttleworth, Sally. "Female Circulation: Medical Discourse and Popular Advertising in the Mid-Victorian Era." In *Body/Politics: Women and the Discourses of Science,* edited by Mary Jacobus, Evelyn Fox Keller, and Sally Shuttleworth, pp. 47–68. New York: Routledge: 1990.

Simmonds, Lorna. "Civil Disturbances in Western Jamaica 1838–1865." *Jamaica Historical Review* 14 (1984): 1–17.

Simpson, David. *Romanticism, Nationalism, and the Revolt Against Theory.* Chicago: University of Chicago Press, 1993.

Simpson, Donald. "Charles Dickens and Empire." *Library Notes of the Royal Commonwealth Society* 162 (1970): 1–28.

Sisken, Clifford. *The Historicity of Romantic Discourse.* Oxford: Oxford University Press, 1988.

Smith, A. D. *The Ethnic Origins of Nations.* Oxford: Basil Blackwell, 1986.

Smith, Adam. *An Enquiry into the Nature and Causes of the Wealth of Nations.* 1776. New York: Modern Library, 1937.

————. *Theory of Moral Sentiments.* 1859. Edited by D. D. Raphael and A. L. Macfie. Indianapolis: Liberty Press, 1982.

Smith, F. B. *The People's Health 1830–1910.* New York: Holmes & Meier, 1979.

Smith, Frank. *The Life and Work of Sir James Kay-Shuttleworth.* London: John Murray, 1923.

Smith, Thomas Southwood. *The Philosophy of Health; or, an Exposition of the Physiological and Sanitary Conditions Conducive to Human Longevity and Happiness.* 1835. 11th ed. London: Longman, Green, Longman, Roberts, & Green, 1865.

————. *A Treatise on Fever and Epidemics Considered with Relation to their Common Nature and to Climate and Civilization.* London: Longman, Rees, Orme, Brown, and Green, 1830.

————. "Use of the Dead to the Living." *The Westminster Review* 2 (1824): 59–97.

Spencer, Herbert. "The Social Organism." In *Essays: Scientific, Political, and Speculative,* vol. 3, pp. 265–307. New York: Appleton, 1891.

Stafford, Barbara Maria. *Body Criticism: Imaging the Unseen in Enlightenment Art and Medicine.* Cambridge, MA: MIT Press, 1991.

Stallybrass, Peter, and Allon White. *The Politics and Poetics of Transgression.* Ithaca: Cornell University Press, 1986.

Stansky, Peter, ed. *The Victorian Revolution: Government and Society in Victoria's Britain.* New York: New Viewpoints, 1973.

Staves, Susan. *Married Women's Separate Property in England, 1660–1833*. Cambridge, MA: Harvard University Press, 1990.

Stedman Jones, Gareth. "Rethinking Chartism." In *Languages of Class: Studies in English Working-Class History, 1832–1982*, pp. 90–178. Cambridge: Cambridge University Press, 1983.

Stocking, George W., Jr. *Victorian Anthropology*. New York: Free Press, 1987.

Stokes, E. T. "Bureaucracy and Ideology: Britain and India in the Nineteenth Century." In *Transactions of the Royal Historical Society*, Series 5, 80 (1980): 131–55.

Stokes, Eric. *The Peasant Armed: The Indian Revolt of 1857*. Oxford: Clarendon Press, 1986.

Strachey, Ray. *The Cause*. 1928. Reprint. London: Virago, 1978.

Supple, Barry. "Legislation and Virtue: An Essay on Working-Class Self-Help and the State in the Early Nineteenth Century." In *Historical Perspectives: Studies in English Thought and Society*, edited by Neil McKendrick, pp. 211–54. London: Europa, 1974.

Taylor, Barbara. *Eve and the New Jerusalem: Socialism and Feminism in the Nineteenth Century*. New York: Pantheon, 1983.

Tennenhouse, Leonard. *Power on Display: The Politics of Shakespeare's Genres*. New York: Methuen, 1986.

Tennent, Sir James Emerson. *Social Economy: An Address*. London: Emily Faithfull, 1860.

Thompson, E. P. *The Making of the English Working Class*. New York: Alfred A. Knopf, 1966.

Tisdall, Evelyn E. P. *Mrs. Duberly's Campaigns: An Englishwoman's Experiences in the Crimean War and Indian Mutiny*. London: Jarrod's, 1963.

Transactions of the National Association for the Promotion of Social Science 1 (1858).

Tribe, Keith. *Land, Labour, and Economic Discourse*. London: Routledge & Kegan Paul, 1978.

Vaughan, Robert. *The Age of Great Cities: or, Modern Society Viewed in its Relation to Intelligence, Morals, and Religion*. 1843. Reprint. New York: Garland Press, 1985.

Vizram, Rozina. *Ayahs, Lascars and Princes: The Story of Indians in Britain, 1700–1947*. London: Pluto Press, 1986.

Walkowitz, Judith R. *City of Dreadful Delight: Narratives of Sexual Danger in Late-Victorian London*. Chicago: University of Chicago Press, 1992.

Waller, John O. "Dickens and the American Civil War." *Studies in Philology* 57 (1960): 535–48.

Walzer, Michael. "On the Role of Symbolism in Political Thought." *Political Science Quarterly* 82 (1967): 191–204.

Watt, Hugh. *Thomas Chalmers and the Disruption, Incorporating the Chalmers Lectures for 1940–44.* Edinburgh and London: Thomas Nelson and Sons, 1943.

Webb, R. K. *Modern England: From the Eighteenth Century to the Present.* New York and Toronto: Dodd, Mead, 1968.

Webb, Sidney, and Beatrice Webb. *English Local Government from the Revolution to the Municipal Corporations Act: The Manor and the Borough.* 2 volumes. London: Longmans, Green, 1908.

———. *English Poor Law Policy.* London and New York: Longmans, Green, 1910.

Weber, Max. "Bureaucracy" and "The Nature of Charismatic Authority." In *Max Weber on Charisma and Institution Building,* edited by S. N. Eisenstadt, pp. 18–79. Chicago: University of Chicago Press, 1968.

Welch, Alexander. *The City of Dickens.* Oxford: Clarendon Press, 1971.

Weylland, John Matthias. *Round the Tower: The Story of the London City Mission.* London: S. W. Partridge, 1874.

Williams, Raymond. *Keywords: A Vocabulary of Culture and Society.* New York: Oxford University Press, 1976.

———. *Marxism and Literature.* Oxford: Oxford University Press, 1977.

Wilson, Angus. Introduction to *The Mystery of Edwin Drood,* by Charles Dickens. 1870. Reprint. Harmondsworth, England: Penguin Books, 1987.

Winstanley, Michael J. *Ireland and the Land Question, 1800–1922.* London and New York: Methuen, 1984.

Wohl, Anthony S. *Endangered Lives: Public Health in Victorian Britain.* Cambridge, MA: Harvard University Press, 1983.

Workman, Gillian. "Thomas Carlyle and the Governor Eyre Controversy." *Victorian Studies* 18 (1974): 77–102.

Yeo, Eileen Janes. *The Contest for Social Science in Britain in the Nineteenth and Twentieth Centuries: Relations and Representations of Gender and Class.* London: Virago, forthcoming.

Youngston, A. J. *The Scientific Revolution in Victorian Medicine.* New York: Holmes and Meier, 1979.

INDEX

abstraction: in history of representation, 4–5; and New Poor Law, 10, 11, 109–10; and origin of domains, 9, 19. *See also* abstract space

abstract space, 19, 25–26; in Chadwick's *Sanitary Report,* 37, 193n. 42; and class, 34; description and history of, 27–31, 43, 52–54, 190n. 11, 191nn. 23, 26; and government, 31–37; and Ranyard's Female Bible Mission, 50–52, 196n. 66; and social body image, 15, 26, 27, 37–38, 40–42; and social machine image, 26, 27, 37–40

Act of Union, 66–67, 71, 201n. 20, 202n. 22

Acton, William, 92–93

Adorno, Theodor W., 3

aesthetic domain, in Disraeli's *Coningsby,* 138–39

Alison, W. P., 40

All The Year Round (Dickens), 160

Althusser, Louis, 13

analytic equality, theory of, 29

anatomical realism: decline of, 97; in Kay's *Moral and Physical Condition . . . ,* 75, 81–88; limitations of, 75, 87–88, 95; versus literary realism, 204n. 8; origins and description of, 74–75, 78–81, 96–97; and prostitution problem, 76, 88–97; and social reform, 10, 75, 82–88

anatomy, study of, 78–80

Anatomy Act of 1832, 80

Anatomy of Ireland (Petty), 193n. 46

Anthropological Society of London, 221n. 46

Anti-Corn Law League, 76

Argentina, investments in, 218n. 24

Aristotelian philosophy, 9

arithmetic, political, 29

Augustine, Saint, 190n. 11

Austen, Jane, 214n. 4

autonomy, relative, definition of, 13

B., Marian, 45–46, 196n. 62

Babbage, Charles, 26, 38–40, 49, 50, 193n. 43